ABILITY

LIABILITY

The Legal Revolution and Its Consequences

PETER W. HUBER

Basic Books, Inc., Publishers

NEW YORK

Library of Congress Cataloging-in-Publication Data
Huber, Peter W. (Peter William), 1952–
   Liability: the legal revolution and its
consequences.
   Includes index.
1. Torts—United States.   2. Liability (Law)
—United States.   I. Title.
KF1250.H8   1988   346.7303   88–4768
ISBN   0–465–03920–0 (cloth)
ISBN   0–465–03919–7 (paper)

Copyright © 1988 by Peter Huber
Printed in the United States of America
Designed by Vincent Torre
90 91 92 93 FG 9 8 7 6 5 4 3 2 1

For Sophie and those who came before.

CONTENTS

PREFACE

MUCH of the business of law is mystification and misdirection. Long words are better than short ones; more words, better than fewer. If the concept is really important, render it in Latin.

These familiar lawyerly techniques have been used to remarkable effect in recent years to transform the law of accidents. By now the public senses that something is badly awry. But few understand how we got to where we are, or who brought us.

This book is an attempt at demystification, so I cannot expect it to be warmly received by all my brothers and sisters in law. Most of them, for one reason or another, find something to commend in a vast system of law, created by lawyers for lawyers, that touches almost every aspect of our daily lives. One way to repel outside inspection is to present the issues as enormously subtle and complicated. But they are not.

This is the story of the revolution in liability law. It occurred in the last thirty years. It has benefited almost no one but the lawyers who run it. It has reached a point where even the most progressive and urgently needed reforms will be hard to accomplish, because the framework of law needed to support them has eroded so badly.

The majority of Americans already recognize the need for reform. But reforms will go wrong, if they go anywhere at all, unless they are built on an understanding of how we arrived at our present pass. Perhaps a simple account of a great revolution that has done much harm can help in setting things right.

ACKNOWLEDGMENTS

I AM deeply grateful to Bill Hammett and the Manhattan Institute for generous and patient support of this project. Walter Olson provided invaluable feedback and tireless editorial assistance at all stages; my debt to him is larger than I can express. My thanks also to Susan Borecki, Leslie Kyman, and Bob Mathew for dedicated research assistance. Our mutual friend has been of great help, too, but he is numbered among the giants and so remains unfootnoted and nameless.

LIABILITY

1

Uncommon Law

I T IS one of the most ubiquitous taxes we pay, now levied on virtually
everything we buy, sell, and use. The tax accounts for 30 percent of the
price of a stepladder and over 95 percent of the price of childhood vaccines.
It is responsible for one-quarter of the price of a ride on a Long Island tour
bus and one-third of the price of a small airplane. It will soon cost large
municipalities as much as they spend on fire or sanitation services.

Some call it a safety tax, but its exact relationship to safety is mysterious.
It is paid on many items that are risky to use, like ski lifts and hedge
trimmers, but it weighs even more heavily on other items whose whole
purpose is to make life safer. It adds only a few cents to a pack of cigarettes,
but it adds more to the price of a football helmet than the cost of making
it. The tax falls especially hard on prescription drugs, doctors, surgeons,
and all things medical. Because of the tax, you cannot deliver a baby with
medical assistance in Monroe County, Alabama. You cannot buy several
contraceptives certified to be safe and effective by the Food and Drug
Administration (FDA), even though available substitutes are more dangerous or less effective. If you have the stomach upset known as hyperemesis,
you cannot buy the pill that is certified as safe and effective against it. The
tax has orphaned various drugs that are invaluable for treating rare but
serious diseases. It is assessed against every family that has a baby, in the

amount of about $300 per birth, with an obstetrician in New York City paying $85,000 a year.

Because of the tax, you cannot use a sled in Denver city parks or a diving board in New York City schools. You cannot buy an American Motors "CJ" Jeep or a set of construction plans for novel airplanes from Burt Rutan, the pioneering designer of the *Voyager*. You can no longer buy many American-made brands of sporting goods, especially equipment for amateur contact sports such as hockey and lacrosse. For a while, you could not use public transportation in the city of St. Joseph, Missouri, nor could you go to jail in Lafayette County in the same state. Miami canceled plans for an experimental railbus because of the tax. The tax has curtailed Little League and fireworks displays, evening concerts, sailboard races, and the use of public beaches and ice-skating rinks. It temporarily shut down the famed Cyclone at the Astroland amusement park on Coney Island.

The tax directly costs American individuals, businesses, municipalities, and other government bodies at least $80 billion a year, a figure that equals the total profits of the country's top 200 corporations. But many of the tax's costs are indirect and unmeasurable, reflected only in the tremendous effort, inconvenience, and sacrifice Americans now go through to avoid its collection. The extent of these indirect costs can only be guessed at. One study concluded that doctors spend $3.50 in efforts to avoid additional charges for each $1 of direct tax they pay. If similar multipliers operate in other areas, the tax's hidden impact on the way we live and do business may amount to a $300 billion dollar annual levy on the American economy.

The tax goes by the name of *tort liability*. It is collected and disbursed through litigation. The courts alone decide just who will pay, how much, and on what timetable. Unlike better-known taxes, this one was never put to a legislature or a public referendum, debated at any length in the usual public arenas, or approved by the president or by any state governor. And although the tax ostensibly is collected for the public benefit, lawyers and other middlemen pocket more than half the take.

The tort tax is a recent invention. Tort law has existed here and abroad for centuries, of course. But until quite recently it was a backwater of the legal system, of little importance in the wider scheme of things. For all practical purposes, the omnipresent tort tax we pay today was conceived in the 1950s and set in place in the 1960s and 1970s by a new generation of lawyers and judges. In the space of twenty years they transformed the legal landscape, proclaiming sweeping new rights to sue. Some grew famous and more grew rich selling their services to enforce the rights that they themselves invented. But the revolution they made could never have taken place had it not had a component of idealism as well. Tort law, it is widely and passionately believed, is a public-spirited undertaking designed for the protection of the ordinary consumer and worker, the hapless accident victim, the "little guy." Tort law as we know it is a peculiarly American institution. No other country in the world administers anything remotely like it.

From Consent to Coercion

Tort law is the law of accidents and personal injury. The example that usually comes to mind is a two-car collision at an intersection. The drivers are utter strangers. They have no advance understanding between them as to how they should drive, except perhaps an implicit agreement to follow the rules of the road. Nor do they have any advance arrangement specifying who will pay for the damage. Human nature being what it is, the two sides often have different views on both these interesting questions. Somebody else has to step in to work out rights and responsibilities. This has traditionally been a job for the courts. They resolve these cases under the law of *torts* or civil wrongs.

But the car accident between strangers is comparatively rare in the larger universe of accidents and injuries. Just as most intentional assaults involve assailants and victims who already know each other well, most unintended injuries occur in the context of commercial acquaintance—at work, on the hospital operating table, following the purchase of an airplane ticket or a home appliance. And while homicide is seldom a subject of advance understanding between victim and assailant, unintentional accidents often are. More often than not, both parties to a transaction recognize there is some chance of misadventure, and prudently take steps to address it beforehand.

Until quite recently, the law permitted and indeed promoted advance agreement of that character. It searched for understandings between the parties and respected them where found. Most accidents were handled under the broad heading of *contract*—the realm of human cooperation—and comparatively few relegated to the dismal annex of tort, the realm of unchosen relationship and collision. The old law treated contract and tort cases under entirely different rules, which reflected this fairly intuitive line between choice and coercion.

Then, in the 1950s and after, a visionary group of legal theorists came along. Their leaders were thoughtful, well-intentioned legal academics at some of the most prestigious law schools, and judges on the most respected state benches. They were the likes of the late William Prosser, who taught law at Hastings College, John Wade, Professor of Law at Vanderbilt University, and California Supreme Court Justice Roger Traynor. They are hardly household names, but considering the impact they had on American life they should be. Their ideas, eloquence, and persistence changed the common law as profoundly as it had ever been changed before. For short, and in the absence of a better term, we will refer to them as the founders of modern tort law, or just the *Founders*. If the name is lighthearted, their accomplishments were anything but.

The Founders were to be followed a decade or two later by a much more sophisticated group of legal economists, most notably Guido Calabresi, now Dean of the Yale Law School, and Richard Posner of the University of Chicago Law School and now a federal judge on the Seventh Circuit Court of Appeals. There were many others, for economists seem to be almost as numerous as lawyers, and the application of economic theory to tort law has enjoyed mounting popularity in recent years as tort law has itself become an industry. An economist, it has been said, is someone who observes what is happening in practice and goes off to study whether it is possible in theory. The new tort economists were entirely true to that great tradition. Indeed, they carried it a step forward, concluding that the legal revolution that had already occurred was not only possible but justified and necessary. Mustering all the dense prose, arcane jargon, and elaborate methodology that only the very best academic economists muster, they set about proving on paper that the whole new tort structure was an efficient and inevitable reaction to failures in the marketplace. Arriving on the scene of the great tort battle late in the day, they courageously congratulated the victors, shot the wounded, and pronounced the day's outcome satisfactory and good.

Like all revolutionaries, the Founders and their followers, in the economics profession and elsewhere, had their own reasons for believing and behaving as they did. Most consumers, they assumed, pay little attention to accident risks before the fact. Ignoring or underestimating risk as they do, consumers fail to demand, and producers fail to supply, as much safety as would be best. As a result, manufacturers, doctors, employers, municipalities, and other producers get away with undue carelessness, and costly accidents are all too frequent. To make matters worse, consumers buy less accident insurance than they really need, so injuries lead to unneeded misery and privation and some victims become public charges.

With these assumptions as their starting point, the new tort theorists concluded that the overriding question that the old law asked—how did the parties agree to allocate the costs of the accident?—was irrelevant or worse. The real question to ask was: How can society best allocate the cost of accidents to minimize those costs (and the cost of guarding against them), and to provide potential victims with the accident insurance that not all of them currently buy or can afford? The answer, by and large, was to make producers of goods and services pay the costs of accidents. A broad rule to this effect, it was argued, can accomplish both objectives. It forces providers to be careful. It also forces consumers to take accident costs into account, not consciously but by paying a safety-adjusted price for every-thing they buy or do. And it compels the improvident to buy accident insurance, again not directly but through the safety tax. It has a moral dimension too: People should be required to take care before the accident and to help each other afterward, for no other reason than that it is just, right, and proper to insist that they do so.

The expansive new accident tax is firmly in place today. In a remarkably short time, the Founders completely recast a centuries-old body of law in an entirely new mold of their own design. They started sketching out their intentions only in the late 1950s; within two short decades they had achieved virtually every legal change that they originally planned. There were setbacks along the way, of course; the common law always develops in fits and starts, with some states bolder and others more timid, and the transformation of tort law was no exception. But compared with the cau-tious incrementalism with which the common law had changed in centu-ries past, an utter transformation over a twenty-year span can fairly be described as a revolution, and a violent one at that.

The revolution began and ended with a wholesale repudiation of the law of contract. Until well into the 1960s, it was up to each buyer to decide how safe a car he or she wanted to buy. Then as now, the major choices were fairly obvious: large, heavy cars are both safer and more expensive; economy cars save money but at some cost in safety. In case after case today, however, the courts struggle to enforce a general mandate that all cars be *crashworthy*. That term is perfectly fluid; it is defined after the accident by jury pronouncements; it is defined without reference to prefer-ences and choices deliberately expressed by buyer and seller before the transaction. A woman's choice of contraceptives was once a matter largely under the control of the woman herself and her doctor, with the FDA in the background to certify the general safety and efficacy of particular drugs or devices. Today tort law has shifted that authority too from the doctor's office to the courtroom. Balancing the risks and benefits of childhood vaccination was once a concern of parents, pediatricians, the FDA, and state health authorities. But here again, the views of the courts have become the driving force in determining what may be bought and sold. Not long ago, workplace safety was something to be decided between employer and employees, often through collective bargaining, perhaps with oversight from federal and state regulators, while compensation for accidents was determined by state workers' compensation laws. Today the courts supervise a free-for-all of litigation that pits employees against both employers and the outside suppliers of materials and equipment, the latter two against each other, and both against their insurers.

What brought us this liability tax, in short, was a wholesale shift from consent to coercion in the law of accidents. Yesterday we relied primarily on agreement before the fact to settle responsibility for most accidents. Today we emphasize litigation after the fact. Yesterday we deferred to private choice. Today it is only public choice that counts, more specifically the public choices of judges and juries. For all practical purposes, contracts are dead, at least insofar as they attempt to allocate responsibility for accidents ahead of time. Safety obligations are now decided through liability prescription, worked out case by case after the accident. The center of the accident insurance world has likewise shifted, from *first-party* insurance chosen by the expected beneficiary, to *third-party* coverage driven by legal compulsion.

Paralleling this shift from consent to coercion has been a shift from individual to group responsibility. The old contract-centered law placed enormous confidence in individuals to manage the risks of their personal environments. The new, tort-dominated jurisprudence prefers universal rules with no opt-out provisions. Tort law now defines acceptable safety in lawn mower design, vaccine manufacture, heart surgery, and ski slope grooming, without regard to the preferences of any individual consumer or provider. If the courts declare there is to be a safety tax on a vaccine at such and such a level, the tax will surely be paid, whatever other arrangements the buyer or user of the vaccine or the FDA, let alone the manufacturer, may prefer or can afford. In a similar spirit, the old law relied on the political branches of government to make those safety choices that only a community as a whole can responsibly oversee. The new again prefers control through the instrument of the lawsuit. Safety standards have been entirely socialized, but in a peculiar sort of way that freezes out not only private choice but also public prescription through all government authority other than the courts. The new accident insurance is likewise furnished on a universal and standardized plan, whether or not one or another of us might prefer a different set of policy terms or a different insurance carrier.

Though we have gone a great distance, there is no reason to believe that the journey is over. In the first place, the momentum of accumulated logic is likely to keep the system moving for the indefinite future, as newly established legal principles are deployed to open up fresh areas of litigation. There is also great financial momentum in the system. The tens of thousands of plaintiffs' lawyers who advertise for clients, dig up the cases, marshal the evidence, and take the claims to court, now have considerable economic muscle on their side. In 1988, asbestos lawyers were beginning to collect fees that will total about $1 billion, and were looking, so to speak, for new places to invest this money. Among the candidate targets were fiberglass and other insulators, tobacco, and various chemicals. The early claims against the Dalkon Shield intrauterine contraceptive device funded second- and third-generation lawsuits against other IUDs, spermicides, and morning sickness drugs. The lawyers who started careers as small-town traffic accident litigators were later to take on automakers, municipalities, taverns, and distilleries. As the Founding generals won their victories, the ranks of their followers swelled. And as the armies grew, the perimeters of the tort empire were pushed out further still. Despite occasional initiatives in state legislatures, and interminable hand wringing in Congress, no armistice seems imminent.

The statistics confirm this picture of restless, ceaseless expansion. The number of tort suits filed has increased steadily for over two decades. So has the probability that any given suit will conclude in an award. And the average size of awards has grown more rapidly still. Multiplied together, these three trends produce the universal tort tax so pervasive in our world today.

Begin with the number of cases. Traffic accident claims, which account for about 40 percent of all tort cases today, have held steady or even declined as states have passed no-fault laws. But other cases have been on a steep rise. Cases where appliances, factory machinery, chemicals, automobiles, and other products are blamed for injuries increased fourfold between 1976 and 1986. More medical malpractice suits were filed in the decade ending in 1987 than in the entire previous history of American tort law. One survey found that damage claims against cities doubled between 1982 and 1986. In the space of a single year, between 1984 and 1985, claims filed against the federal government grew from 41,000 to 54,000, and the amount demanded from $112 billion to $149 billion, an increase of over 30 percent by either measure.

The plaintiff's probability of winning has also risen steadily. The likelihood of success rose from 20 to 30 percent in a product case in the 1960s to more than 50 percent in the 1980s, with similar increases in other classes of lawsuit, again excluding traffic cases.

Finally, there has been sharp growth in the size of awards. The average judgment in all tort cases rose from an inflation-adjusted $50,000 in the early 1960s to more than $250,000 in the early 1980s—a fivefold increase. The inflation-adjusted median award—the amount exceeded in half of all judgments—has been rising steadily too, by more than 80 percent in the same period. Average verdicts against cities rose almost tenfold, to $2 million. The first jury verdict exceeding $1 million came in 1962; in 1975 there were fewer than twenty; today there are over 400 a year, an increase that could not possibly be ascribed to inflation alone. Inflation-adjusted awards in medical malpractice cases have doubled about every seven years.

It is always possible to manipulate and rearrange statistics, and tort law statistics are no exception. Many defenders of the new jurisprudence, including some who helped catapult tort law to the triumphant position it occupies today, have become notably modest, in recent years, about the success of their crusade. Insisting all the while that the legal changes they brought about were necessary, important, and all for the common good, they also suggest that not much has changed at all, at least not in the litigation statistics. They come up with modest-sounding figures on the rise in litigation, most commonly by lumping together traffic accident cases, which have been notably stable, with others, where the real turmoil has occurred. But anyone who cares to wade through the numbers in detail will find the conclusions unambiguous. We are living in an altogether new legal environment, created in little more than twenty years, and profoundly different from what existed in this country and in England for six centuries before. Tort law, once a remote and sleepy province of the law's empire, has become one of its most bustling and dynamic centers of activity.

Backfire

If you pay a steep, unsettling, and broad-based tax, you expect something in return. The Founders promised the world that their tax would bring measurable progress toward two deeply held social goals: protecting life and limb, and helping the injured when accidents do happen nevertheless. How well has the tort tax achieved these goals? The record is a mountain of pretentious failure.

High taxes drive up some prices, and the new tort system has certainly done that. Taxes drive other things off the market altogether, and that too has happened. The immediate impact of the new legal rules has been a marked increase in price and a decline in the availability of a wide range of goods and services. That much was expected, indeed welcomed, by the Founders. Hazardous goods should cost more, they felt, to reflect the risk; too-hazardous goods should not be sold at all.

What was unexpected was the propensity of the tort tax to fall where it is least needed and most difficult to bear. Contrary to all original expectations, the first major casualties of the new legal regime have been many of the methods by which society pursues safety itself. Hospital emergency-room services are perilous in liability terms because emergency-room patients are in trouble to begin with. Vaccines are hazardous (again, from the legal perspective) because the children who receive them are susceptible to a host of diseases and reactions often indistinguishable from vaccine side effects. Running a municipal police department, ambulance service, town dump, or waste cleanup service invites litigation because these activities are aimed at situations that are risky from the beginning. Selling an antimiscarriage drug, contraceptive, abortion, or obstetrical service is legally dangerous because pregnancy itself is risky for both mother and child. And modern tort law has written an altogether new conclusion to the parable of the Good Samaritan, making it unwise to stop at the roadside accident without first checking in with your local insurance agent and lawyer. In its search for witches, the modern tort system has undoubtedly found a few and reduced them to ashes. But too many wonder drugs have also been gathered into the flames.

How could a tort system so committed to increasing safety have landed some of its first punches on the very persons who work on the front line of helping others? Why does it so often fail to distinguish risks that are part of the problem from risks that are part of the solution? The answers are complex. For one thing, juries have often (and quite understandably) proved unskilled at distinguishing the various parties found at the scene of the crime. They are too prone to arrest the firefighter along with the arsonist, the ambulance driver along with the drunk who made the ambulance necessary in the first place. Another part of the reason lies in a slip between theoretical cup and real-world lip. The Founders were committed to deterring hazardous practices. But judges and juries were, for the most part, committed to running a generous sort of charity. If the new tort system cannot find a careless defendant after an accident, it will often settle for a merely wealthy one. But the wealthy defendant is more often part of the safety solution than the safety problem.

The larger fallacy in the Founders' grand scheme was the idea that the most attractive defendants would stick around to be sued, in case after case, after it became clear what was happening. As our right to sue the butcher, brewer, and baker after the sale has grown, our freedom to make the purchase in the first place has declined. The purveyors of meat, beer, and such withdraw only partially, by demanding a higher price; the purveyors of rare drugs, Yellowstone hiking, and rural obstetrical services have often been driven from the market altogether. An unbounded and impossible-to-waive right to sue necessarily overtakes and destroys the right to make deals with people who place a high premium on staying in business and out of court. While the consumer has indeed acquired a new and sometimes valuable right to sue, he has done so only by surrendering an older right, the right to contract, which in the long run is worth far more.

What about the aim of providing more and better insurance against accidents? It has fared no better than the goal of improving safety, and for much the same reason. How much insurance we get depends not only on how much we want to buy but on how much others are willing to sell. The Founders sought to increase the demand for liability insurance, and they undoubtedly did just that. But at the same time they decimated the supply. The net effect was less insurance all around.

The key to providing private insurance is to seek out reasonably narrow, well-defined risk groups, whose membership can be precisely described and whose future claims can be predicted with some accuracy. If an insurer cannot distinguish the young Corvette enthusiast from the middle-aged driver of a weekend Oldsmobile, high-risk drivers will stock up on bargain coverage while low-risk drivers will cut back, and the insurer will eventually have to charge everyone something approaching a Corvette rate. Less insurance will be sold as a result. Every major change in legal rules implemented by the Founders aggravated problems of exactly this kind, by requiring a looser definition of risk and responsibility, which led to higher rates, which led to lower coverage.

As it became less and less clear whose policy would have to pay for whose injury, liability insurance became scarce. In more than a few markets it disappeared altogether. For day care centers, orthopedists, neurosurgeons, and countless others, insurance became wholly unavailable at any price. Some insured activities were discontinued, which turned the shortage of insurance into a shortage of goods and services. Some among the bolder liability targets chose to go bare, deliberately undercapitalizing and underinsuring their operations, and then daring the tort system to do its worst. Many others wound up doing what amounted to the same thing on a more modest scale, still carrying some insurance but far less than they needed or wanted. The liability insurance crisis has hit the smallest enterprises the hardest. While larger players always survive the assault one way or another, the smaller ones often cannot. The system does succeed in paying some of the people some of the time, and on occasion paying them handsomely. But though munificent for a very few, it has been profoundly destabilizing for many more. The financial security of most people, most of the time, has declined.

In both its safety and its insurance effects, the new tort system is highly regressive; those who have the least to begin with are hurt the most. The affluent woman in this country today goes abroad for the IUD, once-a-month pill, or for the exotic eye drug driven off the U.S. market by liability too heavy to be borne; the poor woman stays at home and does without. The highly skilled worker need not be concerned when employers retrench their hiring because of liability concerns; the borderline worker has everything to lose. The well-to-do escape contagious disease entirely or survive with expert medical care; those who live in crowded squalor are far more likely to succumb to an unchecked epidemic that only aggressive distribution of vaccines or medicines could halt. The city dweller continues to enjoy ready access to specialty medical services; her less fortunate country cousin travels great distances or does without.

The insurance picture is more regressive still. The mandatory accident insurance required by modern tort law is funded by an excise tax on goods and services, but its benefits, such as they are, are strongly linked to income and social status. The car—and the implicit insurance contract that must go along with it—is sold at one price, whether the buyer is the president of the First National Bank or its janitor. Yet when disabled in a crash, the president can expect to receive a far higher award than the janitor for loss of future wages. The deal may be a good one for the president (though she undoubtedly has obtained comprehensive direct insurance elsewhere); for the janitor it is a cruel fraud. We would find it unthinkable to require all citizens to pay the same rate for a type of life insurance that gave far higher benefits to affluent beneficiaries. Nor would we charge the same fire insurance premium for a bungalow in Watts as for a mansion in Beverly Hills. Yet that is precisely how modern tort law operates. A more regressive scheme of social welfare could hardly be imagined.

Although the legal revolution has assumed the mantle of public interest, it has paradoxically put a damper on communal enterprise as well. Many things that can only be accomplished collectively are no longer even attempted, because the private right to sue has eclipsed the public power to act and serve. Sometimes the consequences are comparatively minor, as when public transportation is curtailed or a public beach shut down. Sometimes they are grave, as when a mass vaccination initiative is delayed or abandoned altogether. And again the worse-off are hit harder. The wealthy community always finds a way to ship its smokestack factories and wastes elsewhere; the poor one, when prevented by the courts from reaching an understanding with its own citizens, must entirely surrender the communal benefits that such activities make possible.

Across the board, modern tort law weighs heavily on the spirit of innovation and enterprise. The Founders confidently expected that their reforms would provide a constant spur to innovate. The actual effect has been quite the opposite. The old tort rules focused on the human actors, inquiring whether the technologist was careful, prudently trained, and properly supervised. The new rules place technology itself in the liability dock. But jurors, who generally can reach sensible judgments about people, perform much less well when they sit in judgment on technology.

Under jury pressure, the new touchstones of technological legitimacy have become age, familiarity, and ubiquity. It is the innovative and unfamiliar that is most likely to be condemned. One feature after another of the new system presses in the same direction. Consider the gilt-edged safety warnings that the new tort rules demand. Honing a warning to a fine point of perfection requires years of market and litigation experience, which means that established products now do comparatively well in tort suits based on warnings, while innovative challengers are vulnerable. The new rules also force providers to sell not only a product or service but also an accident insurance contract with it. But the availability of reasonably priced insurance depends on the accumulation of actuarial experience—something that all established technologies have but no truly innovative one ever does.

As a result of these and other similar forces, it is far safer, in liability terms, to sell an old, outdated oral contraceptive than a new IUD or sponge. It is more prudent, at least from the legal perspective, to stick with the tried-and-true technologies for car frame design, or aircraft engines, or vaccine formulation than to experiment boldly with something new. Does a pesticide manufacturer wish to steer clear of the courts? Any lawyer knows that the best legal bet is an old, familiar chemical, which has been used for years by every farmer in the community, rather than the latest exotic breakthrough in genetic engineering. Is the electric power company seeking at all costs to avoid liability? It will find coal to be the safest possible fuel in those terms, and uranium the most dangerous, though the ranking of actual risks may be the reverse.

The result is to ingrain a bias against innovation at all levels of the economy—for which we pay a heavy price, not just in money and in our nation's competitive position in the world, but in safety once again. The lay mind is accustomed to equate familiarity with safety, but newer, more often than not, is in fact safer than older. Life expectancy in this country has increased at the astonishing rate of three months per year throughout the twentieth century, not because of the proliferation of litigation but because of the constant press of technological innovation—innovation that is now being slowed and sometimes even reversed by the ongoing legal assault.

Wrong Signals

Modern tort law has likewise failed in what one might call its educational objective, its aim of signaling to consumers which courses of action are riskiest. What the modern law has done with warnings again richly illustrates the problem. Of course it makes sense for the manufacturer of a lawn mower or a potent drug to alert users to the risks. But warning is such an obvious and attractive concept that insufficient warning has become a catchall rationale for liability when no other comes readily to mind. This has been carried to the point where tort law now presses hard for warnings that go into mind-numbing detail and overstate actual risks. An excess of detail undercuts the value of the warning in practice; to warn of everything is to warn of nothing, and in a torrent of new data the really crucial bits of information are likely to go unread. Overstatement is worse still. An overly lurid warning that causes a man with hypertension to put aside a prescribed medication, or an older, overweight woman to reject an IUD and go back to the pill, or a mother to forgo vaccinating her young child, can cause considerably more harm than the omission of a warning of some obscure side effect that does occasionally materialize. Public health professionals across the country work tirelessly to encourage childhood vaccination. Meanwhile, tort verdicts against vaccine manufacturers have been based on the premise that a more draconian warning was desirable precisely because it might have caused parents to spurn the professional advice. And other consumers learn to adjust for overstatement by ignoring warnings altogether. There was a fable once about crying wolf, but it apparently went unheeded when modern warning doctrine was being framed.

The law's larger message to the consumer is false still. A cardinal though unstated principle of the modern rules is that it is wrong to blame a victim, or indeed anyone who lacks the funds to pay, for to do so means to give up the quest for victim compensation. The impulse here is surely generous. But accommodating it requires systematic evasion of the truth. It means sending women the message that their own hygiene or sexual habits are not all that important a risk factor in uterine infection or infertility; responsibility lies with the remote corporations that make contraceptives and tampons. It means sending workers the message that lung disease is primarily a function not of their own decision to smoke heavily on the job, or of the acts of their employer who happens to be shielded by workers' compensation laws; responsibility lies instead with the distant company that originally made the insulation. It means pretending that the responsibility for protecting U.S. servicemen and downwind civilians when a war is being fought or weapons are being tested lies not with the Pentagon, which also enjoys legal immunity in these matters, but with government contractors who make herbicides or fighter jets or help to conduct weapons tests. It means telling the individuals close to the accident that they are rarely in a position to make the difference in terms of safety; the ones with real control are the faraway institutions. Such beliefs have been indispensable in accomplishing the objectives of the new tort system. They have been repeated so often in the courts, and then in the press, that many now accept them as true. But they are all in fact dangerously false.

The new tort message is one of misinformation in matters not only of safety but also of financial protection. The notion that tort liability provides a reliable safety net for accident victims would be an exceptionally cruel myth if potential victims took it seriously. Anyone who forgoes buying her own insurance on the assumption that liability offers an adequate substitute is living in a dream that will assuredly become a nightmare if an accident ever occurs. Beyond doubt, liability is a huge and certain expense for American business. But there is a vast gulf between payments in and disbursements out, because of the lottery-like mechanics of litigation and the huge overhead required to run the courtroom casino. For the injury victim, as for the patrons of other casinos, it would be most inadvisable to spend or rely on any winnings before they are firmly in hand.

The Founders can hardly be faulted for their intentions, which were honorable, or their dispositions, which were kindly. But they were remarkably naive and optimistic about the legal system in particular and the world in general, and much further from omniscience than they so earnestly believed. Theirs was a tidy, linear world where simple stimuli in the courts would produce simple responses among producers and insurers. They thought they were dealing with a mule, which if prodded judiciously in the rear would proceed forward. But the beast was really an octopus, with no discernible rear to speak of, and capable of the most unpredictable reactions from the most unexpected directions.

Reassembling the Pieces

The liability tax that looms so large and baleful today is a recent invention, not an ancient legacy shrouded in the wisdom of the ages. Bringing it under control does not require tampering with a venerable body of law. The tampering has already taken place.

Nor, however, does reform necessarily mean a simple return to the traditional line of tort law as it stood, say, thirty years ago. That is neither feasible nor desirable. Times have changed and with them public attitudes and the wealth of our society. We have the resources to encourage safe practices and to take care of people who are nonetheless hurt in accidents. Common decency dictates that we should. The question today is not whether, but how.

The details will require some elaboration, but the principle can be stated succinctly. The individual's best protection against the hazards of living, physical or fiscal, is to be found not in the measures that can be taken after an accident, but in the freedom to make considered, binding choices beforehand. Security lies in prudent planning aimed at avoiding misadventure if possible, and obtaining direct, first-party insurance against any remaining risks in the knowledge that some level of risk is unavoidable. It lies in advance agreement with other individuals or the community as a whole to provide for our mutual benefit and security.

So the answer is not to abandon contract, as the Founders did so briskly and casually, but to modernize it. The time-tested legal tools that promote informed private or public choice about risk and safety, and the use of direct insurance against the hazards that remain, promise far better than the liability spiral we are riding today. Private contract can be resurrected in new forms that channel incentives toward more care by providers and better insurance against accidents. The rebirth of contract can reconcile the generous and protective impulses of an affluent modern society with the venerable legal principles of cooperation and consent. It is never too late to admit that a wrong road has been taken. This is particularly true when the road leads to a poisonous swamp.

But to understand what such a journey back to contract could look like, we must first reexamine the legal path away from it that we have so recently and so very hastily traveled.

2

The Death of Contract

IN 1958 Chester Vandermark bought a new car from the Maywood Bell Ford dealership near Los Angeles. Six weeks and 1,500 miles later, Chester was driving his sister Mary to Joshua Tree in the California desert. "[T]he car started to make a little shimmy or weave and started pulling to the right. . . . I tried to pull back, but it didn't seem to come, so I applied my brakes gently to see if I could straighten her up, but I couldn't seem to pull her back to the left. So, I let off on the brakes and she continued to the right, and . . . all of a sudden this pole was in front of me and we smashed into it." The car's brakes had failed. Both Chester and Mary were seriously hurt.

They sued Maywood Bell, among others. The dealership indignantly disavowed all responsibility. Its contract with Vandermark, after all, was quite explicit. "Dealer's obligation under this warranty is limited to replacement, without charge . . . of such parts . . . acknowledged by Dealer to be defective. . . . This warranty is expressly in lieu of all other warranties, express or implied, and of all other obligations on the part of Dealer."

The case moved up the slow legal escalator and finally reached the California Supreme Court in 1964. Maywood Bell was in for a rude shock. "[T]he fact that [the dealer] restricted its contractual liability to Vandermark is immaterial," the court announced. "Regardless of the obligations it assumed by contract, it is subject to strict liability." The contract terms, in short, were quite irrelevant; Maywood Bell was liable for the accident because it served as "an integral part of the overall producing and marketing enterprise that should bear the cost of injuries resulting from defective products." And with that, some of the most sweeping changes the common law has ever witnessed were formally underway.

Consent and Contract

Tort means "wrong." If Smith deliberately punches Baker while Baker is drinking peacefully in a bar, or accidentally drives into Baker after they both leave, Baker can hit back or he can sue. Tort law has historically tried to encourage the second, more civilized remedy. Careless accidents, like deliberate assaults, disturb society's calm and order. The legal system aims to restore the equilibrium and discourage self-help in matters of revenge or restitution.

Not all painful or harmful acts are torts, however. *Consent,* or its absence, distinguishes many harmful acts from tortious ones, or at least it used to. Under legal rules that prevailed in this country for centuries, and for centuries before that in the English common law from which we inherited ours, courts viewed the barkeeper who sold Baker a beer very differently from the drunk who took a swing at him. The beer might perhaps injure Baker every bit as much as the blow. But his willingness to buy and consume the drink made a crucial difference. The old common law took the concept seriously enough to render it in Latin: *volenti non fit injuria*—"to one who is willing, no wrong is done."

Consent in fact divided much of the civil law into two distinct territories. One governed contracts, the other torts. If Baker and Smith agreed on their future rights and obligations to each other, they had a contract. Consent cemented the agreement in the first place. And that then made it fair to enforce the deal later on. Consent distinguished Baker's dealings with the accommodating bartender from his altercation with the belligerent drunk.

Most accidents and injuries were covered by contract, not by tort. Tort rules applied, of course, if Smith and Baker collided on the highway as utter strangers. But aside from collisions on the road, mishaps between strangers are comparatively rare. Workplace accidents are preceded by a contract between willing employer and employee; surgical accidents by a consensual doctor-patient relationship; airplane crashes by the voluntary purchase of a ticket. Chester Vandermark and Maywood Bell landed together in court only because they had earlier come together amicably in the sale of a car. And their contract unquestionably *did* cover responsibility for accidents; it spelled out that Maywood Bell would be liable for the replacement of defective parts, and nothing more.

Nobody wants the accident, of course, but everyone enters the deal aware that it may happen anyway. No doubt we'd prefer to get food, shelter, transportation, and medical care without paying any safety price for them; we'd rather not pay a cash price either. But neither option exists in the real world, or so at least the old law stoically presumed. The common sense of the day suggested that the contingency of an accident should be addressed ahead of time, when tempers are cool and minds clear. The old rules therefore placed great weight on the initial agreement. Buyer and seller were allowed to set the terms of their own deal, on questions of safety just as on questions of price. The courts viewed the Chester Vandermarks of this world as intelligent adults, whose freely made contractual commitments were to be respected and enforced as bargained for.

The contract rules that applied consistently until the time of *Vandermark* were of ancient provenance, and grew over the centuries from slender beginnings to imposing grandeur, like a California redwood. It is worth sketching their history, if only to appreciate how quickly and carelessly the old legal monument was hewn down.

It was in the late 1300s, during the latter years of the reign of King Edward III, that the modern theory of contract began to develop. Until then, the civil law had primarily governed estates in land. With the growing mercantile trade of the late middle ages, the courts began to hear complaints against persons who professed to having a particular skill—innkeeping, surgery, carpentry, butchery—but did not deal honestly or exercise proper care in their pursuits.

So there gradually developed a new basis for lawsuit, known as *trespass for deceit*. If a person promised to build you a house but did a bad job of it—roof caving in, crumbling foundation, no chimney for the fireplace—you could sue. As they always do, the common-law judges borrowed from their own history. Your rights had been trampled on by the incompetent carpenter, they now reasoned, in much the same way as your rights would have been offended if a stranger wandered onto your estate without invitation and camped on the land—hence the use of the word *trespass*. By the year 1436, an English court would confidently declare: "If a carpenter makes a [promise to] me to make me a house good and strong and of a certain form, and he makes a house which is weak and bad and of another form, I shall have an action of trespass on my case. So if a doctor takes upon himself to cure me of my diseases, and he gives me medicines, but does not cure me, I shall have action on my case. . . . And the cause in all these cases [is] that there is an under-taking and [it becomes for the court] a matter in fact."

The earliest contract cases recognized no remedy if the builder or the doctor had promised to build the house or cure the disease and never bothered to show up for work at all. In the fifteenth and sixteenth centuries, common-law courts developed the *writ of assumpsit,* which reflected a new recognition that harm could be done because someone had done nothing, after promising otherwise. Extending the protection of law to private commercial relations in this way hastened the demise of feudalism and the rise of capitalism. With the writ of assumpsit, which became the cornerstone of modern contract law, we arrive at the very definition of contract. It comes down to us from nearly a half millennium of use: A contract is a promise or set of promises, freely made between willing parties, which the law will then enforce.

Contract law—the whole idea of making persons stick to their agreements and promises—is thus rooted in a notion of consumer protection. It reflects the idea that unless the law holds people to the bargains they make, the unscrupulous and irresponsible will exploit the conscientious and trustful. And it serves to put the powerful and the humble on the same plane. Great lords and ladies may not need a court's help to keep a carpenter from defaulting; they control many future building commissions and a whole apparatus of local power as well. The yeoman householder may have nothing but the law on his side. It is surely one of the greatest ironies of modern law that latter-day reformers have come to see contracts as nothing more than a stacked game in which producers hold all the cards, a mere pretext for the oppression by the weak of the strong. History teaches otherwise.

Every first-year law student begins her study of contracts with the 1929 case of eighteen-year-old George Hawkins, who was distressed by a "small pencil-sized scar" on his hand. His doctor, Edward McGee, a quack of the lowest order, convinced George that a little surgery would work wonders. McGee performed a graft, taking the new skin from Hawkins's chest. When he was finished, the scar on Hawkins's hand had been replaced by an unsightly hairy growth, and the once functioning hand was now unusable. Hawkins sued.

The case was an easy one under the law of the day: Hawkins won. How much? The value of what McGee had promised but failed to deliver, of course—a usable hand with neither hair nor pencil-sized scar. It was quite irrelevant that no known surgical techniques of the day could have provided a scar-free hand. Contract rules were unequivocal and they were symmetric. If the seller promised nothing in the way of safety or success, that was just what the buyer got. But if the seller promised the moon, as McGee foolishly did, he would have to deliver or convey the equivalent in money.

The same principle extended to every contract. An employee either "assumed the risk" of performing the job or spelled out the terms of job safety and compensation for injury as part of the employment contract. The buyer of a drug, house, horseless carriage, or scar-free hand did the same. To be sure, there might be legitimate disagreement about what the contract really provided. The common law recognized that in regular dealings between buyer and seller, or employer and employee, certain obligations were assumed by common though unwritten consent. If nothing else was said, for example, the employer was assumed to have committed itself to provide safe tools and a fair warning of unusual dangers in the workplace. But the general rule was that contract was king. If they worked at it, the parties could allocate risks and responsibilities in any way they might choose.

In the eyes of the old law, then, a deal was really a deal. The rule of *caveat emptor*—"let the buyer beware"—prevailed, as it had in both England and America since time immemorial. But the rule would more accurately have read *caveat emptor et vendor;* the seller was bound by the terms of the deal too. McGee, after all, came to grief by promising more than he later delivered. A manufacturer selling a product, an employer purchasing a service, or a doctor providing one could insist that the deal was on only if the other party agreed to bear the costs of any accident. By the same token, the buyer, the employee, or the patient could demand a guarantee of satisfaction or success before proceeding. One way or the other, agreements routinely did address health and safety risks.

Indeed, for a long time such agreements were thought to be protected by the Constitution itself. Article 1 of the Constitution contains a clause forbidding the states to pass any law "impairing the obligation of contracts," as well as other clauses that have been interpreted to guarantee "substantive due process," whatever that opaque phrase may mean. The courts' enforcement of these provisions has atrophied for reasons we need not explore here. But there was a time when the constitutionally guaranteed freedom of contract had real meaning. Or so the U.S. Supreme Court declared in a now notorious decision handed down in 1905.

Eight years earlier, New York State had passed a law forbidding bakery employees to work more than sixty hours a week or ten hours a day. The law was intended to protect the health of bakers who worked long hours in the heat generated by the ovens. Joseph Lochner, a bakery owner in Utica, resented the restraint and challenged the law. The controversy worked its way up to the Supreme Court, where Lochner prevailed. "The [New York] statute," Justice Peckham declared, "necessarily interferes with the right of contract between the employer and employees. . . . The general right to make a contract . . . is part of the liberty of the individual." Bakery workers were fully "able to assert their rights and care for themselves without the protecting arm of the State interfering with their independence of judgment and of action." If a baker—or equally well, as the Court sagely noted, a "printer, a tinsmith, a locksmith, a carpenter, a cabinetmaker, a dry goods clerk, a bank's, a lawyer's or a physician's clerk, or a clerk in almost any kind of business"—chose to kill himself on the job, that was entirely his own affair, and his employer's; the State of New York had no right or power to interfere.

Contract principles in this rugged world could operate very harshly. In 1937 the Massengill Company of Bristol, Tennessee, began looking for a palatable solvent for distributing medicine's first miracle drug, sulfanilamide. After less than two months of research, it settled on and began to ship a mixture of diethylene glycol and water flavored with raspberry extract. The formula, never tested in animals, promptly killed 100 people. The president of the company was politely apologetic, but not much more. "My chemists and I deeply regret the fatal results," he declared, "but there was no error in the manufacture of the product. We have been supplying legitimate professional demand, and not once could have foreseen the unlooked for results. I do not feel that there was any responsibility on our part." And he was quite right, at least under the strictest buyer-beware principles. If users of the drug had wanted a guarantee of its safety and effectiveness, they should have demanded one before buying. No such guarantee had been provided. As it happened, the tort law for medicines was already in flux, and the families of some of the Massengill victims did have their day in court. But countless other victims of similar accidents did not. For the most part, a deal was a deal, even when it worked out appallingly for one side or the other.

Harsh though they could be, the contract rules governing health and safety were mechanical, precise, and simple enough to remain largely undisturbed for many centuries. Treating most human interactions as consensual affairs of contract, rather than gratuitous incidents of tort, greatly simplified the law. Above all, rigid respect for contracts kept people out of court. Most transactions were covered by what came to be known as private law, created by the parties themselves and formalized in contract. Public law, whether written by legislatures or by the courts, governed only at the margins and intersections, where there was no private law to follow. Private law formed a structure as inviolable and as complete unto itself as a cathedral. In cases like *Lochner,* the courts guarded its sanctity by preventing public law from invading and desecrating the hallowed grounds.

The Climate for Change

The law today could not be more different. A modern-day baker lets her employees off work when the government so dictates; a modern-day Massengill pays dearly for its terrible mistake. Contracts are no longer sacrosanct; indeed, in matters of health and safety, contract terms count for nothing at all. The intervening revolution has been as profound and far-reaching as any in the history of the common law.

The first modest changes took root between about 1900 and 1920. Responding to a series of scandals involving poisonous food and drugs, Congress passed the Pure Food Act in 1905. The courts, entirely on their own initiative, soon adopted a complementary set of changes in the tort law. The new rule that eventually emerged was straightforward: If Smith said nothing to the contrary when selling food or drugs, he implicitly promised Jones that the product was fit for human use. If Smith had any reservations about that fitness, he had to spell them out expressly. In lawyers' argot this was called an *implied warranty*—an unwritten promise of "fitness for intended uses."

The logic was simpler than the legal jargon. The country had entered an age of some general affluence. For perhaps the first time in American history, most people were reasonably well fed and had access to some measure of beneficial medical care. Few were now so desperate that they would knowingly buy food or drugs unfit for human use. These social changes alone suggested that silence in the sale of such products acquired a new meaning. If nothing was said, the shared understanding between buyer and seller would be that food or drugs sold for human use were fit for that purpose. Or so the courts would assume if the matter later came to be litigated. No sale was flatly barred; if a cook wanted to buy a barrel of rancid food, perhaps in order to pick through it in search of unspoiled pieces, he could still buy it so long as he had been given fair warning. But absent such warning, the risks stayed with the seller. Contract was still paramount, but warnings for the first time became an integral part of the contract.

By the late 1950s and 1960s, the time was right for a second wave of tort-law reform. This was again a period of rising affluence, in which the quality and safety of goods loomed larger than in earlier times of want. Pioneering writers like Ralph Nader sounded the early alarms. Health, safety, and environmental protection had been neglected, not only in matters of food and drink but also in the design of cars, toys, power plants, pesticides, and consumer products of every description. The most visible impact of this critique was a spate of new legislation rivaled only by the New Deal laws in scope and complexity. Congress added to the federal food and drug laws in 1956 and 1962, rewrote the Clean Air and Clean Water acts, and created powerful new arms of government to monitor health and safety: the Environmental Protection Agency (EPA), the National Highway Traffic Safety Administration (NHTSA), the Nuclear Regulatory Commission (NRC), the Consumer Product Safety Commission (CPSC), and the Occupational Safety and Health Administration (OSHA), among others. Alongside these systemwide enactments were countless ad hoc measures addressing such dangers as flammable fabrics, lead-based paints, food colors, leaky pipelines, medicine bottles, railroads, and aircraft.

This time, however, the parallel developments in tort law were no longer to be a matter of incremental adjustments. The Founders were beginning to grow in number and gather strength for an unprecedented intellectual assault. The earlier judicial innovations had mostly consisted of trimming a presumption here and there; the new tort theorists hewed away at the old system root and branch.

One advantage they enjoyed from the beginning was in not having to work through a refractory political process, or even to explain their reforms to the unwashed public at all. The right to sue your doctor for malpractice, for example, is not expressly provided for in any written statute; it exists only because the current crop of judges says it does. Their say-so commands respect because generations of judges before them have said much the same thing. Judges who want to preserve the authority of the law they make need not seek any mandate from the people. But they do have to proceed cautiously, or at least appear to, for the public legitimacy of the common law derives from its antiquity and apparent stability. Where there is no handy scripture of precedent to cite—or worse yet, where the precedent points in the wrong direction—it is critical to find support in the commentaries of legal academics and theoreticians.

With remarkable self-confidence and tenacity, with abiding faith and determined proselytizing, the Founders set about to create the new body of sacred writings and catechetical formulas necessary for the legal schism and reformation they had in mind. Accidents are socially costly, they pointed out, and the law should encourage accident prevention by the most economical means. To that end, liability should fall not on the person most "at fault" in some traditional sense, but on the one who could prevent any given accident at the lowest cost. And just who might that be? Most often, those who provide goods and services, not those who consume them. Corporations, hospitals, city governments, universities, and other institutions, unlike the individual consumer they serve, are accident experts. They could compile scattered accident reports and discover recurring safety problems that individual users might never suspect. They could warn consumers of likely hazards, redesign products, or keep dangerous items out of the hands of irresponsible buyers. Even when there was no immediately feasible way to eliminate a hazard, billing producers for accidents would spur them to search constantly for improvements in their wares. By a happy coincidence, ultrastringent producer liability would further other desirable goals as well. It would ensure compensation for injured parties who can ill afford to shoulder the costs of accidents. And very strict rules would also be simpler to administer because they would sweep aside distracting questions of individual right and wrong, care or carelessness, innocence or fault.

Or so the Founders sincerely believed. And on this mixture of logic, dogma, faith, and superstition, untroubled by much in the way of empirical observation, they set out to establish a shining new legal kingdom.

Flypaper Contracts

In the course of the 1960s and early 1970s, judges across the country embraced the new creed, first in their hearts, then increasingly in their rulings. The central problem they faced was that tort law did not cover much territory. Most transactions were matters of contract, and most contracts allocated risks in ways not approved by the Founders. The first and most important step, then, was to bury the old notion of contract.

This interment had to be performed one spadeful at a time. Jurists could not peremptorily discard centuries of common law simply because new tort theory and deeply felt sympathy told them that doing so would be wise social policy. Instead, the displacement of the old contract by the new tort law proceeded in a series of much smaller steps, each appearing as no more than a trifling adjustment to long-standing rules. Enough small steps, however, will take you from here to Peru. In this instance the trip turned out to be, by the normally sluggish standards of the common law, one of breathtaking speed. It took roughly twenty years, from about 1960 to 1980, to rewrite the common law of accidents from beginning to end.

The courts started profitably with the subject of silence. In the old days, if the buyer and seller of a lawn mower said nothing at all about safety, the buyer took all the risk. This followed a more general principle that every term of a contract has to be expressly affirmed by both sides before it comes into existence. But it is almost as fair to decree the opposite: If a contract says nothing about safety, the parties on both sides presume the best, not the worst, and if an accident happens the *seller* is responsible.

That, at least, was what Helen Henningsen maintained. Her husband, Claus, bought her a new 1955 Plymouth Plaza 6 Club sedan from the Bloomfield Motor Company, a Plymouth and De Soto dealer in Highland Park, New Jersey. Only days later, Helen was driving along when "[s]uddenly, she heard a loud noise 'from the bottom, by the hood.' It 'felt as if something had cracked.' The steering wheel spun sharply in her hands; the car veered sharply to the right, and crashed into a highway sign and a brick wall." The insurer declared the vehicle a total loss.

Helen sued Bloomfield Motors and Chrysler. She claimed that either or both had been negligent in manufacturing or preparing the car for sale; unfortunately she had no solid evidence of negligence to present, nor could she even show that any of the car's parts were defective. But Helen also claimed that the sellers had given her husband an implied warranty that the car was properly manufactured and safe. There was no disputing that neither Chrysler and Bloomfield Motors had provided anything of the sort *expressly* in the sales contract; Bloomfield's contract promised only to replace any defective parts. But the New Jersey Supreme Court ruled for Helen nonetheless. "Under modern marketing conditions," the court declared, "when a manufacturer puts a new automobile in the stream of trade and promotes its purchase by the public, an implied warranty that it is reasonably suitable for use as such accompanies it into the hands of the ultimate purchaser."

The implied warranty of safety had first been sighted by keen-eyed jurists in food and drug contracts several decades earlier. During the 1960s, after *Henningsen,* courts began detecting its presence in one product area after another: not just cars but appliances, cosmetics, and machinery of every description. A new general rule emerged: Courts would presume that silence on the question of safety meant that the seller of a consumer product promised the moon. Any accident caused by a defect would be billed accordingly—to the product manufacturer rather than the buyer, to the doctor rather than the patient, to the building contractor rather than the homeowner. The courts hadn't yet abandoned the basic idea that risk could be allocated by private contract; they had simply changed the rules on how they would read, not the contract's fine print, but the altogether empty spaces beneath.

It is curious to consider, however, what a cheap article ink is, and how far it can be made to go. Those empty spaces could be filled with more print, and they soon were. Many sellers were not at all eager to accept more liability for accidents. If the courts were going to read a no-accident guarantee into their silence, sellers would take pains to speak up. The lawn mower contract would say, in large and conspicuous type, that the device was very dangerous, that it frequently amputated toes and fingers, and that its manufacturer had no intention whatsoever of paying the hospital bills, which surely would arrive in short order. And in the law's unending battle of words, *express disclaimers* still trumped implied warranties every time. Sellers began to use them in torrents.

The Founders welcomed the arrival of express disclaimers much as a pack of chimpanzees welcomes a python, with much howling and chest pounding and waving of arms and throwing of rocks. The main reaction seemed to be outrage that anyone would dare to block the march of progress quite so brazenly and unapologetically. It was especially galling to be stopped by a barrier as flimsy as parchment.

So there began a lengthy siege of the paper battlements, an arms race of verbal escalation and counterescalation between rival legal battalions. The objective for the reactionaries was to write disclaimers of liability that would stick. The objective for the reformers was to get over, under, or around disclaimers one way or another. It wasn't really a balanced contest, because the reformers had by then captured the courts, and the courts always had the final word. What followed roughly tracked the lyrics of "Fifty Ways to Leave Your Lover," the song popularized by Paul Simon a decade later. "Don't be coy, Roy, Just slip out the back, Jack, Just drop off the key, Lee, And set yourself free." Lawyers, who are almost never coy, are skilled at slipping out the back doors of contracts. And judges are among the most skilled of lawyers.

Sometimes a court would conclude that a disclaimer had not been negotiated properly or had not been brought conspicuously enough to the buyer's attention, even if it did appear on the contract. Another trick, popular for a while, consisted of discovering what was said to be a prior breach of the contract by the seller, often on some trivial or technical point, which ostensibly then left the court free to tear up the entire contract as written (including any disclaimer, of course) and construct an entirely new "agreement" from scratch. Yet another verbal sleight of hand was to read the contract with great care and claim to discover some internal conflict, which could then be said to nullify the document in its entirety. As one pair of commentators put it, the decisions of this period acquired "as their only common bond a certain uniqueness of approach that results in the almost mystical disappearance of the disclaimer or limitation in question. . . . [O]ne gets a picture in reading these cases of lights going off, talismanic phrases being mumbled in the dark, and the light flashing back on just in time to show the consumer exiting with a check in his pocket."

This death-by-painful-scrutiny method for killing contracts worked well enough for a while, but it contained the seeds of its own downfall. Each disclaimer case taught the losers another lesson, and they grew increasingly skilled at spelling out just what they wanted to sell (a lawn mower, say) and what they did *not* care to sell (an insurance contract). A battle of words, inevitably to be won by the wrong side, would spell a rather ignominious end to the whole new tort crusade. Different and more potent solvents were needed to clear out the paper-clogged channels and guarantee a free flow of liability. So the courts turned their attention from the terms of the contract to the competence of the contracting parties. And that, without doubt, was the end.

Standardized contracts between a large corporate seller and a small consumer, new tort scholars and judges now declared, were not really agreements at all; they were mere contracts "of adhesion," and should be dismissed out of hand. A single frail individual could hardly hope to hold his own in a deal with a large, knowledgeable institution. Joe Consumer never bothers to read the contract accompanying his airline or bus ticket, his toaster, or his car; even if he did, General Motors, General Electric, and United Airlines would laugh if Joe proposed to renegotiate the terms one by one. The consumer was now viewed much as a fly near flypaper, ever in danger of sudden death by glue, no different in any important respect from the unwitting pedestrian who suddenly found himself adhering to the fender of a stranger's car.

The flypaper theory of contracts was infinitely powerful. Take-it-or-leave-it contracts of course typify virtually all mass-market sales of consumer products and services. Used skillfully, the theory allowed judges to get rid of almost any unwanted language they chose, anywhere they might find it. Adhesion theories could transform any deal, no matter how seemingly consensual, into the legal equivalent of a car accident.

It was the flypaper theory that finally introduced the California Supreme Court to Chester Vandermark, whom we met at the beginning of this chapter. With its ruling in that case, California finally and explicitly threw out contracts altogether, declaring that no conceivable disclaimer of safety would be availing. The contract was "immaterial." Maywood Bell was liable for the accident because the court *said* Maywood Bell was liable, and that was that.

Other courts soon followed the California lead. Tired of scrubbing away at contractual language they disliked, they simply discarded the offending documents altogether. Safety disclaimers were sweepingly denounced as "unconscionable," "contrary to public policy," or "inconsistent with natural justice and good morals." That an individual consumer might freely choose to bargain away her divinely given entitlement to safety was a possibility that would not be contemplated in the new legal order. Contract terms concerning the safety of a car, or a lawn mower, or an airplane were no more enforceable than a Venetian merchant's promise to guarantee repayment of a loan with a pound of his own flesh. Contract, in short, was not contract anymore, at least not when questions of safety were at stake. Contract was just the overture to the symphony of tort.

In barely a decade of steady work, the Founders and their disciples thus dismantled many centuries of law governing consensual relations in the sale of goods, in professional services, and in employment. To be sure, express disclaimers remained a familiar part of the landscape, like tattered scarecrows. But they no longer frightened many litigants. Hospital patients would continue to sign detailed forms surrendering any and all thought of future lawsuits. The skier's lift ticket might still have a similar "agreement" stamped on the back, as might an airline ticket. The lawn mower, contraceptive pill, toaster, or vaccine might still come with all sorts of disclaimers, followed by lists of "wherebys" and "wherefores." Sellers might still insist that they promised nothing at all in the way of safety, or that they warranted the product only against certain kinds of defects or consequences, or that they limited their liability to replacement, repair, or refund. Consumers might still agree at the outset that that was precisely what they agreed to and accepted. But none of this would count for anything at all when the matters came to be addressed in court. As Grant Gilmore put it in his famous monograph, *The Death of Contract,* contract had been absorbed back into tort.

So like Marley, partner to Ebenezer Scrooge, the risk contract was dead. There was no doubt whatever about that. The register of its burial had been signed by the clergyman, the clerk, the undertaker, and the chief mourner. In matters touching on health and safety, contract was dead as a doornail.

As we shall see, however, its troubled ghost had not altogether departed the scene of its earlier habitation.

3

A Search for New Rules

I N 1794, the great French chemist Antoine Lavoisier was led to the Paris guillotine and executed in the prime of his life. "It took but a few seconds to cut off Lavoisier's head," one of his countrymen remarked. "It will take France a century to grow another like it."

The judges who had sentenced and executed the law of contract had not one head to replace, but a million. Every sale of a car, toaster, or cigarette lighter, every hookup of an electric or gas customer, every ticket for an ocean cruise or roller coaster ride, every college admission, hotel room rental, or tonsillectomy, is based on contract. The old law depended on buyer and seller to decide privately beforehand who would pay for what if an accident befell. When the courts abandoned contract, they left a cavernous void that had to be refilled, bucket by bucket, with a new set of public standards, rights, and responsibilities.

When this realization dawned, it came as something of a letdown in legal circles. The attack on contract had been conducted with high optimism. The Founders had announced their early successes as if they were performing on the Pandean pipes, in their own honor, the triumphal march: See the conquering tort law comes; sound the trumpets, beat the drums. Now the conquerors were required to govern, and that was less fun and more difficult. They nevertheless set to work bravely enough, building a new city from the rubble of the old. What emerged from the ruins was a new body of law, based on an entirely new theory of civil obligation. The scholar Grant Gilmore puckishly suggested that it be called *contorts,* in recognition of its mixed parentage. But the Founders were a solemn crowd, and the name never caught on. It should have, for it very aptly described the new legal maneuvers that were now underway.

As we have seen, tort law had been around for ages—even longer than the law of contracts. The very earliest tort law in medieval England provided remedies for intentional wrongdoing—the barroom assault and things of that sort. And if a landowner, clearing his land with all due care, felled a tree trunk that struck a passerby on the adjacent highway, he would have to pay at least nominal damages, even if there had been no actual injury. The insult the passerby suffered in being hit was harm enough. Indirect injuries more remote in time or place were treated less strictly. If another passerby stumbled over the errant log soon after it fell, he could win damages only if he suffered real injury and also showed that the landowner was negligent or had intended to cause harm. And if a passerby *bought* the log from the landowner and managed to hurt himself with it later, tort law was out of the picture entirely; all that counted then was the contract.

The ancients, in short, had fairly modest and limited notions about liability from the beginning. As industrial accidents became more common in the nineteenth century, the courts introduced a new principle of tort that was still more restrictive: Neither direct nor indirect injuries would give rise to liability unless there had been *fault* in some sense of that word. And what was fault? Malicious intent counted, of course. But otherwise, the person seeking recovery would have to prove *negligence.*

Endless pages have since been written about just what the fuzzy concept of negligence means. It is commonly defined with reference to terms that are no more exact, such as ordinary prudence. In 1888, for example, ten-year-old Carl Brown went to play in a railroad yard with his friends. He climbed on a car containing coal and was standing on it with his feet on the drawhead, holding on to the brake wheel, between two stationary cars, when a switch engine kicked several cars against the two stationary cars, catching his foot and crushing it. The railroad had given no signal that the cars were approaching, even though a municipal ordinance expressly required that locomotives ring their bells when moving within city limits. Young Carl sued the railroad, charging negligence. The court agreed. "[I]t becomes the duty of the railway company to use such care to avoid injury to such person as a man of ordinary prudence would have used under like circumstances." "Ordinarily prudent" railroads comply with municipal ordinances.

In the end the layperson's understanding of negligence is as good as the lawyer's, and is all that counts in the jury room anyway. A jury scrutinizes the defendant's character, reconstructs her conduct leading up to the accident, and asks if an ordinarily prudent person standing in her shoes would have avoided the accident by exercising greater care. Did the railway give its employees proper training and supervision? Did the obstetrician take normal, reasonable precautions in helping deliver the baby? Did the maker of a vaccine exercise all the care of an ordinarily prudent manufacturer in that line of business? If so, there was no legal case, no matter how gruesome the injuries that materialized anyway. If not, the defendant was negligent, even if he acted from the purest and kindest of motives. Good faith did not ward off liability. But good care did.

Negligence standards were extended to product manufacturers in the early decades of this century, at least for injuries not covered by any contract. The key opinion was written in 1916 by the great Benjamin Cardozo, then a judge on New York's highest court. Donald MacPherson bought a Model 10 runabout from Close Brothers, a Buick dealer in Schenectady, New York. On July 25, 1911, MacPherson's car was found wrapped around a telephone pole near Saratoga Springs. MacPherson himself was discovered "under the hind axle of the machine," and he was released "with some difficulty." The accident had apparently been caused by the collapse of all twelve wooden spokes on one of the car's wheels. MacPherson had dealt entirely with the independent dealer, but he sued Buick anyway. There was, of course, no contract in the picture, since the two parties had never dealt with each other directly. But Cardozo declared Buick negligent in failing to inspect the car's wheels. "If the nature of a thing is such that it is reasonably certain to place life and limb in peril when negligently made," Cardozo declared, it is a "thing of danger." Irrespective of contract, "the manufacturer of this thing of danger is under a duty to make it carefully."

The *MacPherson* decision injected a bit of tort law at the edges of the marketplace for goods and services. But throughout the mid-1950s, hazardous product or no, the manufacturer would lose only if a person ultimately injured by his product could show negligence or worse. And protection for the immediate buyer of the product, if there was to be any at all, came from her contract, not some independent theory of tort liability.

The negligence standard was frugal. Accidents are vastly more common than accidents caused by negligence. Ordinary prudence, which is what negligence law demands, is what ordinary people ordinarily exercise. The butcher, baker, and fluorescent-bulb maker generally *are* prudent by this standard, as are the majority of surgeons, automotive designers, architects, and others who stand in the foreground or background of life's calamities. In addition, under the old negligence standard courts scrutinized conduct on both sides of the lawsuit. A person who came willingly to a risky situation, such as a fenced-off construction project, assumed the risk of his activities and couldn't blame someone else later for his accident. Nor could an injured party collect if he himself had been negligent in any contributing way.

The system, in short, dealt with most accidents by refusing to deal with them outside the terms of advance private agreement. Oliver Wendell Holmes summarized the philosophy in his 1881 classic, *The Common Law.* "Unless my act is of a nature to threaten others, unless under the circumstances a prudent man would have foreseen the possibility of harm, it is no more justifiable to make me indemnify my neighbor against the consequences, than to make me do the same thing if I had fallen upon him in a fit, or to compel me to insure him against lightning. . . . The state might conceivably make itself a mutual insurance company against accidents, and distribute the burden of its citizens' mishaps among all its members." But the courts of the time would not.

This, by and large, was still the prevailing tort law when contracts were suddenly dismantled and discarded eighty years later.

Strict Liability

The old negligence rules had always been open to the reproach of stinginess. With the death of contract, they now promised to be hopelessly cumbersome as well. The prospect of running an ever-growing number of cases through a full postaccident inquest on how all the players had performed was discouraging; the sheer task threatened to overwhelm the courts, and the outcome would too often be compensation deferred or denied altogether. This was most vexing. The Founders had labored hard to cross the high mountains of contractual language, only to find that the valley of tort below was not exactly flowing with milk and honey.

As we saw earlier, their initial response was to rely on the contractual material already at hand, using it to spin out liability through the implied warranty. If the Mammoth Corporation had somehow *promised* to pay for any and all accidents involving its product, everything else was simple. No one had to worry about whether there had been negligence; somewhere or other down there between the lines the contract itself promised payment. The content was novel, but the forms were reassuringly familiar.

For a while, then, the reinterpretation of contract terms sufficed as a basis for inventing liability standards much stricter than negligence. And a while was all the Founders really needed. Most people are eager to believe good news, even when it is too good to be true. The public and press didn't at all mind the idea that manufacturers had suddenly begun promising (tacitly, mind you) to pay for accidents resulting from all defects in their products, regardless of negligence. Within a few years, this legal notion of "strict" producer liability had become familiar and obvious. At that point, several state courts were ready to discard the roundabout legal fictions and take a more direct route to the same result. In 1962, the California Supreme Court led the way.

For Christmas in 1955, William Greenman's wife had bought her husband a Shopsmith, a new power tool that served as a combination saw, drill, and wood lathe. Greenman was making a wooden chalice on his Shopsmith one day when a piece of wood flew out of the machine and struck him on the forehead. He sued the manufacturer, maintaining that "inadequate[ly] set screws were used to hold parts of the machine together so that normal vibrations caused the tailstock of the lathe to move away from the piece of wood being turned, permitting it to fly out of the lathe." No contract claim was possible: Greenman was not the actual buyer of the lathe, and he had failed, in any event, to comply with California contract rules that require timely notice of a pending claim. By 1962, however, when the case reached it, the California Supreme Court was already growing tired of contracts and all their troublesome formalities and rules. It contemptuously brushed aside the notice requirement as a "booby trap for the unwary." Strict liability, the court bluntly declared, would no longer be rationalized in terms of implied warranties, fictional contracts, or anything of that sort. Product manufacturers would instead be held "strictly liable" to consumers for accidents caused by a "defect in manufacture" of their product.

This was a great leap. The need to find implied warranties and such had been a bothersome and often embarrassing barrier to contractual theories of liability. The need to find negligence had been an equally troublesome barrier to tort theories of liability. Now, at one bound, the courts could leap directly to the desired goal, at least so long as a product defect was at issue.

But there was important work still to be done. Though somewhat obscure on the point, *Greenman* seemed to cover *manufacturing defects,* which are in fact quite rare. *Design defects,* however, were quite another matter, and had not yet been officially incorporated into the new doctrine. So Barbara Evans learned in 1966. Driving her station wagon across an intersection one day, Barbara's husband was broadsided by another car and killed. The 1961 Chevrolet had an X-shaped frame; at the time, other manufacturers still used a box frame. Barbara sued General Motors, claiming misdesign. Her suit was quickly dismissed. "Perhaps it would be desirable to require manufacturers to construct automobiles in which it would be safe to collide," the court of appeals declared, "but that would be a legislative function, not an aspect of the judicial interpretation of existing law." Errors in manufacture were one thing. But in 1966 the courts were not yet ready to examine product design and declare it defective.

Greenman, however, had its own inexorable logic. If General Motors can be held liable for leaving a frame strut loose accidentally, why shouldn't it be liable for leaving it out deliberately? By mid-decade the design defect barrier was beginning to crumble.

David Larsen broke through this last major conceptual wall in 1968, just two years after Barbara Evans lost her case. His 1963 Chevrolet Corvair collided head on with another car, thrusting the steering column into his head. He sued General Motors, complaining that "the design and placement of the solid steering shaft, which extends without interruption from a point 2.7 inches in front of the leading surface of the front tires to a position directly in front of the driver, exposes the driver to an unreasonable risk of injury from the rearward displacement of that shaft in the event of a left-of-center head-on collision." This time, a federal appeals court was ready to move ahead. Thereafter, the court announced, juries would be free to pin liability on defects in design as well as manufacture.

Like so many other changes in the tort rules, the step from manufacturing defects to design defects was presented as the soul of modesty. But with that simple change the courts plunged into a new and daunting enterprise. To begin with, the stakes in design defect cases are much higher. A manufacturing-defect verdict condemns only a single item coming off the assembly line. But a defect of design condemns the entire production, and a loss in one case almost inevitably implies losses in many others. Moreover, design is a much more subtle business than manufacture, and identifying deficiencies is vastly more difficult.

Before long, juries across the country were busy redesigning lawn mowers, electrical switches, glass and plastic bottles, pesticides, and consumer and industrial products of every other description. A product can be defectively designed because a safety device has been omitted (e.g., a paydozer without rearview mirrors) or because certain parts are not as strong as they might have been (e.g., a car roof is not strong enough to withstand a rollover, or the impact of a runaway horse that lands on the roof after a front-end collision). A jury can find that a single-control shower faucet is defective because if one turns it on all the way to one side, it will allow only hot water to spray, or that children's cotton sleepwear is defective because it has no flame-retardant chemicals added. Sears lost a $1.2 million judgment to a man who suffered a heart attack caused (he alleged) by a lawn mower rope that was too hard to pull. The Bolko Athletic Company paid $92,500 for defectively designing the second base on a baseball diamond; a concrete anchor, the jury concluded, was unsafe for amateur-league players. Recent cases have attempted to extend strict liability (at least for the condition rather than the design of a product) to persons who sell used goods, even ordinary citizens selling cars through the classified ads, though so far most courts have declined to take this seemingly logical step.

Drugs and pharmaceutical devices were among the last products to be swept up in design defect litigation. Until well into the 1970s, most courts accepted that potent drugs often have unavoidable side effects, and they declined to repeat the difficult balancing of risks and benefits already conducted by the FDA. But this line was crossed in the end as well. Courts began to find design defects in contraceptive pills (one brand contained more hormone than another, making it both more effective and riskier), vaccines (the live but weakened polio virus is both more effective and more dangerous than the killed virus), morning sickness drugs, and intrauterine devices.

Blaming the Product, Not the People

The courts thus slipped gently from telling people how to behave to redesigning cars, tractors, drugs, and second bases. The single-minded new search for product defects left no room for inquiry into the human element of accidents. Larsen, injured in a car manufactured by General Motors, did not have to prove that the company employees had been negligent in their work; he only had to persuade a jury that the car itself ended up defective for whatever reason. But if the car maker's negligence or good care didn't matter, why should the driver's? Symmetry seemed to suggest that it shouldn't, so the once broad defense of "contributory negligence" was abandoned too.

A driver pushed his Mercury Cougar to more than 100 miles per hour and was killed when one of its Goodyear tires exploded. The tires were designed for a maximum safe speed of 85 miles per hour, but Goodyear and Ford were held liable nonetheless; the product was defective in failing to protect against foreseeable consumer negligence of this sort. A Pennsylvania farmer ordered a skid loader but specifically asked the International Harvester Company to remove a standard protection cage around the driver's seat so that the loader could pass through his low barn doors. Harvester honored the request; the operator was later crushed in an accident that the standard-issue cage would have prevented. A court ruled the loader defective as delivered. The preferences, foolishness, or wickedness of third parties no longer counted for much either. An unknown psychopath deliberately placed cyanide in a bottle of Tylenol capsules; the subsequent suits turned only on whether the bottle was defective in failing to protect against the peril. A labor dispute inspired some arsonists to firebomb a Puerto Rico hotel, killing a hundred guests; the subsequent suits focused on the alleged defectiveness of the building's design and materials in succumbing to this kind of attack.

Where once it had inquired into the frailties of the people who manufactured, used, or abused a product, the law now focused relentlessly on the product alone. The legal inquiries began to take on the color of an inquisition, with the product as the lonely heretic. A car, contraceptive, or lawn mower was either correctly and safely designed or it was unreasonably dangerous and defective. A plaintiff no longer had to contend with the natural ebb and flow of jury sympathy between two human parties. She merely had to impugn a product. And in weighing the case against the product, the original contract between seller and buyer could not, of course, count at all.

Both Weapon and Tool

In his whimsical poem "The Objection to Being Stepped On," Robert Frost recounts how he accidentally "stepped on the toe of an unemployed hoe," whereupon the implement "rose in offense" and struck Frost a blow "in the seat of [his] sense." Yes, there was once a prophecy that weapons would one day be beaten into tools. "But what do we see? The first tool I step on / Turns into a weap-on."

There is a great insight here. The line between tools and weapons is exceedingly fine. Knives cut, irons scorch, dynamite blasts, poison kills. In the wrong hands or under the wrong foot, the tamest and most domestic object quickly becomes an instrument of assault and battery.

Wherever possible, the old tort law had left it up to each individual to distinguish between weapons and tools in her own private universe. If someone wanted to buy a fast horse, lightweight canoe, sharp knife, or strong medicine, that was her business and her risk, or, more precisely, it was a risk that she and her seller could allocate between themselves as they chose. But new tort theorists had clearly declared that it was for the courts to draw the line between tools and weapons, and to draw it without reference to anything but the implement itself.

Just how does one go about locating a defect in a complex product? Sometimes the job is easy. Defects in manufacture are immediately apparent when we compare the car without a critical bolt in the steering column to hundreds of others that came off the same assembly line with it. In effect, the mass manufacturer establishes his own standards, by which any one of his products can be gauged. Manufacturing-defect cases are straightforward. They are also comparatively rare. Far more difficult are cases in which the product is said to be defective in design, where there is no such simple point of comparison. Fully 80 percent of product liability cases today are of this kind.

The search for design defects often requires a jury to compare real with hypothetical products. What is a jury to do, for example, when a lawyer for a sick child claims that a whooping cough vaccine was defective in that it was based on a whole virus rather than a virus extract? The whole-virus vaccine is the only one sold in this country. An alternative formulation has indeed been tested in Japan, but the FDA does not approve its use here.

And how is a jury to decide whether a whole class of products—say, the intrauterine device (IUD) contraceptive—is inherently defective? The new tort system has apparently reached that conclusion, having driven from the market not only the notorious Dalkon Shield, but also its far safer substitutes, the Copper-7 and the Lippes Loop IUDs. The FDA, Planned Parenthood, and the vast majority of doctors do not endorse that sweeping verdict, but the verdict stands, nonetheless.

It is not enough to identify a safety shortcoming; the jury must also weigh the cost of remedying it. In the early 1970s, the Ford Pinto was to car crashworthiness cases what the Dalkon Shield later became to contraceptive designs. The Pinto weighed under 2,000 pounds and cost less than $2,000. Ford's own tests revealed that its gas tank was vulnerable to rear-end collisions, but the company decided not to spend an extra $10 per car to reinforce the structure—a calculation on which plaintiffs' lawyers subsequently grew very rich. But did they really deserve to? Ten dollars is not much, but full-force rear-end collisions aren't common either, and there are innumerable equally rare hazards that could also be averted for $10 or thereabouts. Protecting against every one of them would cost thousands. But people with thousands to spare don't buy a Pinto in the first place, they buy a Mercedes. What about other cars in Pinto's class? Some certainly had safer gas tanks, but that is not to say they were safer cars. A jury later fined Honda $5 million for its "reckless" act of using lighter-gauge materials than some other manufacturers in a 1971-model vehicle. (The driver of that car admitted he had bought it for its economy.) Toyota lost a $3 million judgment on similar grounds. The subtle message here may be that *all* economy cars are inherently defective for tort purposes. But millions of consumers, all major car companies, and NHTSA, the federal agency that regulates car safety, seem to view the matter quite differently.

With lawn mowers, kitchen appliances, airplanes, and safety valves, the conclusion is almost always the same: Safety is no exception to the golden rule that buyers can pay more and get more. Design is an infinitely variable and subtle process. It is always possible to strengthen an airplane wing or a column in a building; it is always possible to reduce the dosage of a drug or change the method or timing of its administration. But the follow-up questions are the difficult ones. There are questions of function: Will the plane still fly? Will it fly as fast? There are questions of cost: At what point is an incremental benefit in the car's safety no longer worth the price increase it would entail? There are questions of safety itself: Has the therapeutic drug really been improved, or has one risk just been traded off for another, possibly a more serious one?

The rule of thumb for American engineers is that the perfect device will be too late, too heavy, or too expensive. "We make do with the third best," the British said in World War II, "because the second best is always too late, and the first best never gets built." The perfectly safe vaccine, birth control pill, or airplane is also perfectly ineffectual or nonfunctional. Whether the objective is to cure disease, or alter the body's chemistry, or travel at 600 miles per hour, some trade-off between safety and functionality is always in order. Disquieting though these judgments may be, they are what real-world design is all about. In fact, they constitute the full-time business of countless design experts in both industry and government.

To give them their due, principled keepers of the new tort faith never denied any of this. To the contrary, they toiled to incorporate these realities in their new jurisprudence. The intellectual effort took the form of interminable discussion, most of it in densely footnoted law review articles, on how jury guidelines could be precisely crafted to steer the design defect inquest through court. A verbal blueprint eventually emerged. It has since become a standard in jury instructions and appellate decisions.

A jury is to consider, first, "the usefulness and desirability of the product—its utility to the user and to the public as a whole." It should then assess "the likelihood that [the product] will cause injury and the probable seriousness of the injury," considering, of course, "the user's ability to avoid danger by the exercise of care in the use of the product." Here, to be sure, the jury should take into account "the user's anticipated awareness of the dangers inherent in the product and their avoidability, because of general public knowledge of the obvious condition of the product, or of the existence of suitable warnings or instructions." Also relevant are "the availability of a substitute product which would meet the same need and not be as unsafe, [and] the manufacturer's ability to eliminate the unsafe character of the product without impairing its usefulness or making it too expensive to maintain its utility." Finally, the tireless jury must determine "the feasibility, on the part of the manufacturer, of spreading the loss by setting the price of the product or carrying liability insurance."

By 1975, this was pretty much the state of the law. Only a lawyer could love the mind-numbing profusion of words. There was, however, a nagging concern. Perhaps the torrent of verbiage conveyed the right sorts of signals, but could any jury really follow the wonderfully complex directives in any intelligent way? At the very least, trials would have to become advanced seminars in economics, engineering, pharmacology, and industrial design.

They soon did. Experts lined up in hordes, on both sides of the courtroom, to educate juries on the finer points of designing a morning sickness drug, a crashworthy car, or a safe playground swing. The old tort law refused to hear this kind of hired-gun testimony in all but the most exceptional cases. But new, relaxed federal rules of evidence were put on the books in 1975, and just in time as far as the new tort doctrines were concerned. Today one referral service in Pennsylvania maintains a nation-wide list of about 10,000 experts grouped in 4,000 categories, and reports a 15 percent annual growth in its listings. Classified ads in the back pages of legal journals offer counsel on bicycle mishaps, grain dust blasts, play-ground traumas, battery or bottle explosions, hot-air balloon calamities, radiation incidents, and accidents involving lawn mowers, toys, and beer barrels. Car crashworthiness cases now routinely inquire into the relative frequency and severity of the different sorts of accidents that can and do occur with a given model, the probable extent of the injuries, the types of precautions that might have been taken, how those precautions might have impaired overall design and performance of the car, and how they might have affected the vehicle's price and the protection it affords against other types of accident hazards.

By the late 1970s, the technical and economic questions being raised in design defect cases were triggering titanic courtroom struggles. But these struggles remained, all the while, mere parodies of the actual process of real-world design. The original design of a car, drug, or appliance takes years, as does review, when required, by a government agency like the FDA. With or without help from two camps of hired experts, a jury typically has a few days, seldom more than a few weeks.

So the courts were now wholeheartedly in the business of trying tech-nologies, not technologists. But they weren't doing it very well, for fairly obvious reasons. "The theory of the adversary system," George Bernard Shaw caustically observed, "is that if you set two liars to exposing each other, eventually the truth will come out." As the new tort jurisprudence picked up momentum, the paid experts and other hired hands multiplied the numbers far beyond two. But despite all the courtroom frenzy and expense there were few signs that much new truth was emerging.

4

Knowledge of the Law Is No Excuse

A PIPER CHEROKEE airplane took off from an airport in Eugene, Oregon, with a student at the controls and Terry Littschwager, a qualified instructor, as copilot. Douglas Wilson and Arbie MacDonald were passengers. The plane crashed in the Cascade Mountains, and everyone but Littschwager died.

Surviving spouses Donna Wilson and Beverly MacDonald sued the Piper Aircraft Corporation, claiming defective design of the plane. Its engine had failed, they argued, because ice had formed in the carburetor. A better designed engine would have used a fuel injector instead. Piper pointed out that its plane's design had been fully approved by the Federal Aviation Administration (FAA); over 80 percent of planes of similar size also used carburetors rather than fuel injectors. A jury nevertheless returned large verdicts for the plaintiffs.

The Oregon Supreme Court reviewed the case and issued a lengthy opinion. The court conceded, at the outset, "special problems in the nature, and necessary proof, of a 'defect' in a product which reaches the consumer in precisely the condition intended by the designer/manufacturer." The court also noted sympathetically Piper's objection that "a lay jury is not qualified to determine technical questions of aeronautical design." The court went further: It took the very unusual step of reexamining all the evidence that had been presented at the original trial, and concluded that the evidence was not "sufficient to permit the jury to find that the airplane was dangerously defective." But "[w]e have found no cases," the court finally ruled, "holding that compliance [with FAA regulations] is a complete defense. We hold that it is not." So it sent back the carburetor-injector debate to be weighed anew by a second jury.

Public Standards

Since the beginning of the Industrial Revolution, professional associations and government agencies have been setting safety standards that embody the expert consensus on safe designs and practices. In the early days of steam technology, for example, boilers exploded with appalling regularity, killing and maiming thousands of stokers, firemen, and bystanders. Engineering societies eventually settled on standards of proper design and operation for boiler manufacturers and users. Today these standards are well established and universally recognized. Boiler explosions are extremely rare.

Devising or endorsing such standards of good design practice was the mission of many of the regulatory agencies that proliferated in the 1960s and early 1970s. The EPA and NHTSA have joined the FDA and other similar bodies in setting thousands of safety standards for foods, drugs, cars, heart pacemakers, aircraft, pesticides, and much else. Where no government agency issues licenses or sets standards, the gap is usually filled by private, nonprofit, trade associations or insurance groups like the Underwriters Laboratories. The line between the dangerous weapon and the useful tool is thus one that experts in pharmacology, engineering, medicine, and chemistry draw all the time. They do so on the basis of years of careful work and painstaking evaluation. The process lacks the theater of the courtroom, but what it lacks in spectacle it makes up in sober, well-considered judgment.

The Founders might well have used this existing matrix of public standards as the skeleton of their new jurisprudence. The crux of their philosophy, after all, was that private judgment about the protection of life and limb should give way to public standards. The most obvious standards on hand were those prescribed by safety professionals.

As it happened, the courts had long accepted that view, at least in a negative context. By the 1870s if not earlier, the *violation* of a regulatory standard was treated as conclusive proof of negligence. One of the clearest statements of the rule was supplied early in this century. On the night of August 21, 1915, Elizabeth and William Martin had been driving their buggy west toward Tarrytown, New York, when they were hit by a car coming from the opposite direction, driven by Samuel Herzog. The collision threw the Martins to the ground and killed William. Who was at fault? A jury found Herzog to blame, even though the Martins had been traveling that evening without buggy lights, in violation of a local statute. But the court of appeals overturned the jury's decision and ruled against the Martins. "We think the unexcused omission of the statutory signals is more than some evidence of negligence," wrote Justice Benjamin Cardozo. "It *is* negligence in itself. . . . [T]o omit, willfully or heedlessly, the safeguards prescribed by law . . . is to fall short of the standard of diligence to which those who live in organized society are under a duty to conform."

The idea was sensible enough then and still is today: Safety standards are made to be obeyed. Modern courts, like their predecessors, will not permit a jury to reexamine, after a poisoning, whether it really *was* negligent for the Mammoth Drug Company to sell a drug in violation of FDA standards. It is always possible, of course, that the FDA made a mistake; perhaps its rule was overly strict, and so a menace to would-be consumers who needed a more potent prescription than the FDA allowed. But it is unlikely that an inexpert jury will often improve on the FDA's judgment. Nor will Mammoth be heard to argue that it was simply unaware of the FDA regulation. Ignorance of the law is no excuse.

Knowledge of the law, surprisingly enough, is no excuse either. The long-standing rule, still applied without apology in the courts, is that even the most complete conformity to applicable regulations is no shield against liability.

This rule, too, has a venerable ancestry. Ray Mitchell, for example, was a guest of the Hotel Berry in Athens, Ohio, on the night of October 21, 1928. Shortly after midnight that evening, a fire broke out in the building. Mitchell jumped from her window to an adjoining roof, missed the roof, and fell to the pavement below. She sued the hotel, claiming that it had not provided convenient fire exits. The trial court ruled for the hotel, on the ground that the hotel had complied fully with applicable fire exit laws. A court of appeals immediately overruled. "[A]lthough it be shown that the defendant had all the exits required," the court declared, "it is not acquitted of a charge of common-law negligence by proof of its compliance with the statutes."

The logic was uncomplicated, at least in the context of its times. Most activities were so sparsely regulated that full compliance with applicable rules meant little. That a driver was not intoxicated and had obeyed the speed limit hardly proved that he had driven prudently. Perhaps ice on the road dictated special caution; perhaps the driver had rashly stayed at the wheel all night and dozed off; perhaps he did all sorts of technically legal things that prudent drivers nevertheless do not do. In a thinly regulated world, full compliance with the law meant only that a defendant had done the minimum necessary, not that he had behaved prudently in the actual circumstances of the accident.

As regulation intensified in the 1960s and 1970s, however, the array of health- and safety-related rules began to fill up much more of the canvas. The FDA began spelling out every detail of how drugs could be composed, packaged, labeled, and prescribed. The FAA and NRC developed exhaustive standards for the operation of aircraft and nuclear power plants. Where once agencies had operated as occasional exorcists of particularly bad practices or designs, they now took on the function of gatekeeper, meticulously investigating, correcting, and approving entire classes of products before marketing was allowed.

This was wonderful news for plaintiffs, of course, and tremendously convenient for those who wanted the reach of tort law to extend rapidly. When regulations proliferate, so do occasions for violating them. And when rules were violated, the courts continued to apply the old rule of incontestable negligence quite strictly. Whether a regulatory standard had been transgressed in a manner that was wanton and momentous, or merely inadvertent and technical, a violation remained a violation and was virtually conclusive evidence of negligence.

But what did not change in the least, through all this, was the rule concerning compliance. Time and again defendants indignantly pointed out that an expert body had officially blessed the precise formulation of the drug or packaging of the pesticide that the plaintiff now sought to condemn. Time and again the courts brushed the argument aside. Knowledge of the law was still no excuse.

The law today can be simply stated: Advance regulatory approval, no matter how thorough, careful, and complete, counts for nothing definite in the subsequent lawsuit. In January the FDA may conclude that the Sabin polio vaccine is as safe as technically feasible, vital for the public health, and to be used in preference to the Salk vaccine, which is less effective (says the FDA) in conferring mass immunity. In February a jury of twelve stout citizens may conclude that the Sabin vaccine is dangerously defective, that the Salk vaccine is to be preferred, and the jury may carry *that* conclusion through to a multimillion-dollar verdict, including perhaps punitive damages. Standards written by regulatory agencies, industry associations, insurance laboratories, or even Congress itself are given polite but only nominal attention. Juries, and juries alone, are the final arbiters of defective design. It is as simple as that.

If there was ever any doubt about this as the age of ubiquitous government regulation took hold, the courts quickly laid it to rest. A plaintiff under forty years of age lost his sight to glaucoma. At the time ophthalmologists generally agreed that routine glaucoma tests were inappropriate for younger patients. But the plaintiff prevailed on the theory that the doctor should have administered the test anyway. The Dayton-Hudson Corporation paid $1 million in punitive damages to a young girl who was burned after her cotton flannelette pajamas caught fire. The pajamas complied fully with the federal Flammable Fabrics Act, but the victim's lawyer persuaded the jury that the government test was not reliable and that Dayton-Hudson knew it. A lawsuit brought by Karen Silkwood's family against the Kerr-McGee Corporation established that a reprocessor of nuclear materials could be held liable to its employees despite essentially complete compliance with all federal safety regulations. The manufacturer of a birth control pill paid $2.75 million in punitive damages for an allegedly defective chemical formulation, despite complete compliance with all applicable FDA regulations. And as we saw at the beginning of this chapter, the Piper Aircraft Corporation learned the expensive way who (as between the FAA and the jury) has the last word on fuel systems in aircraft engines.

Why doesn't complete compliance with regulatory prescription count for more? The usual explanation is that safety regulation is intended only to set a floor—a minimum standard, necessary but not sufficient. Regulation may address only particular aspects of conduct, manufacture, or design. The regulators may never have contemplated the specific type of hazard that the plaintiff faced. What if they clearly did contemplate that hazard and nevertheless judged it to be regrettable but unavoidable? No matter. Agencies are themselves not to be trusted: They may have tailored their regulations to suit producers rather than consumers. Industry standards deserve even less deference, having been written by unscrupulous captains of industry, the very sorts of people whose handiwork is on trial.

This was a fateful line of reasoning. In discarding the old private law of contract, the courts had committed themselves to take on a myriad of new cases, to be decided, somehow or other, without reference to the standards agreed to privately by the parties themselves. Public standards of some sort were the only alternative. But the people who dreamed up this new occupation for the courts didn't know the first thing about designing a car, a contraceptive, or an airplane engine. Neither did the jurors who were supposed to do the real work of resolving cases. There was, to say the least, great potential for confusion and embarrassment here. Confusion and embarrassment materialized quickly enough.

Condemning the Dalkon Shield was all very well; that particular IUD unquestionably was inferior. But it was then all too easy to condemn IUDs in general, which courts and juries promptly did, in the face of an overwhelming expert consensus that for some women good IUDs are the best contraceptive option around. Or was the real liability message that contraceptives of *any* description are defective? There soon followed multi-million-dollar judgments against birth control pills (which occasionally cause kidney failure or strokes) and against the spermicides used with condoms and diaphragms (blamed for birth defects). In all of these cases, the products reached the end user in precisely the condition the manufacturer and the FDA intended; the residual risks (if they existed at all outside the juries' minds) were unavoidable and worth accepting, or so the experts had concluded. The Ford Pinto obviously had its problems. But so did all other compact cars, which are more compact and inexpensive than others for precisely the same reasons that they are less safe. Here and there, juries began to stamp as defective products like vaccines and therapeutic drugs that, though risky in some degree, were clearly vital to the public health.

The inventors of the new tort, of all people, should have been the least surprised by the mounting randomness and incoherence of jury outcomes. A central tenet of their faith was that the consumer is unqualified to make intelligent choices about safety for himself. That, after all, was why disclaimers of liability were no longer enforced, why contract had been buried deep in the earth with the stake of tort driven through its heart. Private choice, in short, was to be replaced by public prescription. Whose public prescription? Not that of the pharmacologists at the FDA, or toxicologists at the EPA, or mechanical engineers at the FAA, but of the juror, pulled off the voter lists at random, solemnly sworn to his duty, and instantly educated in a contest of courtroom experts—solemnly sworn too, of course, and paid by the hour for their particular form of swearing. The member of the public judged incompetent to make wise choices in the marketplace for himself was now being called upon to make wise choices in the jury box for others. It was a theory of the idiot/genius, incapable of dealing with the objects that lay within his own experience, but infinitely capable of errorless flash judgment when it came to the experience of others.

Warnings Rediscovered

The uneasy perception arose that the new tort system was in wild disarray. Truth be told, the average juror looked at a design defect case about as hopefully as an innocent civilian might look at a crowd of troops whom he was required at five minutes' notice to maneuver and review. What the new liability courts really needed was a way of getting back to the simplicity of the old contract rules without returning to the old contract results. It was time, in short, to dust off contract principles and bring them back into the courtroom under new management.

The solution that gradually took shape was ingenious if short-lived. The courts began to sidestep the grueling process of finding defects in the product itself, its manufacture, or design. They now looked, instead, for defects in the way in which the product had been sold. Tort suits began to center on warnings.

Courts have long been interested in the information that is traded along with a product or service. The old rules generally allowed buyer and seller to work out warnings for themselves. Deliberate fraud or concealment of important information was certainly forbidden. But everything else, including simple silence on important points of safety, was allowed. A promise of safety usually had to be offered or sought out as part of the deal, like the gift wrapping at a department store.

When such promises were made, as we have seen, they were enforced. In 1896, for example, the Apperson family bought a folding bed, which stood upright against the wall during the day and could be lowered at night. The seller expressly assured them that they could raise or lower the bed "with perfect safety." But one night, as Mrs. Apperson lowered the bed, it crashed down and broke her arm. She sued, and she won. The seller had given an express promise of safety. Accepted principles of contract took care of the rest.

But silence on the question of safety was equally permissible, and it cut quite the other way. A Mrs. Robbins was injured by a fat-reducing vibrating machine manufactured by the Georgia Power Company. She had recently undergone surgery but used the belt several times, at its highest speed, and suffered a displaced kidney. Georgia Power had not warned of any risk. No matter, the Georgia court of appeals ruled in 1933. "A person having the machine for sale violates no duty to the person to whom it is delivered to be used for the purpose intended, in failing to warn him as to any danger in the use of the machine."

Silence on matters of safety thus generally worked against the victim of any subsequent accident. The rule was not intrinsically unreasonable, but there was much to be said against it as well. In a regular course of fair dealing, a seller like Georgia Power routinely *does* pass on important safety information. It is every bit as fair, and perhaps much simpler, to make *that* the operating presumption, unless perhaps Georgia Power alerts Robbins otherwise at the outset. Even as Mrs. Robbins's suit was being decided against her, many other courts were moving ahead along just these lines. Food and drug cases were the first to switch, as we have seen. By the 1950s, most courts were demanding a proper warning of known risks, and scrutinizing its display, syntax, and emphasis. A seller's warnings had to be "complete, conspicuous and unambiguous"; instruction manuals had to be carefully written, and had to warn against tampering and improper repair.

All of which coexisted quite comfortably with the most traditional notions of contract. Responsibility still turned on agreement and consent; the courts were simply sharpening the requirement that to be effective, consent must be informed, or at least consciously uninformed. Georgia Power was still free to sell a dangerous vibrator so long as it flagged the risk to Robbins, or at least alerted her to the fact that no promise of safety was being made. Robbins could then take the vibrator, risks and all, or walk away.

Ironically enough, warnings fell into some disrepute as the liability revolution gained momentum in the early 1960s. Warnings are just shades away from disclaimers of liability, part of the written or verbal give-and-take that surrounds the actual transaction. Warnings, in short, are an integral part of contract. And contract was anathema to the Founders. Early crusaders like the lawyers representing Chester Vandermark and Claus Henningsen were fighting fierce battles to nullify disclaimers and all they implied. Small wonder, then, that the law of warning was not hugely popular among Founders at the time.

But a short decade later, the mood had shifted considerably. The new rules of strict liability were now firmly in place, but theory was not working out as originally planned. Practitioners of the new tort desperately needed a pliable new rationale for liability, one that would achieve desired results without recourse to unworkably complicated trials, one that could establish liability without stigmatizing useful products as defective, and one flexible enough to take into account the particular circumstances of particular users. A new theory of warning, it now appeared, might fit the bill.

It was assembled quickly enough. A product's design, the new logic ran, includes not only the product itself but also its labeling and packaging. The best possible contraceptive, car, or toaster may still be defective (in the eyes of the law) if the seller fails to warn of residual hazards, even though there is nothing wrong with the device itself. A court can then engage strict liability rules without actually impugning the product, or even considering its composition, manufacture, or design. To be sure, the manufacturer of this admirable product must pay a multimillion-dollar verdict this time around, for lack of adequate warning. But next time (no doubt) the warning will have been perfected and all will be well.

It was an elegant stroke. No longer did a jury have to condemn a product or service that clearly seemed desirable, or solemnly elevate its own engineering or medical judgment above that of the professional engineer, doctor, or federal agency that approved the aircraft, car, pesticide, or drug. If the consumer's simple lack of information was what made a product defective, better warnings could easily remedy the problem. The idea promised a new simplicity as well. Juries were once again being asked to do what juries could obviously do well—to put themselves in the shoes of the ordinary consumer, and ponder what she knew and when she knew it. Unlike product designs, warnings are indisputably *supposed* to be understandable by a member of the general public.

For one brief, shining moment, it appeared that the new tort advocates could have it both ways. Sympathetic plaintiffs would be allowed to win, yet good products would not be falsely condemned as inherently bad. And trials would become far simpler to boot. It seemed too good to be true. It was.

The How-You-Pronounce-It Law of Warning

Things started out smoothly enough. For plaintiffs, the new emphasis on warnings was immensely convenient. Come to court with someone who has been badly injured—by the lawn mower that cut off the foot, the doctor who performed the heart surgery, the vaccine administered two days before the baby went into convulsions. Declare that no adequate warning of this particular hazard was provided in advance. And what is "adequate"? That part is easy: Any warning that did not actually prevent the accident in question couldn't possibly have been enough. After all, no one who truly understood what lay in store would ever have bought the mower, the surgery, or the vaccine in the first place. Then total the bill. Plaintiffs did not always win this way—not by any means. But they won often enough, and from the lawyers' perspective bringing such claims to court was ridiculously easy.

Typical of this legal genre was a 1979 ruling involving Eli Trujillo, a service station worker. Trujillo tried to mount a Uniroyal tire on what he thought was a sixteen-inch-rim wheel. The wheel was in fact sixteen and a half inches. Trujillo couldn't get the tire mounted correctly, so he took it off, relubricated it, and tried again, this time inflating the tire to 48 pounds, well above design pressure. The tire exploded and Trujillo was seriously hurt. He sued, claiming that Uniroyal had failed to warn of the risk of overinflating the tire on the wrong-size rim. A New Mexico appellate court agreed. Trujillo had indeed made a mistake, but with better warning he might have exercised greater caution. The tire was defective as packaged.

Providers of things medical became especially popular and frequent targets of such suits. Most jurors intuitively understand that potent medicines and complicated surgical procedures cannot be totally risk-free. But a different (and therefore arguably better) warning is always possible. Warnings offered similar openings against countless solvents, cleansers, pesticides, and household chemicals. Many are often unavoidably toxic; indeed, toxicity is often what makes such products perform their intended functions. But warnings, once again, can always be written differently, and who is to say that the tragic accident at hand might not then have been avoided?

Almost immediately the courts concluded that inadequate warning, like defective design, need not be defeated by the victim's own foolishness or culpability. A warning was either good enough or it wasn't, and the large social objectives of deterrence and compensation dictated that this inquiry be sweepingly broad, not stifled by the particular circumstances of particular cases. Moreover, producers were expected to tend to the weak and straying lambs in their customer flock, not just those full of strength and vigor. A teenager poured highly flammable cologne over a lighted candle "to make the room smell better"; the cologne manufacturer paid for failing to warn of the scent's flammability. An eager swimmer dove headfirst into a four-foot-deep, aboveground pool; the manufacturer paid for the "inadequate warning" posted on a small sign on the edge of the pool. A mother filled her baby's mouth with peanut butter and the infant choked on the thick spread; a case for the jury on inadequate warning yet again. For its alleged failure to give adequate warning against use of a playground slide by small children, the City of Chicago paid $1.5 million to a two-year-old child. A California champagne drinker collected from Almaden Vineyards for its failure to warn that champagne corks can become high-speed missiles. A telescope manufacturer paid for inadequate warning on the need to use the telescope's "sun filter" attachment. A prankster successfully sued the owner of a building when injured in the course of a burglary by an unwarned-of hazard (a painted skylight) on the roof.

Of course the defendant's careful compliance with government-prescribed labels was not going to count for much either. Richard Ferebee was a worker at the federal agriculture research center in Beltsville, Maryland. He contracted pulmonary fibrosis, a serious lung disease, as a result of long-term exposure to dilute solutions of paraquat, a herbicide manufactured by Chevron. The EPA had spelled out the exact terms of the warning label to be used, and Chevron had followed the EPA prescription to the letter. In large bold letters, the warning stated: "DANGER. CAN KILL IF SWALLOWED. HARMFUL TO THE EYES AND SKIN." It went on to direct that any skin exposed to the chemical should be washed immediately and contaminated clothing removed. "Prolonged contact," the label concluded, would cause "severe irritation."

Not enough warning, a jury, and then a federal court of appeals, decided. The label inexcusably failed to mention "the specter of long-term lung disease culminating, perhaps, in death." It was conceded that Chevron had no legal right to add to or depart from the EPA-prescribed warning in even the slightest detail, but that was of no consequence. Chevron could get along either by petitioning the EPA for a change in the warning or by "continuing to use the EPA-approved label and by simultaneously paying damages to successful tort plaintiffs."

Logic of this sort offered enormous new litigation possibilities. It is far easier to find something wrong with words than with products. Few who are not experts in the field will confidently declare that the Sabin polio vaccine itself was defective, especially in the face of a contrary judgment by medical experts. But any fool can stand up and announce that the warning supplied was not quite right, and who is to say otherwise? The French, as *Pygmalion*'s Henry Higgins points out, don't really care what they say, so long as they pronounce it correctly. The courts were just taking a leaf from the same tradition.

So what soon developed was a legal process of death by painful semantic scrutiny. Warnings were parsed and dissected until they expired on the table. The ensuing autopsy took many different forms, but the conclusion all too often was that the verbal corpse had been diseased. In Ferebee's case, the warning failed to refer specifically enough to the risks of long-term exposure to the lungs. A court ruled against a helmet manufacturer for failing to warn precisely and specifically that the helmet would not protect against a blood clot from a violent head-to-head crash. The manufacturer of a birth control pill warned of possibly fatal side effects but was held liable for failing to itemize stroke as a sometimes nonfatal risk. The manufacturer of the Kut-Koat furniture stripper warned that the solvent was flammable but inexcusably failed to spell out that its *vapors* were flammable too.

A string of vaccine cases brought the how-you-pronounce-it theories to their fullest flower. When the national swine flu vaccination program was initiated in 1976, the federal government took enormous pains to warn every one of the 40 million adults who were vaccinated of the possible risks. The warning form noted a risk of "severe or potentially fatal reactions." It invited questions. It spelled out everything the government actually knew about the vaccine's risks at the time; indeed, it implied a notably *greater* risk than was then known. Robert Petty, like other recipients of the vaccine, signed a consent form stating that he had read the warning and understood "the benefits and risks of flu vaccination." A week after his vaccination, Petty experienced aching, numbness, and tingling in his muscles and joints. An initial diagnosis of congestive heart failure was later corrected to "serum sickness." Petty recovered, and promptly sued the federal government, claiming that he had not been adequately warned of the risks. A jury awarded $213,000 in damages.

A court of appeals approved. "[T]he generality of the warning," it wrote, "was insufficient to encompass the specific risk of serum sickness. To be sure, there is a logical symmetry to the argument that acceptance of the risk of death implies acceptance of the risk of something less extreme. . . . [Nonetheless,] the generality of the warning, especially in the context of the government's unprecedented promotional campaign, was insufficient to have enabled Petty to give an informed consent to receiving the vaccine. . . . The risk of death may be conceptually remote, whereas a more specific warning detailing the known risk of serum sickness and its symptoms would alert recipients more concretely. . . . [T]he vagueness of the generic warning is not mitigated by the invitation to ask questions."

When courts could not find reason to quarrel with the exact phrasing of a warning, they condemned the manner of its dissemination instead. In May 1970, slightly more than two weeks after she had received a dose of Wyeth Laboratories' oral polio vaccine, eight-month-old Anita Reyes contracted paralytic polio. She was completely paralyzed from the waist down, her left arm atrophied, and she lost control of bladder and bowel. Wyeth claimed—probably correctly, though the jury found otherwise—that Anita's polio was caused by a wild strain of the virus. But everyone agreed, in any event, that Wyeth's vaccine was uncontaminated and furnished exactly as intended. So if the little girl was to be paid, it seemed that it had to be on the basis of improper warning.

The vaccine, unfortunately for Anita, came with a package circular that fully warned health officials of the risks inherent in the polio vaccine. Before her daughter's vaccination, Anita's mother signed a disclaimer, releasing the State of Texas, which had administered the vaccine, from all liability. But the form she signed did not repeat the warning Wyeth had supplied to the state health officials. Here, then, was the opening; the rest was obvious. Anita's father sued Wyeth and won $200,000. Wyeth had given a fully adequate warning, but to the wrong person. The court accepted that as a "general proposition" a manufacturer of prescription drugs is required to warn only the prescribing physician. But here the vaccine had not been dispensed with "individualized medical balancing of the risks." Wyeth was therefore required to convey the warning to the actual recipient of the vaccine, and it had failed to do so.

You-warned-the-wrong-person logic created another large breach in the fortifications of the defense. The Massachusetts Supreme Court applied it to birth control pills, where the warning went to the prescribing doctor but not directly to the patient. The Ferebee paraquat case used the same notion, but in reverse. The court conceded that Ferebee himself had entirely ignored the warning that was given and would have ignored any other warning too. But his supervisor might perhaps have read and heeded a different warning, and *that* was enough. The manufacturer of a dump truck's hydraulic lift included appropriate warning in the instruction manual, but was held liable for failing to place the same warning on the truck itself to reach those who might not read the manual. A manufacturer of radial tires warned in both its manuals and its advertising against mixing radials and nonradials on the same vehicle, but nevertheless paid $500,000 for failing to stamp the warning on the tires as well, to alert buyers of secondhand cars.

As warning law expanded, lawyers stumbled on a happy solution to a problem that had vexed them for some time. Must manufacturers of food processors, cars, vibrators, or peanut butter really warn against every conceivable use, abuse, and misuse of their product? Bizarre accidents can happen with almost any product or service, and—as defendants cogently and repeatedly argued—it is impossible to warn in detail about every imaginable misadventure. Now the new tort theoreticians thought they had arrived at a simple answer. Warnings would be required for all "reasonably foreseeable" risks. This turned out to be a wonderfully circular test. Foreseeing the future depends largely on remembering the past. This means that an accident involving bizarre behavior *becomes* foreseeable as soon as it has happened. Is it really foreseeable that a teenager might pour cologne over a lighted candle to make the room smell better? It certainly is once it's been done, and the case does not come to court until it has. "Do you believe in baptism?" a rustic was once asked. "Believe?" he replied with some surprise. "Why, I've seen it done." The foreseeability test quickly came to depend on faith of a very similar kind.

The Ghost of Contracts Past

The courts were getting excellent mileage out of the new warning theories, but they were losing ground on important matters of principle. The very definition of a product defect was subtly changing, and slowly being consumed by its verbal child. A product was now considered defectively dangerous if its risks were "beyond that which would be contemplated by the ordinary consumer." And warnings were what shaped the consumer's contemplation. The new consumer-contemplation test echoed earlier theories of consent and assumption of risk. Product defects, it seemed, now depended once again on what the consumer understood, wanted, expected, or agreed to. Thirty years earlier, when language was plainer, these matters had been bluntly called questions of contract.

A first problem for new tort litigators was the ghost of their Christmases past. Only a few years earlier, they had killed off contract by insisting that it can't possibly make any difference, since no one reads all the paper anyway. It was now the defendants' turn to dust off the old lessons and carry them back into court.

The mother of the polio-afflicted Anita Reyes, for example, had a seventh-grade education and spoke mainly Spanish. At trial she was asked about a card she had signed at the clinic.

Q. And did you read that [card] before you signed it?
A. No, I didn't read it. I just signed it.
Q. Have you taken Anita back for further immunization since?
A. Yes.
Q. What has she been immunized for or vaccinated for since May 8, 1970?
A. I don't know. They just put it on there.
Q. You just take her and they do it?
A. Yeah. They are the ones that know what they are going to put next.

Explaining away this kind of record on the way to approving $200,000 for failing to warn Mrs. Reyes herself (as distinct from clinic officials who *had* been fully warned) required some undignified judicial contortions. It was all too clear that Mrs. Reyes was not directly warnable. She did not even testify at trial about what she would have done, had proper warnings been provided. That, however, was unnecessary, the court of appeals lamely declared, as the testimony "would have been both speculative and self-serving." In the end, the court simply announced a "rebuttable presumption" that people in Mrs. Reyes' position "would have read an adequate warning." The court reached its intended destination all right, but appeared ridiculous in getting there.

The larger problem was dismally familiar. If consumer contemplation was to be the new touchstone for liability, and warnings were touted as the key to what the consumer contemplates, then manufacturers were going to provide them in abundance. By making warnings the new center of their attention, the courts were exposing themselves, once again, to a paper war that the wrong side was bound to win in the end. Lawyers and judges could fight back for a while with the how-you-pronounce-it or who-you-warn gamesmanship. But each time a court condemned a warning, or its manner of delivery, the lesson was assimilated. Defendants lost cases, but they quickly won experience.

Warnings became progressively more elaborate. If a warning stamped on the product was not enough, a separate written warning would be provided, or vice versa. If a signature on a liability release form that described the hazards of the operation would not suffice, a videotape of patient and doctor carefully discussing and agreeing on the procedure and its attendant risks might. Sooner or later, warnings would crystallize in a form and phrasing that could not be wished away by the courts. What lay ahead was nothing less than a humiliating retreat to the old contract-based notions of liability. The warning had served new tort objectives well when it was missing or inadequate. Its presence, however, proved enormously inconvenient.

By the cruelest of ironies, the courts were finally forced to face up to the problem in dealing with the most dangerous of all known consumer products, the cigarette. Having come down hard on countless vaccines, therapeutic drugs, small planes, contraceptives, and small cars, the courts finally drew the line at condemning tobacco. One court after the next declared that the smoker who had puffed away in the face of all warnings for thirty years would not later be allowed to sue for his cancer.

The cigarette cases were exceptional in this regard, and even here, it began to appear by the late 1980s that plaintiffs were going to break through sooner or later. But across the board, new tort proponents were being slowly squeezed in a vise of their own creation, crushed by their own contradictory assumptions about the consumer. Is the consumer ignorant, helpless, and incapable of making choices for himself, as the Founders argued on their way to discarding contract law in the first place? Or is he alert, cautious, and quick to assimilate and heed information given, as they contended when the warning law was being written? By this point he was both. Once again, the new tort theorists had come to view the consumer as a sort of idiot genius of a most peculiar kind, now incapable of reading the manufacturer's disclaimers and warnings when they were given, but absolutely fluent and competent with them when they were not.

The ghost of contract had thus returned in its full spectral horror. For centuries, contract had been applied to deny recovery when there was no promise of safety. When implied warranties were discovered in the early 1960s to create new safety obligations, manufacturers parried with express disclaimers. Now, when new tort advocates attempted to pin liability on shortcomings in warnings, manufacturers responded by offering warnings in abundance. For the third time in as many decades, new tort objectives ran head-on into the compelling logic that informed consumers could make their own safety choices and should then be required to stand by them.

5

The New Town Meeting

IN THE COURSE of the Vietnam War, U.S. forces sprayed millions of tons of Agent Orange to destroy enemy cover. The herbicide contained minute traces of dioxin, a potent poison. In the years after the war, veterans and their families searched for an explanation of the various physiological and psychological ailments that plagued them. They eventually fixed on Agent Orange as the culprit. On January 8, 1979, they sued seven chemical companies and the U.S. government.

Federal Judge Jack Weinstein consolidated more than 600 separate suits into one of the largest class actions ever formed in the history of personal injury litigation. He accredited a committee of plaintiffs' lawyers to represent 2.4 million people, a population the size of Arkansas, comprising U.S. veterans, their wives, their children born and unborn, Australian and New Zealander veterans, and a few civilians. On May 7, 1984, only hours before the trial was to begin—and nine years to the day after a helicopter evacuated the last American troops from Saigon—the vets settled their claims against seven chemical company defendants for $180 million.

The Old Law of Nuisance

The old law dealt with most pollution under the heading of *nuisance*. Nuisances included smoke, vibration, the noise of a howling dog, and the fouling of water by cattle. In the seventeenth century this kind of environmental tort was labeled *annoyance*, a term that accurately conveyed the kinds of injury at issue.

The courts of the day viewed these complaints very skeptically. Nuisances, by their nature, are wide and thin. They affect whole neighborhoods, so that inviting one litigant into court invites a crowd, though no individual plaintiff suffers more than a trifling injury. Nuisance is also, often enough, a subjective matter. One man's noise is another's music, one woman's source of soot and smoke is another's cheery fireplace or barbecue, one's asthma aggravators another's picturesque meadow, one's ruined landscape another's industry and livelihood. Without some sort of legal charter permitting a modest measure of routine public inconvenience or hazard in the pursuit of ordinary business, those who specialize in doing will be perpetually at the mercy of those who specialize in objecting. Judges were not the least bit eager to adjudicate an endless series of these parochial disputes over minor inconveniences. They insisted that a nuisance had to be serious if it was to be considered in court at all. *De minimis non curat lex* was the rule—"the law does not concern itself with trifles."

Nuisance litigation was discouraged by procedural obstacles as well. A single neighbor vexed by Smith's smoky factory would generally find a lawsuit not worth the time. A group of similarly affected neighbors might have consolidated their claims into a single action and paid one industrious soul among them to pursue the case, as they might jointly have paid a mosquito sprayer to abate another kind of common nuisance. But the old law firmly rejected consolidations and proxy actions of this kind.

The law did, however, act with vigor against risks that threatened serious harm to individual victims. The main body of law here dates to an 1868 English decision. Fletcher owned a mill in Lancashire and built a reservoir on his land. The water broke through into an abandoned mine shaft and flooded along the connecting passages into Rylands's adjoining mine. Fletcher was free of all personal blame, but the Law Lords, the body of peers that serves as the highest court in Great Britain, nonetheless held him liable. "[T]he person who for his own purposes brings on his land and collects and keeps there anything likely to do mischief if it escapes, must keep it at his peril, and [is] answerable for all the damage which is the natural consequence of its escape." The ruling was carefully limited to "nonnatural" uses of land—in this instance, building a water reservoir in coal mining country. But the words "at his peril" were pregnant with meaning. They implied a very strict standard of liability.

U.S. courts gradually adapted the *Rylands* rule to an array of cases fitting the original mold, against landowners who accumulated water in an unnatural reservoir, used dynamite, stored flammable liquids in quantity, or kept dangerous wild animals, at least when they did such things in a populated area unsuited to such activities. Low-level nuisances might well be an inevitable part of the human condition. But *ultrahazardous activities,* as they came to be called, were a huge escalation in the nuisance weaponry, like a switchblade on the playground. The cozy, customary standard that brushed aside low-level nuisances as too trivial and widespread to bother with emphatically did not apply. Perhaps there is no way to ban such activities entirely or (what is much the same thing) require the consent of each potential victim beforehand. Some ultrahazardous activities surely are socially desirable, as when a dangerously decrepit building is the blasting target. But we can at least keep the level of violence down to the absolute minimum by making the blaster pay for any damage, whether or not he has been negligent.

The cases that fell under the *Rylands* aegis had simple links between cause and effect: There is nothing subtle or uncertain about the effects of a dynamite blast, or a flood from a burst reservoir, or an attack by a wild animal escaped from its pen. The accident itself was well defined in space, the few plaintiffs involved were seriously affected, and the suit that resulted was correspondingly narrow and self-contained.

Rylands operated as an important check on certain abnormally risky activities. But most activities, by definition, are *not* abnormal for their time and place, just as most human conduct is, by the very definition of the word, not negligent. Nuisance law, like negligence law, thus kept most of the world out of court most of the time. Contract law defined the inner limits of the tort law—the universe of privately consensual activities too discrete, personal, and insular to be reached by the law of torts. A less explicit but equally compelling notion of the social contract defined the outer bounds—the universe of essentially public risks too broad-ranging, diffuse, and multifaceted to be managed in the courts. This conformed to the time-honored view that courts are best at rescuing individuals from wrongs done to them, while legislators are best at striking a balance between contending social benefits and burdens.

In this area, as in so many others, the old law was pragmatic rather than doctrinaire in defining where private freedom of action must give way to the public right. It was not that acute hazards were bad and diffuse hazards were good; if society as a whole wanted to close down or relocate a smokestack or a town dump, the elected arms of government were free to do so. But the courtroom was not a gladiatorial arena for titanic clashes between broad sectors of society. It was a more intimate tribunal, interesting itself in cases where some individual had been placed in abnormal jeopardy against his will.

The Socialized Offense

An altogether different scientific, social, and then legal culture evolved in the 1960s. The rise of the environmental movement brought to prominence new concerns about the dangers of industrialization. In 1962 Rachel Carson described how the overuse of pesticides could have devastating environmental consequences, and with that one shocking book, American culture was irreversibly changed. Of all the alarms sounded by the environmentalists, one had by far the most profound impact on the law: concern about the possible health effects of diffuse but toxic chemical exposure.

There was a genuine kernel of scientific truth in the new public fears. We know today that many once mysterious diseases can be linked to microscopic assaults on the body. In the late 1950s and early 1960s, epidemiologists established the first solid links of cancer to smoking, drinking, and certain workplace chemicals. Bruce Ames, a brilliant microbiologist at Berkeley, then developed a fast and simple way to test the chromosome-damaging potential of various toxins on bacterial cultures. The Ames test, soon used everywhere, suggested that a great many other alarmingly common chemicals in food, air, water, cosmetics, and pharmaceutical products might also cause disease.

Scientists, led by Ames himself, got over the initial fright quickly enough. They came to realize that the carcinogenic potency of different chemicals varies widely, and that the risks from measurable but still unimaginably small traces of industrial poisons are tiny in comparison to many other hazards that assail us. But the public was not about to forget the frightening lessons so recently learned, especially while some reputable scientists continued to assert that even a single hit of molecular-level damage might trigger serious disease. It remained all too easy to multiply the near-zero risk by the near-infinite breadth of exposure to arrive at terrifying though wholly imaginary body counts.

Most important, from the legal perspective, was that the new research insights blurred the old intuitive lines between seemingly minor annoyances and obviously grave risks. Scientists, reputable or otherwise, could now somberly discuss a cascade of possibles—if few probables—by which the trivial might be transformed into the tragic. A diffuse, low-level toxin in the air could now be analogized to a dangerous wild animal escaped from its enclosure or the directly harmful shock from a blasting operation. Indeed, in the press the accepted metaphor for chemical hazards came to be the "toxic time bomb," an image that suggested violent if unpredictable danger. The moment had come for personal injury law, in its restless and unending expansion, to invade the formerly sleepy kingdom of nuisance law.

An irony at the outset was that some of the theoreticians' favorite arguments, so carefully and lovingly developed for products, now suddenly cut the wrong way. When their attention had been on defective products, the Founders had extolled the value of spreading costs thinly, over large numbers, rather than letting them fall on a few. But industrial pollution does just that too, spreading small harm widely while providing what is often a much-needed benefit to a few. The Founders had earlier embraced the most utilitarian of cost-benefit and risk-utility reckonings. But these were precisely the tools the *old* law had invoked in refusing to address widely dispersed, low-level injuries: better for 10,000 people to suffer the minor harms of stinging eyes and sooty windowsills than for 200 workers to suffer the major harm of unemployment. In reforming the law of product liability, the Founders had earlier brushed aside matters of consent: If a product did more harm than good, individual consent was irrelevant. But consent, or more particularly its absence, suddenly seemed all-important when the discussion shifted to the victim of pollution.

So the Founders and their successors now quietly shelved their old arguments and wheeled out some new ones. Their emphasis now became libertarian and individualistic. It is immoral for one person to impose unconsented-to burdens on another. The operator of a polluting power plant or factory does violence to the individual's private space and personal autonomy. Though social benefits as well as costs might be at stake, they should not sway a court: Even if aggression is economically productive, it is still morally wrong, unjust, and contrary to natural law and right, and the perpetrator should be made to pay.

On the strength of such logic, an entirely new environmental jurisprudence was quickly invented. The first of the old limits to disappear was the once strict requirement that the court give careful, skeptical scrutiny to the seriousness of a nuisance. Even a hazard as diffuse as a tall smokestack, science now taught, might be worse than serious for the unfortunate victim whose fleeting exposure one day happened to trigger lung cancer. True, we might have no idea who, if anyone, would actually be injured. But that just meant that everyone in sight was a potential victim and deserved a day in court. The new principle that began to emerge was that chemical manufacturing, waste disposal, nuclear power, and the transport of all hazardous materials are ultrahazardous plain and simple, no matter where the operations are located or what precautions may be taken. In the spirit of *Rylands,* liability for any harms to bystanders should be absolute. The only contestable issues would be whether the injury had been caused at all.

And with that, the second stage of the new tort revolution was underway. The demise of the old threshold of harm, itself rather like a bursting reservoir, flooded the legal landscape with the waters once placidly confined within the narrow *Rylands* enclosure. The courts had first taken the limited legal theories of the past, meant to apply to front-yard sorts of environmental mischief, and stretched them to cover the inner space of intimate contractual relations; now they extended them to the outer space of the public square, with its myriad low-level mass contacts. *Public risks* and *environmental torts,* once all but excluded from the tort system, quickly became the vibrant hub of a whole new field of litigation.

The whole world may be seen in a speck of soil or a drop of water. A breath of air or a glass of water contains a billion trillion molecules, among which is a diffuse collection of chemical flotsam certain to include at least a few hundred molecules of every mass-produced synthetic chemical, from every human source on earth. Diffusion and dispersion guarantee that every activity flows and mixes with every other. No matter how strict our religious observance or civic hygiene, we are all bombarded on a molecular level with bits of pig, dog, and rodent, as well as biological matter even more vile. Each campfire or radium-painted watch dial, each filling station pump or can of turpentine, sends out chemical ripples that spread and reverberate indefinitely, touching an ever-increasing number of people ever more softly. The environment knows no bounds.

Which meant that the environmental lawsuit could not know any bounds either. The modern history of *toxic-tort* litigation has thus been the record of an ever-widening circle.

The first-generation cases were product liability suits. Most involved therapeutic drugs, which are potent by design, deliberately administered, and hardly ever free of side effects of some sort. Thalidomide, diethylstilbestrol (DES), and high-dose X-ray therapy were among the earlier targets. The key variables of a lawsuit—exposure, toxicity, and actual injury— were comparatively easy to ascertain.

The second-generation toxic-tort cases arose in the workplace. Occupational exposures are often high, last for many years, and affect a fairly well-defined population. In moving from drugs to the workplace, the toxic-tort clientele grew dramatically. Few people are exposed to potent therapeutic drugs, and exposure is, of course, contained by the boundaries of the human body. Nearly everyone works, and the workplace is a much larger space. In August 1982, when it filed for bankruptcy, the Manville Corporation faced 16,000 personal injury claims and its total liability was estimated at over $2 billion. Asbestos cases began to level off in the late 1980s, but other occupational suits are now on the rise. Millions of employees are at some risk from dust (which affects textile workers, grain handlers, and construction workers), radiation (airline pilots, X-ray technicians, uranium miners), toxic chemicals (factory workers, carpenters, building cleaners, artists, and many others), pesticides (farm workers), and even secondhand smoke (office workers, nightclub singers, bridge tournament organizers).

The third-generation environmental litigation that began to unfold in the early 1980s overflowed even these capacious limits. The substances at issue were familiar enough—asbestos, dioxin, radiation—but they were now spread over huge territories: school buildings (asbestos insulation), towns (dioxin in road spraying), even entire states or multistate regions (fallout from nuclear tests). Exposure levels were thousands of times lower, and the populations exposed were concomitantly larger and less well-defined. The toxic tort once bounded by the human body or the factory walls now encompassed rivers, municipal water supplies, lakes, outdoor air, and entire communities, cities, and watersheds.

The first large toxic-tort case thrust onto the nation's attention arose from the Hooker Chemical Company's ancient waste dump at Love Canal, New York. In 1978, nearby residents were alerted to alarming concentrations of chemicals in the soil and groundwater. President Carter declared a state of emergency and ordered the relocation of 710 families. In 1985, more than 1,300 current and former residents of the area settled with Hooker for $20 million. Love Canal became a symbol of the costs of environmental neglect and spurred the passage of the massive federal Superfund legislation.

Other hazardous-waste suits followed in rapid succession. Their scope is suggested by the way they are now commonly catalogued, not by the name of an individual plaintiff but by the town or community and how many millions of dollars were won in judgment or settlement. Jackson Township, New Jersey—$16 million; Triana, Alabama—$24 million; Woburn, Massachusetts—$8 million; Times Beach, Missouri—$19 million; Toone, Tennessee—$12.7 million. Each new award seemed to establish a floor on which the bargaining in the next case would begin. Plaintiffs' lawyers in the Los Paseos neighborhood in South San Jose, California, characterized their 1987 settlement as "far more significant" than Love Canal. Lawyers for residents of the Denver suburb of Friendly Hills confidently predicted that they would win a judgment "far higher" than the settlement in Woburn. The numbers of claimants grew geometrically, and the awards rose apace.

Federal rules of procedure were amended in 1966 to facilitate just this kind of escalation. The new rules permitted a radically new device called the *common question class action*. Today, a single class representative is permitted to initiate suit for a group. She notifies class members by mail of the initiation of "their" lawsuit and, in a process familiar to Book-of-the-Month-Club members, offers them the chance to opt out if they wish. Other than a toothless plea that classes should be kept "manageable," the rule contains no limits on how large they may be.

Practitioners of the new tort soon recognized the opportunities. Class actions would add salutary deterrence of marketplace misconduct, so they were efficient. They would bring more compensation to huge numbers of new claimants, so they were just and compassionate. Class actions, in short, would allow more suits by more people over more things. And that was surely good.

A standard life cycle for the toxic-tort suit soon emerged. Once a few pioneers braving hardship conditions had opened up a new legal territory, thousands of plaintiff-come-latelies could follow in relative security, as the corporate and governmental defendants, falling back in disarray, were overwhelmed like the Indians by sheer numbers.

The first-generation radiation cases, for example, involved a few claimants injured by medically administered X-rays; the second, a few hundred employees suffering workplace exposures in uranium mines and fuel reprocessing facilities. The third, directed at such things as fallout from aboveground atomic bomb tests, now cover thousands of plaintiffs demanding billions of dollars in compensation. Chemical litigation followed a similar history. A first settlement in the Triana, Alabama, case, for example, involved 1,100 claimants; a second round swept in 7,000 more plaintiffs who lived somewhat farther from the pollution source but had otherwise identical claims. The first-round asbestos cases involved insulation workers; later rounds pulled in school districts, building contractors, and municipalities; today, plaintiffs' lawyers are taking aim at car brakes, home furnaces, hair dryers, and countless other mass-market products that still use the mineral for its unique insulation properties. Dioxin litigation started narrowly with incidents of accidental spills or confined exposures in factories. The later suits encompassed entire communities. One early $19 million settlement covered 128 claimants in Times Beach, Missouri. This only spurred an additional 1,500 claims by other nearby residents. Agent Orange, which was also a dioxin case, then brought 2.4 million claimants to court, named and unnamed, born and yet to be conceived.

In the space of twenty years, pollution law had been rewritten in its entirety. The old nuisance law drew a tight line on where litigation would end and other forms of governance begin. The new assumes the other branches of government are asleep. The old acknowledged that most activities went on with reasonable safety most of the time; the new assumes the worst. The old focused on narrow, bilateral justice, shunning crowds; the new deals wholesale with classes and masses. The old played an extremely modest role in government; the new acts as substitute regulator, prosecutor, social-insurance program, and rewriter of the grand social compact that governs us all.

Rounding Up Defendants

Tort law does not make money, however; it only finds it. A court judgment, no matter how wise or generous, is valueless if entered against someone without the cash to pay it. But often the most obvious candidate to bill for an injury—the drunk driver or arrested mugger, the careless child or neighbor—is in just that position. As the Founders took charge and expanded the horizons of the plaintiffs' universe, they were too often stopped short by this plebeian reality. If their tort law charity barbecue was to be a success, people of substantial means would have to be invited in numbers as well, to supply the food. As they say down on the farm, the best way to make a silk purse out of a sow's ear is to start with a silk sow.

Just how is the guest list on the defendants' side of a typical lawsuit drawn up? Defendants are, of course, only supposed to be liable for injuries that they cause. But causal chains stretch far and wide. If Baker arms himself and shoots Jones, it is easy enough to conclude that Baker caused the injury and should be held accountable. More debatable liability targets are Baker's brother, who furnished the pistol, the local gun dealer, who sold it, or the Smith & Wesson Company, which manufactured it. Going after Baker's mother-in-law, whose persistent nagging sharpened his misanthropic tendencies, would seem to be going too far. Somehow, people and causes sufficiently far removed in time and place don't count, and shouldn't if trials are to be held in courtrooms rather than stadiums. The question here, as on the plaintiffs' side of the courtroom, is just where to draw the line.

The old tort law drew it tightly. Judges of the day had a passion for uncrowded courtrooms on both sides of the aisle.

The simplest techniques of crowd control were those applied in the law of contracts, which, as we have seen, dominated most of the legal landscape. If Smith sold a carriage to Baker, the contract obligated Smith to Baker but not to anyone else, and certainly not to Burton who might subsequently buy the carriage from Baker. This principle was grandly labeled *privity of contract*. Less tidy but functionally similar rules applied to accidents not covered by contract. For a long time, tort law was more willing to address *direct* than *indirect* injuries. But for the legal profession's love of pedantry, the homely direct-indirect distinction would probably have survived to this day. What took its place was a bit of legal jargon more scientific-sounding but not the least bit more precise: *proximate cause*.

Helen Palsgraf learned as much in 1928. Palsgraf, a custodian and housewife of modest means from Brooklyn, was standing with her two daughters on a New York railway platform. A train pulled up and two men ran to catch it. The first leaped aboard the moving train; the second, carrying an unmarked package, jumped up afterward. One guard reached forward to pull him in, while another pushed from behind. The man's package fell on the rails and exploded when hit by the train's wheels. The package, it turned out, was filled with fireworks. The shock caused a set of scales on the platform to fall on Palsgraf, who, a week later, developed a stammer and stutter, apparently as a result of the shock. She sued the railway company, claiming negligence by the guards. But without success. Perhaps the guards *had* been negligent, Justice Benjamin Cardozo ruled. But their error was just too remote from Palsgraf's injury for her suit to survive.

Strict requirements of this character provided effective crowd control. The ironsmith who missed a nail in the horse's shoe might be held liable for the loss of the shoe, and perhaps the loss of the horse too. The loss of the rider was a longer shot, and no one would think of holding him liable for the loss of the battle, let alone the kingdom. Could his negligence be said to have caused the greater losses? Certainly. But taking legal notice of that fact would stretch the concept of liability beyond all workable bounds, or so the courts of the day generally ruled.

The only important exceptions involved rare instances of truly joint action. Some notions of group liability have ancient roots. The atomistic community under the Saxon organization of England was a *tithing,* a group of ten families of freeholders. A *hundred* contained ten tithings. A notable feature of the hundred was group responsibility for certain defaults. Under the ancient English law of *hue and cry,* for example, all who heard a loud outcry that a felon was being pursued were bound to join in the pursuit until the malefactor was taken. Another English statute, the Riot Act, provided that if any twelve persons or more were unlawfully assembled and disturbing the peace, the sheriff could command them to disperse ("reading the Riot Act"); their failure to do so would render them all guilty of felony.

Less exotic concepts of joint liability were incorporated into tort law early on. It has long been accepted that if Baker and Burton go out together and burn down Smith's barn, Smith can sue them both together and hold them *jointly and severally* liable for his resulting injuries. Smith can then collect any part of his award, up to the full amount, from either of the guilty parties. When Smith has been paid in full, Baker and Burton can stay in court and fight things out further among themselves, if they care to.

In its traditional application, the venerable rule of joint liability had limited effect. It ensured that one major wrongdoer could not easily escape liability simply because another was also on the scene. But rarely did the rule force those whose sins had been minor to answer for those whose sins had been great. Joint liability, unlike the spirit of the feudal rules that applied to an entire community, was not a theory of group liability. English courts, and later American ones, worked hard to delineate where the consequences of negligence ended and life outside the courtroom could proceed without the help of lawyers.

The Socialized Defense

The Founders had a quite different vision. If accidents were to be deterred and victims compensated, someone was going to have to be held liable. It was immensely frustrating to discover, as the Founders often did in the early days, that under the established etiquette none of the eligible invitees to a legal dance were worth suing. Large institutions and corporations that might absorb costs, prevent accidents, and do all the other things the Founders were determined to encourage were often far removed from an accident and adept at keeping their distance.

Given their objectives, the Founders had an aversion to the lean, hungry, and lonely defendant. Like Caesar, they much preferred to be surrounded by fat men, and in numbers. So they really had no alternative. As the hold-someone-liable culture took hold, the short arm of the law would have to be lengthened, in a process of extension rationalized by whatever means might be expedient.

As elsewhere, the Founders started their work with the legal material most readily at hand, the law of contract. Helen Henningsen's 1960 suit against Bloomfield Motors started the process. As we saw earlier, the New Jersey Supreme Court in that case discovered an implied warranty under which Bloomfield had promised Helen's husband, Claus (without ever actually saying so), a certain degree of safety in the car. But the claimant was not Claus, it was his wife, Helen, who—under venerable privity-of-contract principles—had no contract with Bloomfield at all. There was no way around this. So the New Jersey Supreme Court cleanly discarded privity-of-contract limits altogether.

And with this simple stroke, the Founders' universe expanded radically. It was now possible to have a legally binding contract—and all the contract's attendant duties and responsibilities—with someone you had never met or dealt with in any way. At precisely the same time, of course, contract duties themselves were blossoming as the courts freely discovered one implied promise of safety after the next. "What followed," wrote one leading commentator, "was the most rapid and altogether spectacular overturn of an established rule in the entire history of the law of torts."

This expansion, though of high importance, marked only a transitional victory. It was crucial for the Founders to deny their opponents the kingdom of contract, but the crown did not rest easily on their own heads either. Courts would soon tire of the burdensome chore of unearthing new implied warranties and burying old express disclaimers. Before long, they would be seeking a way to move the whole process over to the realm of pure tort law. And in that realm, the selection of candidate defendants was still cramped by parsimonious notions of proximate cause.

Here again, there was new doctrine to be poured into the bottles of old legal precedent. Justice Benjamin Cardozo's landmark *MacPherson* decision of 1916 had already declared that a buyer of a negligently manufactured car could sue not only the dealer but also the original manufacturer, not under a theory of contract but in tort. The decision, however, had been tailored to familiar market realities. Most consumer products pass quickly down an easy-to-trace chain of intermediate and very temporary "owners" on their way from manufacturer to end user. The Buick Motor Company knew all along that its car would end up with someone like Donald Mac-Pherson. Extending liability along the sales chain here was not especially daring; the chain was straight, fairly short, and uncomplicated.

The keepers of the new tort flame grasped this precedent and cited it for all it was worth. Their objective was to trace out causal chains much further than was then permitted by traditionally crabbed rules of proximate cause. The legal pioneers might simply have stretched the old legal vocabulary to new practical limits, but a new dogma called for a new dialectic. Proximate cause, everyone agreed, was obsolete terminology based on ungenerous conceptions of what the tort system should provide. The new tort theories assumed that most accidents could be foreseen and prevented. This suggested that people should be held liable for all *reasonably foreseeable* consequences of their actions, in much the same way as they were being required to warn of all foreseeable risks. If the ironsmith could reasonably foresee that for the want of the nail the entire kingdom would be lost, then he could properly be called upon to pay for the same. Only in this way would the tort system properly encourage smiths of the realm to be careful in their work.

And so, one set of words displaced another. The legal academics who put forward the new foreseeability test were proud of their idea and announced it with pomp, as if exulting in the powers of an extraordinary new telescope. Nothing grew the least bit more precise. But more people could now be sued more often, and that, of course, was the whole idea.

While the father is one of only two proximate causes of the son, he can surely foresee any number of more remote descendants further down the family line. In like manner, the truly proximate causes of an accident are usually few, but the family tree then quickly becomes complicated. If the sins of an injury-prone world were to be visited on all previous generations, the courts would have to become experts at unraveling the genealogy of accidents.

The incentives for conducting the search were certainly there. Orphan injuries, which lack financially responsible parents, are all too common. Many originate with the victims themselves, or with their close family members, or in the malevolence of Nature, which deals out rain storms and birth defects equally to the just and the unjust. Others are the progeny of common criminals or uninsured drunk drivers. Still others are caused by defendants who enjoy statutory immunity from suit, like employers, who are supposed to make payments only through workers' compensation programs, or the military.

The easiest lineage to trace was often that of the product that served as the instrumentality of disease, death, or crime. A Maryland court held the manufacturer of a "Saturday night special" liable to Olen Kelley, a store employee who was shot in the chest during an armed robbery. A Michigan court ruled that a manufacturer could be held liable for selling a slingshot to children. Most of the asbestos cases, which grew out of employee exposures in World War II shipyards, were directed not at the government employer, which enjoyed statutory immunity, but at manufacturers of the mineral. Veterans barred from suing the brass who made the real decisions about Agent Orange in Vietnam, or about open-air atomic bomb tests in the Southwest and in the Pacific, instead sued the contractors who furnished the herbicide or the bomb paraphernalia. A manufacturer was sued successfully for installing a telephone booth in a place where a drunk driver could and subsequently did collide with it, injuring the person inside. A pawnshop that sold a pistol later used in the murder of an automobile-dealership employee paid $1.9 million to the widow.

The logic was always the same: People don't kill people; guns, cars, appliances, and airplanes do, or, more precisely, the sellers or manufacturers of those sometimes lethal objects do the killing. And if not the product itself, then one of its constituent parts, perhaps. Sooner or later, somewhere or other in this kind of chain, there is bound to be a solvent defendant able to foot the bill and likely to be improved by the chastening experience of a lawsuit.

But when there was no apparent murder weapon in sight, new tort lawyers were equally willing to dispense with the props and shift the dramatic spotlight to the human players on stage. States have paid for the crimes of a paroled prisoner and an escaped convict. The Torrington, Connecticut, police department paid $2.6 million for its failure to arrest a suspected wife beater who later injured his spouse. Landlords began to pay regularly for failing to protect their tenants from muggers and rapists. Under similar theories of *negligent security,* the courts extended liability to libraries, supermarkets, restaurants, schools, laundromats, commuter train stations, and summer camps. People exposed to AIDS through their sexual partners began suing too—not their partners, who were usually impoverished, nor obviously the virus's Creator, but third parties like school districts, prisons, the American Red Cross (for having unwittingly distributed contaminated blood), and hospitals (for having transfused it). Then there arose a novel theory of *negligent hiring.* A security guard at a Miami bank went berserk, killing a fellow guard; the widow of the slain guard recovered $300,000 from the bank on the theory that it should have uncovered the risk and protected against it. In 1983, the Minnesota Supreme Court upheld a verdict that owners of an apartment complex were financially liable for hiring a manager who was convicted of raping a tenant.

On-the-scene verdicts of this character neatly complemented the instrumentality cases, which invariably pinned blame on some product manufacturer very much *off* the scene of the final accident. Between them, these two sweeping legal principles pretty much filled out the defendants' guest list and dance card. In the fullness of time, alcohol-related accidents allowed the courts to embrace both theories within the same lawsuit.

The traditional rule for alcohol was simple: You could sue the drunk, but not those who helped her become so. A few states enacted dramshop acts under which taverns and liquor stores which sold liquor, especially to minors, could be liable to subsequent accident victims, but most did not. As the new age of tort dawned, however, other states acquired equivalent legislation by the shortcut of judicial decree. In 1984 the New Jersey Supreme Court declared that a social guest's drunken driving and subsequent accident are foreseeable and thus chargeable to the host who served the alcohol. Similar initiatives in Oregon, Iowa, Minnesota, and California were promptly overruled by statute. Meanwhile, a few courts were attempting to trace responsibility back to the distiller; the first such suits arrived in the early 1980s.

On-the-scene liability reached its zenith, however, with the medical profession, which has a known propensity to meddle in accidents of every description. A tormented cancer patient sues the doctor for failing to diagnose the disease promptly enough, skipping lightly, of course, over whether the misdiagnosis made any real difference to the chances of cure. Anguished parents, finding no one to blame for their child's birth defect, sue the obstetrician for failing to provide them with adequate prenatal genetic counseling, resulting in the "wrongful life" of the baby. Psychiatrists have offered still richer possibilities for development of long-arm liability principles.

Prosenjit Poddar, a Berkeley graduate student, met Tatiana Tarasoff at the campus's International House in 1968 and stabbed her to death on October 27, 1969. In the intervening year, he had seen a university psychologist, and had confided that he planned to kill Tatiana. The psychologist told the campus police, who took Poddar into custody but released him after extracting a promise that he would leave Tatiana alone. Tatiana's parents successfully sued Poddar's therapist, on the theory that Tatiana should have been warned directly. Psychiatrists have since been held liable when their patient recklessly drives a car into another car, or goes on a shooting rampage in a nightclub. In many cases, the violence occurs months after the treatment ended. By 1986 over 100 psychiatrists, clinical psychologists, and even clinical social workers were defending suits of this kind across the country.

If the costs of aberrant behavior could be pinned on those who attempt to treat psychological disturbance, perhaps those who provide psychological stimuli could be sued as well. After Kenneth Nally committed suicide in 1979, his parents, Walter and Maria, sued the Grace Community Church and some of its pastors, claiming they had discouraged psychological counseling and encouraged the suicide. In late 1987, a California appellate court approved the lawsuit in principle and returned it to a lower court for trial. In September 1974, NBC aired a movie called *Born Innocent,* in which a gang of girls carried out a lesbian rape with a toilet plunger. Some days later, a young girl was the victim of a copycat crime apparently inspired by the movie. The real-life victim sued NBC, though this time without success. On a similar theory, the parents of a four-year-old girl sued the telephone company after their daughter was raped by a twelve-year-old boy who had earlier spent two hours listening to sexually explicit messages on telephone dial-a-porn services.

Not every new claim succeeded, but one thing was quite clear. The foreseeability horizon for liability, like other horizons, receded rapidly on closer approach. The Founders' basic premise—that most accidents have preventable outside causes that can be effectively deterred by litigation— impelled them to take an ever more expansive view of what is foreseeable. In the end, the difference between the foreseeable and the unforeseeable in the courts turned out to be very much like the difference (as defined by legendary National League umpire Bill Klem) between a ball and a strike. There wasn't any until the umpire had called it.

As the law's reach grew longer, the victim's own role in self-protection became increasingly attenuated. Under the old law, for example, the proximate cause of lung cancer would certainly have ended with the victim's own act of lighting up the cigarette. A sexually active woman who later contracted pelvic disease would have had little success in arguing that a contraceptive implant was primarily to blame for her infection. A drunk driver would not have lasted long in his postaccident suit against the manufacturer of his car. But, as we have seen, the old notion of contributory negligence did not sit well with the new tort advocates. Blaming the victim was no way to build up an expansive new program of compensation and deterrence in the courts.

If the victim's own negligence was to be considered at all, the Founders concluded, a much fairer rule would be *comparative negligence.* Responsibility for an accident would be allocated in percentages among the plaintiff and the various defendants, and the victim's recovery would be reduced to the extent of his own fault. Mississippi had in fact adopted the comparative negligence rule as early as 1910. As the new tort revolution took hold, most other states followed suit.

Today comparative negligence principles allow into court a steady stream of wounds that would once have been viewed as self-inflicted. A man mutilated after he deliberately jumped in front of a subway train sued New York City, claiming that the driver should have stopped faster, and walked off with $650,000. The father of a thirteen-year-old who committed suicide at home sued school officials, several of the boy's teachers, and the local police, claiming they should have known of the boy's troubles and prevented the harm. And so a system that had started with the plan of punishing the irresponsible gradually began to reward at least some of them in proportion not to their blamelessness but to how many others were also arguably at fault.

Fearful of scapegoating, the courts piled the sins of the individual onto an ever-wider circle of the community at large. The injuries once ascribed to the gross carelessness of a single drunk driver may today be caused, in the eyes of the law, by the bartender, the distiller, the auto or tire or brake maker, the local police force, the drunk's boon companions, perhaps her psychiatrist, and many more. Behind the implement of harm, the car or gun or chemical or electric power line, stand a line of distributors, manufacturers, and designers. Behind the human factor stand the summed influences of teachers and foster parents, ministers and psychiatrists, social workers and parole officers, bartenders and prescribers of mood-altering pills, advertisers, and purveyors of pornographic and violent entertainment. Behind Nature itself stand the obstetricians and pathologists, climatologists and weather forecasters who should have warned of its fury, and the specialists of every sort—builders of ships, aircraft, bridges, and buildings—whose handiwork should have withstood Nature's assault. Behind the ranks of the parties that did something stand the numerous ranks of those who did nothing but who might have helped matters by intervening.

Group Guilt

All the while, the old rule of joint-and-several liability was alive and expanding in momentous ways in its own right. That venerable rule, as we have seen, allowed the injured victim to collect his entire recovery from any defendant he chose. The rule could afford to be simple; joint liability cases were comparatively rare because causal chains were cut very short.

The new tort advocates were not about to revise *that* happy institution, of course. Apportioning damages according to degrees of fault was all very well in assessing the plaintiff's share in causing his injury. But applying the same principle between defendants was quite another matter.

Joint-and-several liability provided the brass knuckles at the end of the law's ever-longer swing. The drunk driver who hit the child was liable under all theories of cause, old and new. But the big loser under the new rules was the city, for its failure, say, to maintain a more vigilant constabulary. Los Angeles, for example, paid nearly all of a $2.16 million judgment on a 1979 traffic accident after a driver high on drugs ran a stop sign. The city's fault? Inadequate trimming of certain bushes that perhaps obstructed the drugged driver's vision. San Diego paid $1.6 million to a car passenger on the scenic Torrey Pines Road who was left a quadriplegic when a speeding drunk driver crossed the center line on a curve and smashed into his car. The drunk offered his insurance policy limit of $25,000; the city was then sued for faulty road design. A Michigan driver who was found to be 60 percent negligent himself in an accident nevertheless collected $240,000 from the state.

What is now derisively called *deep-pocket liability* was born of the convergence of an old principle—joint-and-several liability—with a brand-new one—the long-arm, socialized defense. Behind every great fortune there is a great crime, Balzac once said. New tort practitioners managed to reverse things entirely. Searching for the fortune came first; a crime would then be found, one way or another, in the vicinity of the cash.

Glen Gregos, a sixteen-year-old boy who was left paralyzed after an accident in a cross-country motorcycle race for novices, was only one more among thousands of beneficiaries of the new money-first principle of liability. The race was sponsored by the American Motorcycle Association (AMA). Glen sued, charging negligence in the design and management of the race and a failure to instruct him in racing technique and evaluate his capabilities. The AMA pointed to a consent form Glen's parents had signed, and insisted they were responsible. Glen was quite content to sue them both—knowing full well that joint-and-several liability principles would permit him to recover all of his damages from the race sponsors and none from his parents. The AMA pleaded to have the joint liability rule set aside, so that it would pay only according to its assessed fault. But with astonishing candor, the California Supreme Court brushed aside the objection that the least culpable among Glen, his parents, and the AMA might end up paying most of the damages. "[E]ven when a plaintiff is partially at fault for his own injury," the court reasoned, "a plaintiff's culpability is not equivalent to that of a defendant."

A troublesome natural barrier to the forward march of liability continued, however, to stymie the advance guard of the new tort army. As candidate causes proliferate outward, they are easily lost in the mists of space and time. An independent handler collects chemical wastes from fifty different factories and dumps them in a landfill. One rare poison leaches into the water supply. Suing the impecunious handler is useless; fortunately, long-arm liability rules make it easy to sue the original generator of the toxin. But who is it? So long as no one really knew, the old tort law refused to impose any liability at all in most such cases. Rounding up the usual suspects was not enough; joint-and-several liability was not a principle of group guilt. Here was one of the toughest challenges yet for proponents of the new tort to overcome.

They seized on an idiosyncratic precedent that arose in California in 1948. On November 20, 1945, Summers, Tice, and Simonson armed themselves with 12-gauge shotguns and shells containing 7 1/2 size shot and went off to hunt for quail. Tice flushed a bird, which rose in flight between the three. Tice and Simonson both fired wildly. One (and only one) of the two managed to hit Summers in his eye—but whether it was Tice or Simonson, no one could determine. So the California Supreme Court invented a new doctrine, which came to be called *alternative liability,* and both Tice and Simonson were held fully liable. The decision contained the kernel of a revolutionary new thought: the notion that it is better to impose liability on someone who has caused *no* harm—at least if he somehow "had it coming" anyway—than to leave uncompensated someone who clearly has been wronged.

A generation later, this small seed was to blossom into an entirely new body of law. In 1972, the idea of group guilt was extended by a New York court to product manufacturers. Thirteen children playing with blasting caps were injured in twelve separate incidents over a period of four years. In each case the explosions destroyed the caps' markings, so no one could tell who had manufactured them. The injured children sued six blasting cap manufacturers, comprising virtually the entire American industry, along with the manufacturers' trade association. They filed a total of 230 separate actions and demanded $200 million in damages. All members of the industry jointly controlled the risk, the New York court ruled. So it would be up to the defendants to prove which one of them had provided the caps involved in the accidents; failing to do so, all would be liable.

A ruling eight years later was to become the leading decision on collective industry guilt. The case grew out of the 1937 discovery, by two British scientists, of a synthetic form of estrogen, DES. DES proved to be effective in preventing miscarriages, and before long, 300 drug companies were marketing it, usually under a generic rather than a brand name. In 1971, researchers discovered a weak but definite statistical link between DES and clear-cell adenocarcinoma, a form of cancer, in daughters of women who had taken the drug during pregnancy. The *DES daughters,* as they came to be known, sued five of the companies that had manufactured DES decades earlier. But no plaintiff could identify which firm had manufactured the medicine her mother had used. Unable to disentangle the causality knot, the California Supreme Court cut it clean through. It simply parceled out liability in proportion to the share of the DES market each manufacturer had held back in the 1950s.

This was a radical advance, and the last one possible in the search for a truly socialized defense. Market-share liability theories are as unbounded, on the defendant's side of the courtroom, as environmental class actions are on the plaintiff's. The roster of undifferentiated defendants recalls the man met with on the road to St. Ives, the one with seven wives, every wife having seven cats, every cat having seven kits, and so forth. If a single unsuitable landfill has been used by seven waste transporters, each of which has seven industrial customers, each of which has seven raw-material suppliers, 400 parties will end up defending the case in court, not counting everyone's insurers. Similar legal theories are now being adapted to air and water pollution, pharmaceutical products, medical devices, and toxic waste dumps.

The New Town Meeting

The socialized offense and defense developed separately, but they were complementary all along. As the right to sue expanded, the obligation to pay of course had to expand apace. As crowds collected on one side of the courtroom, they inevitably had to be collected on the other as well. Today no case is too unwieldy for a court, no exposure too low, no injury too uncertain, no class of actual or potential victims too large, no list of defendants too long. A legal system once concerned with individual justice is now a principal center of social engineering.

At times the population explosion is confined to the plaintiffs' side. Thousands of claimants consolidate their demands against a single chemical factory or drug manufacturer. At times it is only the defendants who proliferate. A single medical malpractice suit targets a small army of doctors, surgeons, nurses, and anesthetists, together with the manufacturers of anesthesiology equipment, drugs, and medical instruments. Sometimes the crowds are assembled on both sides. With Agent Orange, millions of plaintiffs sued eight very large defendants and advanced market-share theories to allocate liability when individual responsibilities could not be traced. The typical toxic dump case today pits hundreds or even thousands of claimants against tens or hundreds of corporations and institutions.

The single effect of these developments has been to extend the courts' control to matters that used to lie outside their grasp. The socialized offense transformed diffuse, widely shared injuries into consolidated claims. The socialized defense accomplished just the opposite: It diffused legal responsibility among large groups. Both developments had the same effect, encouraging more plaintiffs to sue more defendants. The instrumentality principles provided a form of social control over the manufacturers of handguns and alcohol, fireworks and insecticides. The ever-ramifying logic of foreseeability turned the courts into all-purpose, open-ended review boards to monitor the conduct of policemen, psychiatrists, air traffic controllers, and weather forecasters. On-the-scene liability gave courts a handle on how governments, landlords, store owners, and others supervised their premises, public or private. Market-share liability offered control over entire industries. Venerable notions of joint-and-several liability then permitted claimants to pick and choose which particular defendant would ultimately pay.

Matters of public policy, once considered to be so broad-ranging that only the political branches of government could address them, are now routinely squeezed into the mold of a lawsuit and adjudicated like two-car collisions at an intersection. It has been said that defeat is an orphan while victory has a hundred parents. With their fully socialized defense, however, the new tort theorists confidently declared that every disaster has a hundred legal fathers. The old courtroom dramas were styled as two-rider jousting tournaments; the new look more like an Arabian bazaar. The tort lawsuit, until recently a private affair, has become the new town meeting.

6

Resetting the Clock

RAUL MARTINEZ-FERRER, a California physician and surgeon, was worried about his blood cholesterol level. In March 1960 he prescribed for himself a new anticholesterol drug called MER/29. By September 23 he was unable to read; soon afterward he developed severe dermatitis over his entire body and had to stop work for a month. A medical colleague he consulted suspected that the drug was to blame and advised Ferrer to discontinue all medication. Ferrer's dermatitis slowly cleared up and his vision recovered. Sixteen years later Ferrer developed cataracts. He sued Richardson-Merrell, the drug's manufacturer.

In its defense, the company pointed to a California law which provided that any lawsuit concerning an injury "caused by the wrongful act or neglect of another" had to be filed within one year. A California appellate court was unimpressed. Yes, the court conceded, it had been sixteen years since Ferrer took the drug, and the statute did say that one year was the limit. But the statutory clock wasn't going to be allowed to run down quite so quickly. The real rule was that different clocks would run for different symptoms. The cataracts were new and different effects, separate from the original reaction, and they developed much later. Ferrer's suit would therefore be allowed to proceed.

The Short Season

Under rules firmly in place until the early 1970s, plaintiffs had to pick their time carefully. They could not come to court too early or too late. Injury claims, like delicate fruits, could be thrown out as overripe or ordered back to the shelf as underripe. The season of freshness in between was rather brief. These timing rules kept countless cases out of court altogether.

To start with, judges of the earlier legal era were particular and inflexible in enforcing *statutes of limitation* like the one on the California books when Ferrer brought his case. When time ran out, the litigation game was over. It didn't matter how legitimate your claim might be.

Why have such limits at all? The logic was uncomplicated. If I've been injured by what I believe to be your negligence, I need a reasonable amount of time to decide whether to sue, whether you are the right person to sue, and how much money I should ask for. But if I wait too long, it becomes unfair to you. You need timely notice in order to put together an effective defense before the normal ebb and flow of human events washes away the evidence in your favor. And society's broader interest is to resolve disputes, not to memorialize them. Time may not actually heal all wounds, but forgetfulness is a necessary balm if the level of unresolved tension, and uncertainty of rights, is not to mount from one year to the next. As the great Justice Louis Brandeis once observed, it is often more important that things be settled than that they be settled right.

Excessive delay was not all that was forbidden; the old tort law frowned equally on undue haste in litigation. In 1885, for example, a certain Mr. Bealey was manufacturing alkali on the banks of the river Irwell, not far from Manchester, England. His enterprise produced a toxic "vat waste," which he dumped near the riverbank and from which there oozed a greenish liquid of "noxious character." A Mr. Fletcher owned a plant a mile and a half downstream where he manufactured the "very finest classes of paper," using a process that required pure water from the river. Fearing that Bealey's waste-retaining wall was on the verge of collapse, Fletcher went to court. He asked for an order directing Bealey to take measures immediately to protect against the anticipated accident. Come back later, the court airily replied. The feared catastrophe had not yet occurred, and no one could be sure it ever would. Bealey had declared that he intended to prevent any harmful pollution, and in any event the advance of technology might some day provide a way to render Bealey's wastes harmless. If the worst did materialize, Fletcher would have a full opportunity to sue for damages later. The case, in short, was not ripe for decision. Fletcher was sent home to sweat it out.

American courts of the day followed similar rules. Our Constitution expressly restricts federal courts to deciding "cases or controversies." Judges understood this to mean that they could only involve themselves in disputes that had reached a point of concrete and well-defined acrimony. And if the courts were reluctant to issue protective orders prematurely, they were still less willing to award cash prizes too early in the game. No matter how disquieting it might be to live downstream of a precarious waste dump, negligence "in the air" was never any basis for demanding money here and now. And even if the defendant *had* whizzed by at 100 miles per hour, no bystander could ask for money just out of anger, however well justified, at having been endangered; the rule was, no collision, no lawsuit.

Why were the courts so reluctant to act quickly when the wisdom of ages concurs that prevention is better than cure? They may have had in mind other aphorisms that counsel caution and slowness to wrath. The failure to add a stitch in time may sometimes have cost nine, but there was a different sort of economy to consider as well: What may appear to be a real threat of harm often is not, and litigation postponed is often litigation avoided altogether. The rule was also grounded in judicial modesty: If an injury lay too far in the future, a court's preventive order would be too speculative and prone to error. Better to accept with stoicism the fact that accidents may happen and award money damages if and when they materialize.

The old timeliness rules thus operated with the fussy precision of a school bell or the clock at a football game, and offered all the benefits that strict, clear rules bring. The starting bell sounded at a reasonably well-defined time—the day the two cars collided, for example, or when the toxic wastes slipped into the river and corrupted Fletcher's paper operation, and then a fairly precise timepiece started to run. When time ran out, so did the right to sue. Such rules had the great advantage of making life, in court and out, orderly and predictable.

And like other arbitrary rules, the timing rules could also appear frustratingly harsh and unfair. The Marlin Firearms Company, for example, manufactured a new rifle and shipped it to a sporting goods store on May 28, 1946, receiving payment a week later. Three years later the rifle was sold to a young man in Williamsport, Pennsylvania. He lent the weapon to his cousin, Paul Dincher, in July 1950. A few days later, Dincher lost his left eye when the weapon backfired. He sued, claiming that the rifle was designed with too much headspace between the face of the bolt and the rear space of the barrel. A state law required claims to be filed within one year "from the date of the injury or neglect complained of." The act in question here, the court ruled, took place no later than June 6, 1946, when Marlin completed its sale of the rifle. So Dincher was out of court without a chance to present his case. Indeed, his right to sue had expired before he ever laid hands on the rifle. "Except in topsy-turvy land," a dissenting judge thundered, "you can't die before you are conceived, or be divorced before you ever marry, or harvest a crop never planted, or burn down a house never built, or miss a train running on a non-existent railroad. For substantially similar reasons . . . a statute of limitations does not begin to run against a cause of action before that cause of action exists, i.e. before a judicial remedy is available to the plaintiff." But that was the dissent. The majority had no problem with the case.

A Climate for Change

Developments far outside the legal arena then began to undermine the old timing rules. Even as they were learning about the possibly toxic properties of ubiquitous environmental poisons, scientists were also beginning to understand the slow life cycles of disease. Their invisibility and ubiquity aside, the terrifying thing about environmental poisons was their insidious power to reach far into the future. The victim might enjoy year after year of good health, but that might be just a mask concealing the canker within. Counterevidence, and thus reassurance, was next to impossible; no doctor could ever swear that a person was quite free of invisible but latent injury or disease. The most horrifying slow-motion injuries were those that originated in the womb. Daughters exposed to DES, for example, did not begin to show its effects until they had grown to maturity. The scientific community was also beginning to gain solid insight into lethal breakdowns in complex engineering systems and technologies. New techniques of *fault tree analysis* and *probabilistic risk assessment* gave engineers a systematic way to calculate and predict the likelihood of very rare catastrophes in systems like Union Carbide's Bhopal plant, or the natural-gas storage depot in Ixhautepec, near Mexico City, or the Chernobyl nuclear power plant.

By the early 1970s, science thus offered important new reductionist tools for compressing time and causality. Today's diseases could be traced to activities in the 1940s and 1950s. And the consequences of today's activities could be projected forward to disease and catastrophe that would materialize decades later. The chemical factory quietly releasing diffuse poisons into the surrounding air might perhaps be condemning one life every week, but no one would know it for sure until ten years—or 500 lives—later. And even if the factory was releasing nothing at all today, statistical analyses of pipe fractures, tank leaks, and operator errors could suggest that some time in the next ten years, this factory, or another just like it, would suffer a cascade of malfunctions leading to a catastrophic accident with immediately fatal consequences of similar magnitude.

Proponents of the new tort jurisprudence had never been at all fond of the old rigid time limits on litigation. Surely, they argued, a person injured by MER/29 or asbestos should not go uncompensated today merely because the cataracts or cancer took decades rather than weeks to develop. And the responsible corporation should not escape the lash of liability merely because the law had never advanced from the sundial and the astrolabe to more modern ways of fixing timetables. If the important function of tort law was to get the accident bill sent to the right people, technicalities about just when the bill was supposed to be mailed should obviously be swept aside.

Similar logic seemed also to justify some instances of compensation well before any disease materialized. Smith lives on the doorstep of the Colossal Company's chemical or nuclear facility. This in itself is surely disquieting. Before the accident, acute anxiety—"in the air" to be sure, but real nonetheless—can lead to clinically observable health problems. After a toxic release has occurred, the anxiety is still greater, even though the toxin will work its effects (if any) only over many years. And before the disease actually materializes, many things might happen. Smith might die of something else. Colossal might go out of business. The evidence linking Smith's disease with Colossal's enterprise might fade away in the mists of time. Any of these developments would leave Smith uncompensated and Colossal (or others like it) undeterred from future misconduct of the same sort. And all of these concerns are present immediately after a toxic release; many are present even before the accidental release itself. Far better to allow Smith to sue at once. Then both sides will get their just deserts, albeit before the main course has been served, and society will reap the added benefit of salutary deterrence.

At both ends, the logic for relaxing the old strict time limits seemed very attractive, at least to those convinced from the start that there was nothing wrong with liability that more liability could not cure. By the late 1960s, the Founders had already committed themselves to improving social justice and market efficiency through a great expansion of tort law. The ancient and venerable timing rules, in short, were now ripe for sweeping change.

Toward an Infinite Legal Memory

From the start, however, statutes of limitations presented a vexing problem. Unlike almost all other aspects of tort law, these statutes are not ad hoc creations of judges themselves. They are express, written laws, enacted by state legislatures or Congress. And whatever else they may do, judges are not supposed to repeal statutes. This was mightily inconvenient, because few legislators shared the pioneering spirit of the Founders when it came to expanding the kingdom of tort. Eventually, to be sure, the advance of the tort revolution was to reshape public opinion and so bring pressure to bear on legislative bodies. But at the beginning, the courts were still advancing largely on their own. Their previous victories had consisted of moving into unoccupied and undefended territory. But now they faced an area already comfortably settled and walled off by legislative action. What could they possibly do?

Almost anything they liked. Statutes are written by lawyers, and what one lawyer writes another must read. What the deconstructionists later discovered in the field of literary criticism, lawyers had known all along: More creative ingenuity can go into reading a text than ever went into its writing.

The literary method of a good lawyer consists not of denying the text but of altering its application. If the rule book says the clock in the football game is supposed to run for sixty minutes, the lawyer will not argue afterward for changing it to sixty-five. Since the rule book says sixty minutes, sixty minutes it must be. But did the offense really have enough time to scramble into position before the kickoff? Or was a time-out improperly called by the defense or denied to the offense? Or did some seemingly unrelated call by an umpire affect the running of the clock? These questions, of course, are always fair game.

Some judges became exceedingly particular about just what "the injury" mentioned in a statute of limitations really was. A surgeon finishes the operation, closes the incision, and five days later discharges the patient from the hospital, leaving a pair of scissors inside. Common sense says that the two-year clock on suing the surgeon begins to run on the day of the operation, or perhaps the day of discharge from the hospital. But then a claimant will come along who does not suffer damage from the scissors until three years later. The solution? Redefine the injury as the doctor's continuing failure to remember or discover the mistake and alert the patient. That, of course, stops the clock from ticking as long as the patient's name remains in the doctor's file. In the case of Raul Ferrer, the California court of appeals took a slightly different tack. It smoothly declared that different clocks should run for each symptom of Ferrer's reaction to the MER/29 drug. Ferrer had indeed experienced failing eyesight and dermatitis sixteen years earlier, but the cataracts appeared only much later. The early symptoms were "different, independent and relatively innocuous," and that was surely enough reason to clock them on a separate timepiece.

Strained though they were, arguments of this character worked for a good number of litigants who in an earlier day would have found the courtroom doors locked against them. But the loopholes were still too narrow, especially for many plaintiffs with latent diseases that take decades to develop. If they were to pass through the statutory gates, an all-purpose open sesame was needed.

In the end, many judges flatly decreed that the injury did not really exist at all until the victim had discovered it. The tree in the forest, in other words, would be deemed not to have fallen until its owner stumbled across its horizontal trunk. This discovery rule had its start in malpractice cases but soon spread from doctors to dentists, accountants, architects, and product manufacturers.

A fine exposition of the discovery rule in action came in 1979 when a group of Utah residents claimed they had been injured by radioactive fallout from aboveground atomic bomb tests conducted by the military between 1951 and 1963. Federal law provided that "[a] tort claim against the United States shall be forever barred unless it is presented in writing to the appropriate Federal agency within two years after such claim accrues." In an earlier day, the court would routinely have acknowledged that the claim "accrued"—and the two-year clock therefore started to run—when the bombs were detonated or a few days thereafter when the fallout drifted downwind. By 1986, however, discovery rules were well in place, and the quarrel over timing took on the dimensions of a lawsuit in itself.

Judge Bruce Jenkins, presiding over a federal district court in Salt Lake City, addressed the question in a pair of several-hundred-page opinions.

The crucial event for determining whether the suit had been filed on time, he first ruled, was when the plaintiffs discovered their injury. And what amounts to a discovery? Five pages of dense prose later, Jenkins had decided that discovery means "knowledge of an injury," with "knowledge" being considerably more than "suspicion" but a good bit less than "absolute certainty." That having been settled, the question was: When did the plaintiffs acquire knowledge of their injury? Not until a short while before they filed suit, or so they insisted. But such a purely self-serving claim, which every plaintiff would surely make in similar circumstances, could not be accepted unexamined. So another three dense pages of reflection and scrutiny were required, in which Jenkins dissected all available objective evidence bearing on what the plaintiffs knew and when they knew it. This included, of course, a general survey of everything the plaintiffs had read, said, and done during the twenty-five years between the end of the bomb tests and the beginning of their lawsuit.

Judge Jenkins did the job conscientiously, without skimping in the least on factual detail, and finally concluded that the lawsuit was still timely and the trial could proceed. All sides were duly impressed by this display of judicial industry. But there was not the least doubt that on the strength of precisely the same evidence, Jenkins could have reached precisely the opposite conclusion, had he been so inclined.

The beauty of the discovery device, as the bomb case revealed, is that it is infinitely elastic. The old rules afforded little judicial discretion because everyone usually knew when the starting gun had been fired. There rarely is much doubt about just when the scissors were forgotten inside the patient or when the worker was exposed to the asbestos. The detonation of an atomic bomb is an even less ambiguous event, at least for a timekeeper. But fixing the exact day on which John Smith discovered he was chronically short of breath, or Mary Jones knew for sure that she was terrified of the latent effects of a drug she took as a child, requires something of a philosophical discourse on the theory of knowledge. Kafka's hero Gregor Samsa may have awoken suddenly one morning to discover he had turned into a cockroach, but most horrifying realizations, to say nothing of deep-seated fears, dawn more gradually. Often there is no one but the plaintiff herself who can say with any certainty just when discovery occurred—but she is hardly an objective witness. The extreme subjectivity of the trigger raises the most vexing question of all, namely, the victim's own honesty and good faith. Judges—who already had to act as scientists and engineers—now took on the mantle of psychohistorians as well.

The discovery rule encouraged plaintiffs to come forth with dramatic charges of cover-up and conspiracy. I sue you because you sprayed some weed killer on your lawn and I contracted a chronic illness. The spraying and therefore the onset of the illness both took place twenty years ago, but I didn't link them until yesterday, or so I claim. The judge seems dubious—twenty years is a long time, after all. The best way for me to keep my lawsuit alive is to argue that you concealed your misuse of the product or its alarming consequences. How was I to know the full scope of the danger when you were busy covering it up? The cover-up, real or imagined, can take a multitude of forms. Perhaps I asked you, back then, whether your herbicide was safe, and you confidently assured me it was. Since then you have made no move to retract this assurance, carefully concealing the fact (or so I claim) that you misused the product and knew all along that it was dangerous. Under the discovery rule, my lawsuit may well be timely if my story is true. So we must start with a preliminary mini-trial on my cover-up charge.

That first-round battle will have a curious feature: The more you are convinced that your weed killer was harmless, the more likely it is you will lose on the question of timing. The U.S. government insisted before its atom bomb tests, and insists to this day, that the radioactivity releases were too small to harm any downwind civilians. But taking this position, and asserting it firmly all along, played right into the hands of the plaintiffs on the question of timing. They had simply *believed* the government, they claimed, and for that reason alone failed to discover for twenty years that they had been injured. Judge Jenkins embraced this logic wholeheartedly, as have other judges since. It is a logic that holds that the offense doesn't have to start the clock until the defense capitulates on the core issues of the lawsuit.

The heart of a lawyer swells with pride in the contemplation of such cleverness. You are the defendant. To win in the pretrial maneuvering on timeliness, you must demonstrate that my injury and its link to your conduct were obvious and plainly discoverable years ago. To win in the trial proper, you must demonstrate that no such injury or linkage ever existed or could possibly be claimed even today. I, as the plaintiff, must first baldly insist that the injury was subtle, hidden, and quite undiscoverable, and then swear high and low that the injury was clear, definite, and quite obviously caused by your misconduct. Lawyers love this kind of game, because in the fullness of time they will always be paid generously to play both sides.

Judges can find much to love here too, because after the display of advocacy skills, they will do exactly what they please—which, in the age and culture of the new tort, most often means throwing away the clock and getting on with the trial. If it's clear that you did cause my injury, no new-school judge will want to let you off scot-free on a technicality like timing. But if it's not at all clear that you really hurt me, the new discovery rules let the case go to the jury as well, no matter when I file suit. After all, I can't possibly be charged with having discovered something that you earnestly insist never happened at all.

The New Well of Prophecy

As the cold tomb of remembrance began to yield up one live claim after another, so did the well of prophecy. It's a poor sort of memory (the Queen of Hearts once noted) that only works backward; the heirs to the new tort legacy had little trouble doing better. If cases are going to be decided twenty years after the injury, why not also twenty years before? The same telescope that permits us to look far into the past often lets us gaze far into the future.

The old law, as we have seen, shunned claims filed before their time, and the time for suing was generally after palpable physical harm had materialized. This requirement, like almost all other constraints on the right to sue, did not sit well with the tort Founders. They believed that litigation delayed would too often turn out to be litigation denied, neglected, or altogether forgotten. Any of these eventualities would deprive the world, once again, of the deterrence and the compensation that the new legal school was committed to supply in quantity. So the courts began systematically to dismantle the rules barring the premature litigant from the courtroom.

The legal device here was a second discovery rule, though never dignified with that title. It operated much like the first, but now at the front end of the litigation cycle. The claimant's state of mind was again the focus of attention. The idea was simply to recharacterize the distress and anxiety he might feel in anticipation of future harm as an injury in itself, sufficient on its own to support an immediate legal claim. A suit was now ripe for adjudication, in short, as soon as the claimant discovered that he might have been hurt, that he would perhaps fall sick some time in the future, that some day his health might conceivably deteriorate because of something the defendant had already done.

In 1977, for example, servicemen from the Orkin Exterminating Company in Perry County, Tennessee, sprayed the ground around the Laxton family's home with chlordane and heptachlor to eliminate termites. For several months afterward, the Laxtons' water didn't smell right. The Laxtons then discovered that their water supply had been contaminated with pesticide. They had suffered no physical complaints, they conceded, nor had they sought medical treatment. But they had learned that both chlordane and heptachlor are suspected human carcinogens. Mrs. Laxton had been "very worried" and would "call her husband at work, and cry and express concern about the future health of her children." They sued. A jury awarded $6,000 for mental anguish to each of the four members of the family, on top of $6,700 for property damage and expenses incurred in attempting to confirm that the pesticide had no impact on the Laxtons' health.

The Laxtons' case seemed simple and limited, but the principle it stood for was not. Other similar cases began to accumulate. Residents of Jackson Township, New Jersey, for example, were permitted to sue for their fear that they would contract cancer because toxic wastes had leaked from a municipal landfill into their well water. Individually, each decision was framed as a modest extension of previous ones. But the law was being transformed, step by step. At first, courts entertained fear suits only if the feared disease was imminent and nearly certain. After a while, some courts were approving phobic claims if supported by any "reasonable medical basis" for believing that future disease might materialize sooner or later. Still others went on to declare that any exposure to radiation or a toxic chemical would support a lawsuit because it had a "physical impact" at the molecular level, whether or not the victim displayed any visible symptoms.

The logic was soon extended in a subtle and clever way. I've been hurt, the argument now ran, precisely because I greatly fear (but don't really know) that I may have been hurt. The philosopher may choke on this corruption of the Cartesian argument for existence, but any half-competent lawyer can swallow it easily, and the Founders and their successors were no legal slouches. Fear of harm *is* harm, immediate and tangible, whatever else may (or may not) materialize later on. Indeed, the marketplace has already proved as much. Whatever private fear may trouble you, from terrorist kidnapping to losing your good looks, Lloyd's of London stands ready to cover it with the blanket of an insurance policy. The price

Lloyd's charges, when all is said and done, is a professional worrier's sober valuation of anxiety—now the *insurer's* anxiety that the feared risk might some day materialize as harm. With scientists and statisticians on the one hand to give credence to fear, and the insurance company actuaries on the other hand to price it, future accidents could thus be made tangible with marvelous, if wholly illusory, precision. Why not, then, require the party who would be responsible for tomorrow's accident or disease to pay the insurance premium today, or at least the tort system's equivalent? The physical harm might never materialize, but fear of future harm was harm itself, and that was enough for cash immediately.

This, as we shall see in later chapters, was only the comparatively modest beginning—and not by any means the end—of tort claims based on psychic injury alone. But it was no mean start. By the simple device of concentrating on the plaintiff's state of mind, rather than on concrete events in the physical world, the courts had again reset the clock, again extending by years or decades the period during which claims could be filed.

The next step was obvious enough. Accidents can rile people's nerves before they happen just as surely as afterward. Why wait on the sidelines until the toxic molecule or stream of electrons or photons has been released to work its invisible harm? Anyone who does business with an exterminator or home insulator, who travels on a railroad track or highway, or who lives near a chemical factory or waste dump, a power plant, gas pipeline, or construction project, is also at some risk of accidental toxic releases, which may possibly then lead to disease. One's life may as easily be cut short by the distant effects of tomorrow's accident as by the distant effects of yesterday's. If the second fear is enough to get you into court today, why not the first?

The answer can hardly be that the injury from tomorrow's accident is too speculative. If one "possibly" is allowed in bringing a matter to court immediately, there is no strong reason to balk at two. Certainly if *fear* is the linchpin of these suits, people can be just as frightened by the indefinite range of mishaps that could occur tomorrow as by the definite one that happened yesterday. Of course the chain of contingencies is a little longer the day before the accident than the day after, but only a little.

The logic was irrefutable. So before long, there were half a dozen accepted theories by which the accident that might happen tomorrow could be brought into court today. The ancient rules that had once rigidly cut off such suits as grossly premature had all but disappeared. By the early 1980s, the legal academics were inching toward a general theory under which awards would be based directly, without apology or embarrassment, on "enhanced risk" that accident or disease might develop some day in the future.

The Self-Winding Clock

In the space of three decades, the Founders and their followers thus dismantled time limits on litigation that had been integral to the tort system for centuries before. Today, being hit by a molecule can get you into court long before any harm is actually visible. Being hit with a Mack truck, however, is often not enough to start the lawsuit's clock ticking against you. The courts will gravely weigh your claim that you are emotionally distressed by the risks of injury not yet visible. But when it better suits new tort objectives, the courts indulgently treat you as a cockeyed optimist who never notices or worries about obvious and well-known hazards. If you were warned of peril, it is no wonder you suffer emotional distress immediately. If you were not warned, it is no wonder you did not realize your injury and sue until decades later.

These doctrines are all wonderfully circular and self-propelling. At the front end, fear and litigation feed on each other. The courts react to a murmur of anxiety about a new risk and put the litigation machinery in gear. The word gets out, and still more people infer from the flurry of legal activity that there is much to be worried about. So the courts now have a larger quantum of public fear to tackle. No sooner is a possible target for litigation identified than it is transformed—by the very fact of a lawsuit—into an urgent candidate for still more lawyering.

A similar dynamic operates at the end of the day as well. Defects in technology, like negligence in human conduct, depend critically on the context of time, place, and contemporary human capabilities and preferences. The best-designed cars of 1950 are unduly dangerous by 1980 standards; the same is true for almost any medical procedure, industrial process, or home appliance. So the later a lawsuit is filed, the more likely it is that a jury will detect a defect or negligence in the ancient product or conduct under scrutiny. An endless clock on litigation allows each improvement in technology, material, or design to set a new standard against which all earlier undertakings are then judged, so that progress itself becomes a reason for litigation.

There is no doubt that in their wholesale reform of ancient timing rules, new tort advocates achieved exactly what they intended—a vast increase in opportunities for litigation and an increased likelihood of success to boot. The old law used time limits to dissipate the rancor of conflicts. It discouraged a premature rush to court until the clash of tangible interests had reached a point of no return, and it encouraged ancient controversies to rest in peace so that once-fresh wounds would have a chance to heal. Today, real or imagined malefactors are chased eternally down the corridors of time, pursued by potential litigants years before their dirty deed is done and years afterward. The law now concerns itself with activities that took place fifty or more years ago and with injuries that will materialize, if at all, well into the next century. For better or worse, the modern law's timing rules are based on a single, age-old moral aspiration, that the wicked shall know no rest.

7

Sentence Without Verdict

IN 1676, the great English surgeon Richard Wiseman suggested for the first time that cancer might be caused by a sudden, traumatic injury—a blow to the chest, say, or a fall that breaks a leg. The theory remained popular for two centuries. But by the mid-nineteenth century physicians began to recognize that it had no substance. Traumatic injury does not, in fact, cause cancer.

Then workers' compensation laws arrived on the legal scene, first in Germany and other European countries, and eventually in the United States. Court dockets were soon crowded with claims that a blow received on the job had caused cancer some time later.

Scientists and doctors began a vigorous new search for traumatically induced cancer. A typical report in 1928 described an automobile mechanic who was severely struck in the face. The wound healed in two weeks, but eight weeks later the mechanic developed skin cancer at the site of the original injury. The physician reported the case but noted that a cause-and-effect link was "very much doubted." In the ensuing years, medical investigators examined the trauma-cancer link at length, but almost uniformly concluded that it did not exist.

By 1945, doctors were losing all interest in traumatically induced cancer. A 1947 observer accused unqualified physicians who testified in court to causal relationships between trauma and cancer of either "stupidity or cupidity." "Because toads appear after a rain it is not necessary to assume that it has rained toads," he continued, "yet this form of reasoning fills our medical testimony concerning trauma." "Two factors when brought to bear on the same individual very commonly produce cancer of all kinds," another sarcastically observed. "These two factors are a single trauma and insurance. . . . Unfortunate indeed is the man who works for a firm covered by insurance, for even his slightest injury may result in cancer." In 1961 another medical expert declared that the theory of traumatic causation would have been long since abandoned "if it were not for the litigation which keeps it alive."

The doctors were beginning to set aside the whole silly affair, but lawyers had other ideas. The major law journals latched on to traumatic cancer in 1933, and legal writing on the subject burgeoned in the 1950s and early 1960s. A 1962 law review article sagely observed that "the absence of scientific data to prove that a single trauma may cause cancer does not mean that cancer cannot result from trauma"; a few years later another argued that "shortcomings of the medical profession should not be visited upon the victims of industrial accidents." Checks continued to be cashed on the endorsement of such legal reasoning. "Aggravation of cancer or other disease may be inferable despite the lack of medical evidence establishing indisputable causal connection between trauma and spread of pre-existing cancer," the New Mexico Supreme Court explained in a 1958 decision, "whenever the sequence of events is so strong as to establish a causal connection." Judges and legal academics did not in fact abandon their embarrassing attempts at scholarship in this area until the late 1960s. By then, plaintiffs' lawyers had collectively concluded that toxic chemicals offered more promising prospects for achieving similar purposes.

Cause and Effect

It was fated almost from the beginning. As the Founders expanded the tort law's horizons in time and space, they were bound to collide, sooner or later, with the last great barrier that has traditionally separated the tort claimant from someone else's cash. The obstacle here was the element of cause.

Cause has always been the golden thread that links those who can pay with those who wish to be paid in the tort system. Congress need not worry at all about the causes of disease when it raises taxes to fund the Medicare system. But judges, unlike legislatures, have never had general authority to raise revenues from wherever convenient and disburse them wherever needed. A court does perhaps possess the raw power to order anyone to pay for anything. So do the Joint Chiefs of Staff, who (one might add) also have more effective means at their immediate disposal to enforce their wishes. The power just isn't supposed to be used indiscriminately.

The problem with cause is that it is a question of fact, and whatever authority the courts may have over legal doctrine, no judge has the power to make something a fact when it is not. The Founders and their successors, as we saw in the last two chapters, were eager to take on diffuse pollutants, long-latency diseases, and lawsuits among crowds, and they had no trouble reshaping the legal rules to permit as much. But scientists, who sooner or later get the last word on what is fact and what is not, remained frustratingly cautious about such matters. The only scientific certainty with most birth defects, cancer, other chronic disease, and the like is that certainty itself is very elusive. In addressing these afflictions, the honest scientist talks of shifting probabilities and evolving, but still primitive, understanding. Almost everything is possible; proving the negative—that something does *not* cause something else—is exceedingly difficult and time-consuming.

There is always epidemiological evidence, which looks at patterns of exposure and patterns of disease and attempts to establish correlations between the two. But the problems run deep here too. Good statisticians are well aware of the subtle difference between accidental correlation and affirmable causation; drawing such distinctions is indeed the heart of their abstruse profession. A man receives a blow to the chest; three months later his doctor discovers cancer near the spot. There is coincidence here, but no cause and effect. How can anyone be so sure? Only through painstaking studies of large populations over many decades. In time, one finds that the incidence of cancer does not rise after wars, nor is there any statistical increase in cancer among victims of automobile or industrial accidents, boxers, or football players. Traumatic injuries can also be studied systematically in laboratory animals. With trauma, the studies have been completed and the conclusions are now unambiguous. But in many other areas, the scientific picture remains much more cloudy.

Uncertainty, however, was anathema for practitioners of the new tort. Their entire social program depended, in the end, on definite judgments, and precise monetary awards, even when millions of claimants congregated in court, complaining of the most obscure diseases, physical and mental, and pressing claims that spanned decades. The pharmaceutical, chemical, and nuclear industries were either killing people in large numbers or they were not, and if they were, they should be called upon to pay for the same at once. There was no room here for the thought that some matters might be too complex and uncertain to be addressed intelligently in a courtroom.

So pressure developed to stretch out the science and the epidemiology. What was needed was certainty sufficient for the new tort purposes, and if the real scientific thing was not to be found, the illusion of certainty would have to suffice. When the competent scientists backed off and excused themselves from entanglement in the burgeoning legal industry, pseudoscientists, charlatans, and mystics of every description rushed in. The opportunities were everywhere.

There are, for example, over 60,000 significant birth defects in the United States every year. What causes them? A biological accident in the germ cell, a risk inherent in reproduction itself, is probably the most important single factor. But the Almighty cannot be sued. Alcohol, tobacco, and other recreational poisons also certainly play an important role. But the Founders recoiled at the thought of blaming the victim's personal habits. In some number of cases, however, the culprit is a medicinal drug, or a course of medical treatment, or a synthetic environmental poison of some kind. Even as we learn more about the causes of birth defects in general, we do not necessarily draw closer to the power to pin down with confidence the cause in any particular case.

In an earlier day, that would have been the end of the matter so far as the courts were concerned. But as the spirit of the law changed, obstetricians, midwives, and manufacturers of morning sickness drugs and spermicides suddenly began to look like very fair and convenient game.

Mary Oxendine, for example, was born on January 25, 1971, with a shortened forearm and only three fingers on her right hand, fused together.

Eleven years later, in February 1982, her parents filed suit demanding $10 million in compensatory damages and another $10 million in punitive damages from Merrell-Dow Pharmaceuticals. And what had that company done? For twenty-seven years it had manufactured and sold Bendectin, an antinausea morning sickness drug used, over the years, in 33 million pregnancies, including Mary's. Bendectin had been (and still is) approved by the FDA as "safe and effective." But after a three-week trial, a jury awarded Mary $750,000.

As the new tort school took full control in the early 1970s, Bendectin claims burgeoned. In one early case, a jury decided that the child's injuries were *not* caused by the drug but tried to award $20,000 for medical expenses anyway. Merrell-Dow won almost all the early cases, but each trial stimulated a flood of new claims. Eleven hundred claims were consolidated in a single class action. Faced with the staggering legal costs of taking such a case to trial, Merrell-Dow offered to settle for $120 million. Plaintiffs' lawyers foolishly torpedoed the offer. The case was then tried, and Merrell-Dow won again. But hundreds of other claimants had opted out of the class action, and their cases were still pending. In 1987 a jury awarded $2 million to a six-year-old boy born with club feet. Another jury awarded $95 million for another birth defect. As of July, 1987, seventeen juries had considered the Bendectin–birth defect link. Merrell-Dow won twelve times, plaintiffs five. Throughout, the overwhelming scientific consensus, in the FDA and in all respectable scientific circles, had not moved an inch: Bendectin does not, in fact, cause birth defects. "With Bendectin," a *New York Times* editorial commenting on the original class action concluded, "the law has made a devastation and called it a settlement." In 1985, under the mounting pressure of litigation, the drug was pulled from the market.

The reasoning behind the trauma cancer cases seems quaintly amusing today, at least to anyone familiar with the real causes of cancer. But identical errors are regularly repeated today, not just with Bendectin but in cases involving IUDs, spermicides, tampons, herbicides, vaccines, and countless other products. When there is enough doubt, and enough injury, rigorous proof of cause gives way to sympathy for the injured. The litigation opportunities are as boundless as the reservoir of human suffering is large.

Comparatively few women use morning sickness drugs; far more use contraceptives before or shortly after they unwittingly conceive. Katie Wells was born on July 1, 1981, with tragic birth defects. Her mother sued Ortho Pharmaceutical, blaming that company's spermicidal jelly, Ortho-Gynol, which she had used for about four weeks after conception. The active ingredient in the gel is Nonoxynol-9, also used in most other foams, gels, condoms, and contraceptive sponges. The trial judge decided that the statistical studies offered by experts were "inconclusive on the ultimate issue of whether [Nonoxynol] caused Katie Wells' birth defects." Just what did persuade him was never quite clear. But he ultimately declared that defects in Katie's left arm and shoulder and her right hand were caused by the spermicide, while her cleft lip, nostril deformity, and right optic nerve defect were not. A \$4.7 million award was upheld by a federal appellate court. The plaintiffs were not required, that court declared, "to produce scientific studies showing a statistically significant association between spermicides and congenital malformations in a large population" or to defer to two studies by the FDA that had found no link whatsoever between spermicides and birth defects. This time, the *New York Times* editorial was titled "Federal Judges vs. Science." "[T]he Federal judiciary has placed itself opposite the best judgment of the scientific community," said the *Times*. "That [the courts] ignored the best scientific evidence is an intellectual embarrassment."

At the heart of all these cases is the classic *post hoc ergo propter hoc* error of confusing temporal coincidence with cause and effect. Unlikely sequences of events are common, but the cause-effect correlations they suggest are spurious far more often than they are real. To the lay mind, however, a sequence of events that coincides with preconceptions about what causes what can be almost overwhelmingly suggestive. The manufacturer of a polio vaccine thus learned in 1974 that it could be held liable for cases of polio in an area where polio itself was epidemic, so long as there was sufficient doubt about whether the disease was caused by the vaccine or the wild virus. A 1984 case imposed liability for a failure to warn that the swine flu vaccine might cause "serum sickness." There was then, and is now, no reputable scientific evidence that the vaccine causes any such malady. Time and again, courts have declared, through the instrument of generous tort verdicts, that so-and-so causes such-and-such. But as Sportin' Life could have told them, "It ain't necessarily so."

The problems have proved graver still when one weak but definite cause-effect link operates among other much stronger ones. The Dalkon Shield significantly increased a woman's risk of contracting pelvic inflammatory disease (PID). While IUDs were on the market, close to a million women a year developed PID. The Dalkon Shield and all other IUDs have now been withdrawn from the market, but the incidence of PID has nevertheless increased slightly. How is this possible? By far the largest cause of PID is not contraceptive devices but venereal disease caused by sexual activity. Similar numbers cloud any inquiry into the risks of vaccines. Each year about 3.5 million American children are vaccinated three times against whooping cough. This prevents at least 300,000 cases of the disease, saves at least 400 lives, and averts thousands of cases of seizure and pneumonia and a smaller number of cases of serious brain damage. But the vaccine is not perfect; it roughly doubles the usual risk of contracting a rare but serious condition that can result in permanent brain damage. Statistics from one large-scale study suggest that the vaccine causes some 30 cases of brain damage every year, among 600 other occurrences of that condition among children under six years old every year. Since virtually all children are vaccinated, all 600 reactions represent potential lawsuits. Hundreds were in fact filed in the late 1970s and 1980s.

Even more difficult questions of cause and effect surfaced as ambitious advocates pressed outward into the terra incognita of environmental liability. From the statistician's perspective, spurious geographical clusters are no different from spurious chronological correlations. By pure chance, some children will be vaccinated on a Monday and fall sick by Friday even if the vaccine is blameless. Similar rolls of the dice guarantee that unusually large clusters of one disease or another will occur geographically. Juries are easily led astray, however, because the statistics of clustering are horribly counterintuitive.

About 4 in every 100,000 children, for example, contract leukemia every year. A perfectly average incidence of the disease in Woburn, Massachusetts, between 1969 and 1985 would have been six cases in all; there were in fact nineteen. Too many to be a coincidence? The plaintiffs' lawyers thought so and cashed in handsomely (at the expense of local chemical companies) on a claim that it was. But the numbers are far from clear. Take a large map of the United States and scatter 28,000 beads across it at random—the total number of childhood leukemias that occur in this country in a sixteen-year period. Pure chance will almost certainly produce some unusually dense clusters of beads here and there on the map. Now superimpose a second map, showing the locations of the 2,000 largest hazardous waste dumps or chemical factories in the country. Pure chance, once again, will guarantee that some of the leukemia clusters will land close to some of the dumps or factories. A similar degree of overlap is equally likely, one must recognize, if the second map displays the 2,000 largest bowling alleys or amusement parks. But we are predisposed to fear dumps more than bowling alleys, and preconceptions count for everything when there is no solid science to go on.

The most aggressive proponents of the new tort arrived with suspicions and preconceptions in abundance, and marched boldly forward. Some of the less scrupulous learned one invaluable technique early on that proved good for printing money almost any day of the week. In a process familiar to any unscrupulous politician, it is easy to gerrymander clusters of cancers or other ailments and the boundaries of the population being examined to include an unusually high—or low—incidence of disease in much the same way as the boundaries of voting districts can be arranged to bias elections in favor of the party in power. The incidence of a particular disease in a class consisting of a single sick person is 100 percent. The incidence of the same disease in a class of 240 million will exactly equal the national average—0.05 percent, let us say. Almost any statistical picture in between can be drawn simply through careful manipulation of the class selected for scrutiny. Different analysts reached quite different conclusions about the leukemia clusters in Woburn, for example, simply by drawing different-sized circles around the contaminated water system. This worked to confirm the worst suspicions of those convinced at the outset that a particular industry or activity needed more new tort deterrence than it was currently receiving. But more objective observers recognized that nothing was being reliably proved at all.

Misdirection and Merry-Go-Round Liability

The uneasy, sickening perception began to rise that the cluster game was mostly fraud, and that most people in the business secretly knew it. Judges and lawyers like to characterize their business as a relentless search for truth, but litigation is in fact a rather mechanical and bureaucratic process run by people of a bent for such processes. The system as a whole, as the trauma cancer cases demonstrated, is perfectly capable of endorsing the most systematic falsehoods. Cut loose from the discipline of solid science, good engineering judgment, and rigorous proof of cause, the whole enterprise quickly falls into disarray and then, inevitably, into disrepute.

The courts had encountered very similar difficulties before, in their impetuous rush to uncover product defects. It was easy enough to condemn environmental poisons in the abstract, just as it had been easy to decry product defects, whatever form they might take. But applying the principle once it had been trumpeted was distressingly difficult. After a prolonged period of vexation, some courts finally hit upon the happy idea of shifting the burden of proof.

Ray Barker discovered the possibilities early on in a case involving an allegation of design defect. In August 1970, Barker was working at a construction site at the University of California at Santa Cruz, operating a high-lift loader manufactured by the Lull Engineering Company. The device was designed to lift loads of up to 5,000 pounds to a maximum height of 32 feet. In the course of lifting, a load tipped. Barker leaped from the loader but was struck by a piece of falling lumber. He sued Lull Engineering, claiming defective design. The loader, he claimed, should have been equipped with outriggers, mechanical arms extending out from the sides of the machine, as well as a roll bar and seat belts. Lull's experts testified that seat belts would have increased the danger by making exit more difficult and that Barker had operated the loader on a steep slope for which it was unsuited. No competitive loaders with similar lifting capacity were equipped with outriggers. By a ten to two vote, the jury found in favor of the company. Barker appealed, and his case reached the Supreme Court of California in 1978.

"[T]rial judges have repeatedly confronted difficulties in attempting to devise accurate and helpful instructions in design defect cases," the court acknowledged. "[A] product may be found defective in design, even if it satisfies ordinary consumer expectations, if through hindsight the jury determines that the product's design embodies 'excessive preventable danger.'" But recollecting that proof of design defects had proved intractably difficult, the court then made a second, much more radical announcement. "The allocation of [the burden of proof] is particularly significant in this context. . . . [O]nce the plaintiff [shows] that the injury was . . . caused by the product's design, the burden should appropriately shift to the defendant to prove, in light of the relevant factors, that the product is not defective." So the jury's verdict in favor of Lull Engineering was overturned, and the case was sent back for a new trial. Thereafter, in California at least, it would be up to *defendants* to prove that their loaders were *not* defective.

The burden of proof is a marvelously plastic piece of legalese. Barker claimed that the loader was defective in its design; Lull Engineering insisted it was not. With or without a three-day crash course in high-lift loader design, no honest juror was going to pretend that he really knew which side was right. So the outcome had to turn, in the end, on who should win a case when no convincing case had been made. Reversing a tradition as old as the common law itself, the California court baldly announced that if there is no persuasive case either way when the design of a product is attacked as defective, the plaintiff wins.

Other courts, toiling under a growing weight of claims that eluded solid proof, quickly seized on this idea. By the early 1970s, for example, doctors were being sued in increasing numbers for failing to diagnose incipient disease, especially cancer, at a very early stage. An obvious problem was proving that an earlier diagnosis would have made a difference to the patient—a particularly difficult thing to do with cancer, where useful treatments often do not exist. In 1974, New Jersey courts found a simple solution, announcing that thereafter it would be up to the doctor to demonstrate that an earlier diagnosis would *not* have produced a cure.

If burdens of proof could cut so easily through the Gordian knot of product defect and negligence, they could serve equally well to simplify the inquiry about warning. In the Anita Reyes polio-vaccine case, discussed in an earlier chapter, the vaccine manufacturer demonstrated convincingly that Anita's mother was *not* the kind of woman who paid any attention to formal warnings. For a legal traditionalist, that would have been the end of the matter: The failure to warn, if there was one at all, could not have caused the injury. But *that* just couldn't be the right result when an eight-month-old girl had been severely injured. So the court of appeals announced instead a "rebuttable presumption" that people like Mrs. Reyes "would have read an adequate warning" and heeded it.

All of these were important cases in the expansion of liability. But the new deal on burden of proof had its greatest effect when the courts finally thought to use it to get around intractable questions of cause and effect. Who is to say for certain whether or not open-air atomic bomb tests in the 1950s and 1960s caused some cases of leukemia downwind of the test sites? The downwind radiation fallout from the tests was very low, and no scientifically solid showing of injury is possible. But a cause-effect link between the tests and any individual case of leukemia can never be absolutely ruled out either. So the judge hearing that case simply decreed that it was up to the government to prove that the particular cancers had *not* been caused by radioactive fallout from the nuclear tests. It was a perfect solution, at least for everyone but the infinitely wealthy People of the United States, who were being called upon to prove or pay up.

The most ambitious of the new tort brotherhood finally went one step further. Whatever the burden of proof on any one issue, the structure of a trial as a whole still favored the defendant. The various elements of liability—such things as negligence, lack of adequate warning, and causation—still had to be established in turn, and the plaintiff would still lose if the defendant could prove his side on any one critical point. The requirements were serial, each necessary, none alone sufficient. The patient was not alerted to the risk and never consented to it, the doctor had performed the operation negligently, and her negligence had in fact caused the injury.

But why should a court be so particular? If the objective (in some courts at least) is to control the broader sweep of human affairs or to get cash to the people who need it, why not convert the necessary into the sufficient, and impose liability whenever any *one* of these elements was present? Thus emerged, in place of the old ducks-in-a-row theory, an altogether new merry-go-round theory of liability in which the plaintiff could take any one vacant horse and go for a ride.

Sometimes, cause is what's easy to ascertain. There was not much doubt that the fiery deaths in a Pinto *were* connected with the gas tank, or that a person with a bullet in his back *was* indeed injured by the handgun, or that the highway victim *was* injured, indirectly at least, by the alcohol the other driver had imbibed too freely. The accident happened. The product undoubtedly figured in it. And it was then all too tempting to gloss over whether the product was truly defective in any intelligent sense of the word, or whether adequate warning of the risk was provided.

Sometimes the simple element in the case is not cause but negligence or product defect. The Dalkon Shield certainly was a bad IUD. This soon became so apparent that the courts emphasized the fact to the exclusion of all others, which conveniently allowed them to avoid the much more difficult question of whether the Shield had actually caused a particular plaintiff's pelvic disease. And if a doctor indisputably *had* failed to diagnose the cancer at the earliest possible time, the courts were quick to brush aside any argument about whether earlier diagnosis would have helped at all. There had been negligence, after all, and surely that was enough.

The game was played out even more effectively when warnings were placed at center stage. If no one could confidently say whether the hazardous waste dump had in fact caused any harm, the lawsuit would turn on whether the chemical company that sold it thirty years earlier had adequately warned the buyer of a possible risk. If it was obvious that the vaccine was *not* defective, and highly debatable whether or not it had caused the injury in question, the case would turn on whether the victim had been adequately warned of the possibility of harm.

Carried further, the failure-to-warn cases became single-minded inquisitions on cover-up and conspiracy. The flames of the Dalkon Shield, asbestos, Ford Pinto, and Agent Orange disputes were vigorously fanned by accusations of this character, some (though hardly all) of which were quite true. The more spine-chilling the charges of conspiracy, the less attention anyone paid to questions of what actually caused the injury or whether the products could reasonably be labeled defective. Was Agent Orange really a bad risk for U.S. servicemen faced with the alternative of hostile enemy fire concealed by a leafy green jungle? Was asbestos really unreasonably dangerous in the wartime circumstances where it was most extensively used? How should anyone deal with the poisonous synergy between asbestos and tobacco, which multiplies tenfold the risk of either toxin alone? Clever advocacy relegated these central but terribly difficult questions to brief footnotes in elegant legal disquisitions on contracts, warning, and disclosure. Among professional magicians, this trick is known as misdirection.

Through subterfuges of this kind, the courts could achieve almost anything they wanted, at least in the individual case. Rather than manipulate burdens of proof, the courts began to dispense with proof on certain questions altogether. To escape liability, defendants would have to do what plaintiffs once had to do: establish each link in a convincing narrative. When ignorance is king in the courtroom, the burden of proof decides everything; whoever bears it is bound to lose. Burdens of proof do not dispel any ignorance, of course; they just shift its costs. The magic of the burden of proof is that it smoothly converts ignorance about the facts into certainty about the verdict, and the greater the ignorance, the more certain and expeditious the verdict. The merry-go-round theories of liability go further still, yielding a sentence without any real verdict. The process has been described before. The King's messenger, so Alice is told by the Queen of Hearts, is "in prison now, being punished; and the trial doesn't even begin till next Wednesday; and of course the crime comes last of all." "Suppose he never commits the crime?" Alice asks. "That," the Queen firmly replies, "would be all the better, wouldn't it?"

Cashing In on Uncertainty

Legal diversions of this kind produced the desired results, but not through any regular process of law. A merry-go-round provides orderly enough locomotion for any particular rider and horse, but to the observer on the outside it is all a confused blur. Legal conceits can likewise create a semblance of order in the individual case, but when cases accumulate, the chaos inherent in the underlying rules soon becomes all too apparent.

The problems were most obvious with allegedly defective products. What emerged here was a straightforward legal lottery. Five Bendectin cases produced no award at all; a sixth netted the plaintiff a $95 million verdict. A crane manufacturer who was sued in two different states after different operators drove into high-tension wires lost $12.5 million for failure to warn in one state but won summarily (on grounds that the risk was obvious) in the second. Out of eleven early cases against MER/29, the manufacturer won four, the plaintiff won only compensatory damages in four, and the plaintiff won punitive damages in three—one of which was then overturned on appeal. At one point late in the company's legal battles over asbestos, lawyers for Manville staged a series of full-scale trials, presenting the same evidence and instructing mock juries according to the modern rules. Verdicts from five such panels ranged from no liability at all to a large award of both regular and punitive damages. From the perspective of the persistent plaintiff's lawyer, it is a game of heads-you-lose, tails-we-flip-again.

In the environmental cases, the confused state of the legal rules was reflected in the character of the awards and settlements. Money changed hands; there was no doubt at all about that. But the amounts bore no relation to any traditional measures of cause, effect, and harm. Jackson Township plaintiffs recovered for polluted groundwater, even though they suffered no physical symptoms at all; the award covered health monitoring and the expense of hooking up to an uncontaminated water supply. A child born with Down's syndrome within a year of the accident at the Three Mile Island nuclear plant in Pennsylvania collected $1.1 million, though no plausible scientific evidence linked the injury with the accident. The science behind the verdicts and settlements was no stronger at Love Canal, New York, Los Paseos, California, or Toone, Tennessee. The settlements and awards were now explained by referring to a need for future medical monitoring, by invoking the plaintiffs' considerable emotional distress, or by making sweeping pronouncements on the subject of disease phobia.

In all of these cases, plaintiffs came to court emotionally convinced of the merit of their claims. Defendants arrived with a crew of bloodless toxicologists and epidemiologists ready to testify about the state of scientific ignorance, which was all anyone really had. Both sides were equally horrified at the prospect of taking matters to a jury, the plaintiffs fearing that a jury might look at the paltry handful of facts carefully, the defendants fearing that it probably would not. So the litigation risks came to be recognized as much more concrete than the risks from the poisons themselves, and settlements were built not on the physical hazard, which was impossible to pin down, but on the purely legal one. Virtually every case ended as a compromise settlement, with the plaintiffs cashing in on emotion, and the defendants paying dearly to escape from high-stakes legal uncertainty.

The chaotic state of the law invited fundamentally new litigation strategies. A first lucrative way to exploit legal disorder is through a form of guerrilla warfare, in which final victory is promised not to the just but to the persistent. The battle is fought without a front or a timetable, manned by springtime soldiers and sunshine patriots. By 1985, for example, one out of four obstetrician-gynecologists had been sued. Almost three-quarters won their cases, but it cost the physician or insurer an average of $20,000 per claim to do so. Stakes like these often make it prudent to settle claims with no merit whatsoever—especially when the disarray of shifting burdens of proof and merry-go-round theories of liability always keeps open the possibility of defeat, no matter how weak the underlying case by conventional standards.

The guerrilla war can be fought even more effectively against product manufacturers. In the space of a few years, for example, nearly 800 lawsuits were filed against Searle's Copper-7 IUD. Some 470 were disposed of one way or another—one-third with no payment and no trial, the remaining two-thirds with very small settlements. By 1986, Searle had actually been to court for full trials in only ten cases, of which it had won eight. In one 1986 ruling, a federal judge declared that the evidence submitted on behalf of seventeen Copper-7 users who had sued Searle was nothing but a "series of alternative unsubstantiated theories." Series of theories, however, is what modern merry-go-round liability is all about; the cases continued to mount, and so did the expenses. Searle spent $1.5 million defending just four cases that it won outright; the several hundred million dollars in legal expenses that Searle faced were hundreds of times its annual profit on the device. The legal vindication was bittersweet at best.

A second way to profit from the legal uncertainty depends on the frontal assault, in a process the *New York Times* has come to call "Orangemail." This strategy for untold fortune requires a coordinated legal wave, and victory depends on sheer force of numbers. "Hordes of personal-injury lawyers sign up alleged victims of a toxic chemical, creating the prospect of such costly litigation that the manufacturers are driven to settle, even if no connection between injury and chemical can be proved. . . . Agent Orange is orangemail in its purest form. A thousand tort lawyers jumped on the settlement bandwagon, even though the court found their case to be substantially without merit. . . . Yet the makers of Agent Orange faced the prospect of endless litigation, and the risk of losing many cases before juries apt to put compassion ahead of dispassion." As Lenin once said on the subject of tanks, quantity has a quality all its own.

Sometimes, of course, the two methods are combined in different phases of the same campaign. The Bendectin war, for example, included both a 1,000-claimant class assault and hundreds of individual suits that continued after Merrell-Dow won the class action battle. In March 1985, an outbreak of salmonella poisoning was traced to milk pasteurized by a dairy owned by Jewel Companies, a Chicago-based food retailer. Five days after the outbreak, Jewel was named in a $100 million class action lawsuit filed by a handful of self-appointed class representatives on behalf of 20,000 plaintiffs. In January 1987 a Chicago jury ruled for Jewel on all points. But some plaintiffs had opted out of the class trial, and dozens of cases continued to be litigated.

Across the board, the confusion in the rules quickly attracted the legal speculators and arbitrageurs whose business it is to invest skillfully in disorder. It was not necessary to have a solid case on all important points or in every claim filed; it was good enough to have a plausible case in some of them. It was not necessary to win all or even most cases filed: A one in ten chance of winning twenty times your stake produces a very comfortable living if the bet is repeated often enough. There was money to be made on liability futures, and good lawyers knew it. Not every part of the pig was certain to appreciate. But plaintiffs' lawyers, able to play the odds again and again, were assured a very comfortable living by investing in the hog as a whole.

A Question of Control

A "single injury cannot cause a malignant tumor," two doctors observed in 1962. But "we see little hope in the present imperfect state of science and society of ever establishing such a fact to the satisfaction of everyone. The objections peculiar to negative experiments of this kind will always be present; that is, the exact conditions which existed when a particular trauma affected a particular worker on a particular spot were not duplicated. It may be that the relationship of trauma to cancer will be explained not by experiments designed to study this specific problem, but rather by an overwhelming clarification of the etiologies of malignant conditions which will appear with continuing basic cancer research."

That clarification was in fact already developing in 1962. It solidified in the next decade. And as predicted, the result was the disappearance of traumatic cancer claims from the courts. The legal focus now shifted to toxic chemicals, drugs, contraceptives, and radiation. Scientifically, these were much more plausible candidate causes of cancer than trauma. But plausibility is not what courtroom proof is supposed to be all about. And when it came to establishing more, the courts found themselves adrift in a sea of uncertainty and ignorance. Relatively few cancer victims have suffered a sudden trauma near the point of tumor some time before the tumor is discovered, but, fortunately for lawyers, all will have been exposed, at some level or other, to synthetic chemicals or radiation. Today's epidemiologists may be quite certain that the large majority of cancers are *not* caused by exposures of this type, but the courts, once again, are lagging decades behind. The only convincing negative case in such lawsuits is an affirmative demonstration that some *other* factor caused the disease complained of—but such proof is unavailable in a day when the precise origin of most long-term disease is still untraceable.

As the history of the trauma cancer cases reveals, the old tort law was not without its problems. But the judges who administered it were at least modest in their ambitions and determined to keep well in mind their individual and institutional limitations. They declined even to address many of the most difficult questions of cause and effect, leaving it to private contract to allocate responsibility in advance. Perhaps no one really knew whether the polio vaccine might occasionally cause polio, whether dust in the workplace might cause lung disease or a spermicide trigger birth defects, but contractual arrangements could take care of the contingency without ever wading into the scientific controversy. In the cases that judges did examine in depth, the disputes were confined by stricter limits of time and space, and this further simplified the issues. Strict rules of privity and proximate cause kept the causal inquiry short. Suits were brought by individual plaintiffs, not through class actions, which precluded most claims based on very diffuse toxic exposures. Claims could not be pressed long before actual injury had materialized, or long after. To be sure, some trauma cancer cases and other factually unsound cases did slip through the net now and again. But countless other questionable cases did not.

The new tort Founders started from different factual assumptions, and they had a quite different agenda from their more sober predecessors. When all was said and done, their system assumed and required at least one external human cause for almost every misadventure, and preferably more than one to increase the chances of finding a solvent defendant. The facts were eventually stretched to meet the new demand.

In 1975 Guido Calabresi, one of the major defenders of modern tort law, published an elegant essay on the legal question of cause. "[M]any seemingly significant philosophical questions concerning cause become irrelevant to the use of that term in law. To amplify: so far as legal language is concerned, the 'cause' of a disease would depend on how, at any given time, it could be most easily controlled. From this point of view, in the nineteenth century it would have been appropriate to speak of the 'cause' of tuberculosis as the absence of sun and the presence of bad living conditions. . . . With the identification of the Koch bacillus all that changed. At first potentially, and subsequently in practice, efforts directed at *this* causally linked element seemed most likely to control the disease. . . . More recently, the prospect of genetic engineering has again changed the causal language appropriate to this disease. Now one can, in a meaningful way, speak of genetic predisposition as a 'cause' of tuberculosis."

As Calabresi frankly acknowledged, modern tort law, in its wisdom as in its foolishness, was driven by the objective of control. The issue, in the end, was who would reign over the boundless territories of human ignorance. Until modern times, the accepted rule has always been that when in serious doubt, the courts would stay outside the fray. Individuals, regulatory agencies, and legislatures would decide, instead, what is to be done and who should pay when no one is the least bit confident about the right answer. But the Founders had different designs, and grander aspirations for the courts. So the jurisprudence of ignorance expanded beyond all previous bounds.

The old trauma cancer cases are gone, of course. In their place today we have the toxic tort, involving drugs, contraceptives, vaccines, chemicals, pesticides, and power plants. There have been great advances in science, but the legal picture is one of regression. Measured by the volume of scientifically fanciful litigation and the degree of legal artifice needed to usher these cases through the courts, the jurisprudence of ignorance is still on a rapid rise. The scientists have been cautious about their claims, but the courts have not. Vindicating the ancient biblical promise, fools have rushed in where angels fear to tread.

8

Pain and Punishment

LILLY GRAY bought a new Ford Pinto in November 1971. Six months later she set out on a drive to Barstow, California, accompanied by thirteen-year-old Richard Grimshaw. While going up the freeway exit ramp, the car stalled; moments later another car slammed into its rear, driving the gas tank forward and impaling it on a bolt. The passenger compartment was engulfed in flames. Mrs. Gray was killed, and Richard suffered permanently disfiguring burns over his face and body.

He sued Ford. The placement of the Pinto's gas tank behind the rear axle, his lawyer argued, made it unsafe in rear-end collisions. Inexpensive changes would have protected against the danger. Ford responded that the car had a reasonably safe overall design and met federal standards for crashworthiness in effect at the time.

A jury awarded Richard $2.5 million in compensation for his injuries, much of it for the pain he had suffered, and a further stunning $125 million in punitive damages against Ford, which the trial judge cut to $3.5 million. Ford did not bother to contest the award for Richard's pain but it did appeal the punitive award, insisting that it had had no evil motive.

In 1981, a full nine years after the accident, the court of appeals conceded as much but sustained the jury award anyway. California law, it declared, allows punitive damages even if the defendant had no "actual intent to harm the plaintiff or others." All that is necessary is "conscious disregard" for the safety of such persons. "Punitive damages," the court explained, "provide a motive for private individuals to enforce rules of law and enable them to recoup the expenses of doing so." So Ford paid Richard $6 million, most of which went to cover intangible distress, on the one hand, and corporate iniquity, on the other.

The Old Limits

Baseball is 90 percent physical, Yogi Berra once observed, and the other half is mental. As the Founders took charge, the law of accidents soon came to incorporate similar numbers. A jurisprudence once concerned with broken limbs and with who would pay to reset them slowly shifted its emphasis to matters mental and psychic.

As far back as the seventh century, a time when English law set tort damages by statute, the courts were prepared to consider some claims for hurt feelings. The idea was to encourage recourse to the courts instead of retaliation after a blow that might cause little harm but large offense. In one 1696 English case, for example, a daughter sued her mother after the mother pretended the girl was mentally ill, took her to the apothecary, forced medicine on her, and tied her up for two or three hours. The daughter was awarded £2,000, a fortune at the time. By the mid-1800s, the legal consensus among American courts firmly supported this sort of award.

But this history notwithstanding, courts have long been uneasy about all claims centered on mental distress. The concerns have always fallen into three categories: proof, price, and the proliferation of suits.

From the very beginning, judges worried about how easy it is for plaintiffs to feign or exaggerate psychic injury. In a case from the year 1348, in which the parties are remembered now only by their initials, "I de S," a tavern keeper's wife, sued after she successfully dodged a hatchet thrown by "W de S," an irate customer. But the rowdy customer successfully cast doubt on her claim of great emotional trauma, and she was not paid. Physical pain has always seemed like a more objective concept, but in practice it too can be guessed at but not measured. Even if fear or pain can be proved, they are impossible to price. Asking a husband how much money he would accept in advance for the death of his wife is more likely to lead to a puzzled stare, if not a fistfight, than a nuanced damage assessment.

A final concern was that countless lawsuits might be cloned from a single accident. Almost any accident victim other than a hermit in the forest leaves a circle of sorrowing family and friends, not to mention utter strangers shocked when they witnessed the ghastly scene. And with the proliferation of such suits come second-round problems of proof and price: The anguish of the victim's loving daughter may be apparent to all, but what about his black-sheep son, who never had much use for Dad during his lifetime and came to town only to file a claim?

All the while, the law recognized that psychic injuries can be real and that in principle they deserve redress like any others. The law's compromise, until the arrival of the Founders, was a set of simple mechanical rules that broadly allowed a few kinds of psychic damages but flatly denied most others.

One line was firmly drawn against claims where the mental distress had not arisen from physical contact. The traditional English rule, unanimously adopted by U.S. courts, was that negligent infliction of pure mental distress was no grounds for a suit. Unless the victim of negligence had been physically abused, she would have to take care of her own psychic injuries. *Intentional* outrages, where the perpetrator intended all along to cause fear or distress, were quite another matter, but cases of this kind have been comparatively rare.

The old rules, as we saw in connection with barriers to premature litigation, also demanded some concrete physical injury as a precondition to opening the courthouse doors. If Baker had lost his arm in a car accident, he was allowed to seek compensation for the earnings he would lose in years to come. If bitten by a dog, he could ask for damages to compensate for his reasonable anxiety about the risk of rabies. But a definite physical injury—the lost limb or the dog bite—was essential at the threshold.

Finally, the courts placed a narrow and peculiar set of limits on claims for certain intangible interests in family and friendship. Under the rubric of *loss of consortium,* a husband was allowed to sue for the loss of his wife's or child's services—with the valuable economic nature of those services being an essential predicate. This was a day, one must recall, when the wife was viewed as the husband's servant and property, and the older children often served as the father's apprentices, stable boys, or handmaidens. Sexist and paternalistic though these ideas now appear, the rules they spawned were logical enough for their cultural times.

Like all the other old rules, the rule against damage for pure emotional distress could operate very harshly. On March 25, 1934, Susie Waube watched horrified from the window of her home as her daughter Dolores was struck and killed by a car negligently driven by Amber Rose Warrington. Less than a month later Mrs. Waube died, allegedly from the shock. Her husband sued for the death of his wife; the Wisconsin Supreme Court flatly rejected the claim. A negligent driver had no responsibility for "physical injuries sustained by one out of ordinary physical peril as a result of the shock of witnessing another's danger." Imposing such liability would be "wholly out of proportion" to Warrington's culpability, "would put an unreasonable burden upon users of the highway, open the way to fraudulent claims, and enter a field that has no sensible or just stopping point."

Similar limits operated when the defendant's state of mind was at issue. If plaintiffs could at times collect a bonus for the mental dimension of what they had endured, defendants could at times be forced to pay a premium for their maliciousness, callousness, or fraud—for the aggravating aspects of *their* mental state in the incident. Like awards for psychic distress, punitive awards have an ancient and respectable pedigree. The full-blown principle turns up in a 1763 case of illegal entry. The jury was held justified in going beyond "the small injury done to the plaintiff" in order to punish "a most daring public attack made upon the liberty of the subject" through entry and imprisonment pursuant to "a nameless warrant." Unlike criminal fines, which they otherwise resemble, punitive damages are paid to the plaintiff rather than to the state, and they are assessed according to a civil jury's unwritten standards on a case-by-case basis.

Once again, however, the old tort law was suspicious of punitive awards, and for many of the same reasons. Like psychic damages, punitive damages have an open-ended, anything-goes quality that can too easily stoke the ambitions of eager plaintiffs, the zealous advocacy of their lawyers, and the vindictive or sympathetic passions of juries. Proving a defendant's knowing turpitude is every bit as difficult as proving a plaintiff's inward anguish, horror, or humiliation. Pricing turpitude correctly is still more difficult. And punitive damages again raise the danger of proliferation. A single negligent act, say of product misdesign, can spawn repeated punitive awards in different courtrooms, and the payment of punitive awards often sweeps in a host of peripheral bystanders. When assessed against a corporation, for example, punitive damages are paid by stockholders, not by the responsible executives, and often not even by the stockholders who owned the company when the original mistakes were made.

For these reasons, the old tort law hemmed in punitive claims with limitations even more severe than those surrounding claims for psychic injury. Punitive damages had to derive from conduct that went far beyond ordinary negligence, with the most common standard being *outrageous misconduct.* The defendant had to have acted if not with outright malice, then with a truly wanton disregard for others' safety. And the focus was on individual culpability: It was unheard-of for the punitive principle to be transmitted from one party to another by association. An employer might be made to pay compensatory damages for outrageous acts by its employees who should have been supervised or restrained, but it would never have to pay punitive damages simply in its capacity as employer.

The old rules confining claims for both psychic distress and punitive damages were thus reasonably clear and notably strict. On both sides, cultural restraints provided a last, practical barrier against awards of this character. Juries of that stoic era usually viewed with suspicion a plaintiff's necessarily self-serving testimony about how he had suffered emotionally; victims were expected to be made of sterner stuff. And if the defendant was held in high social esteem, as producers generally were, the chance of a punitive award was slight. In a day when accidents occurred frequently and the victim was, as often as not, thought to be responsible for watching out for himself, punitive damage awards proved exceptionally rare.

Changing the Climate

The more principled Founders had little interest in damages for either pain or punishment, at least not when the new tort manifesto was first being drafted. It was precisely because accidents are normal and inevitable, the early theoreticians had written, that their statistically predictable costs could be absorbed by producers (and eventually consumers collectively) with little muss or fuss. The vaccine maker would continue to sell its lifesaving product, adding a small margin to the price to insure against the unavoidable side effects of vaccination. Stringent liability would work not because producers were vicious, but because they were mostly virtuous; the stability, prosperity, and efficiency of their operations made them logical candidates for the role of social insurer. Far from increasing the level of acrimony and distrust in the courts, the new rules were supposed to cool the passions by regularizing the process; the plaintiff-consumer would collect his routine award from the bloodless defendant-insurer with no more ill will than if he were filing a claim on his own insurance policy. The tort system would tick along unemotionally, more like a mundane tax audit than a crowd-stirring murder trial. Or so the Founders expected and promised.

But reality has a logic of its own. It was all very well for judges and academics to argue, in their richly footnoted, 100-page opinions and law review articles, that holding the vaccine maker liable in no way implied that it bore any sort of moral guilt for the paralysis of its victims. But the courts are influential and respected teachers who shape public opinion as much as they follow it. For centuries the public had been conditioned to view the tort system as one that identified fault, admonished those responsible, and succored the victims. In the public's mind, someone who is hailed into court and ordered to pay a huge damage award has surely misbehaved in some reprehensible way; someone ordered to pay a whole series of awards is quickly branded as a habitual miscreant.

Each step down the new tort road reinforced this emergent public attitude. Standard-form contracts were to be tossed out as a trick played by the powerful on the powerless. Government and professional safety standards could count for guilt but not innocence because producers might have rigged them behind the scenes. The content of warning labels could matter only in a negative way for similar reasons.

Educated by its courts, the public increasingly came to view accidents as malign and calculated intrusions on the settled order of things. The exploitive producers of the world, from the gigantic multinational firm down to the factory-like hospital with its assembly-line surgeons, were not only thick-skinned and well insured, but close to malevolent in their callousness: They *knew* accidents like this were going to happen, but they still declined to take measures needed to prevent the latest one. As for their consumer-victims, now seen to be uninformed and easily misled, they were the sort of vulnerable and much-put-upon people who suffer intensely from life's reverses and require much help in recovering from them.

Well before they arrived in the jury box, typical citizens were thus sensitized to claims of unusual distress, on the one hand, and callousness, on the other. The new tort rules provided ample scope for them to exercise both their generosity and their indignation.

The New Lamentations

As we saw in earlier chapters, the Founders and their successors had already done some ground-breaking work at the site where others now set about erecting a worthy legal monument on the foundations of psychic injury. Invoking plausible fears of future disease had first proved useful in circumventing timing rules, which would otherwise have barred sympathetic claims as premature. The specter of cancer phobia had been invoked to justify paying off claimants who could not convincingly prove injury of any other form. If fear or distress could sustain a million-dollar award when the accompanying physical injury was suspect and uncertain, distress surely could justify even more cash when the accompanying injury was clear and definite.

Every trial that involves serious injury today will include extended discussions of the victim's pain. The plaintiff routinely summons expert testimony from physicians, impressively illustrated with charts of nerves and tension points, along with records of prescriptions for sedatives and orthopedic devices. To add the requisite visual impact in the era of television, there is often a "day in the life" videotape of the plaintiff, or a person whose injuries are said to be similar, painfully struggling through daily chores.

Once the jury's mind has been focused on the gravity of the phenomenon of pain, the question becomes how to monetize it. A trick of the trade known as the *golden rule* or *job offer* is highly effective. Jurors are urged to consider how much they would demand in exchange for having to suffer the plaintiff's pain, either gratuitously or as part of a job that required them to endure it. The *per diem* is a variation on the same theme. The lawyer suggests a modest per-minute or per-hour figure for what suffering should be worth—a cent a minute, say—which is then converted into a six-month total of $310,000 by performing the appropriate multiplication. When the victim has died within minutes or seconds in a car or plane crash, the approach changes to one more alarming, and the nature rather than the duration of the deceased's last moments is considered central.

These methods work. Since the early 1960s, average awards have been rising much faster than either medical costs or wages. An estimated 30 to 40 percent of awards in personal injury cases today are attributable to psychic distress of one sort or another, and the fraction is rising steadily. In a 1953 California decision, a seaman whose foot and ankle were crushed received $50,000 for the pain. A 1962 plaintiff who suffered serious skull injuries won $240,000; a 1965 New York plaintiff who suffered uncontrollable muscle spasms and pain after a negligently performed operation was awarded $350,000. A plaintiff who lost both legs in a car accident won $400,000 for the pain in 1978; a 1973 plaintiff who was severely burned in an auto accident received $2.5 million. In 1986, an eight-year-old girl left paralyzed and brain-damaged after she fell out of a Jeep won a $23.7 million verdict, including $6 million for pain and suffering. (The jury concluded that the girl's mother was 75 percent responsible in failing to lock the door and to restrain the child with a seat belt, but the award was issued nevertheless.) In July 1986, a New York court awarded $65 million to a Brooklyn woman who lost most of her small intestine when a hospital failed to diagnose an obstruction in her stomach, $58 million of which was for pain and suffering.

These cases, like Richard Grimshaw's Pinto accident, all involved concrete physical injuries at the core of the case. The new development was qualitative only; psychic damages that had once been awarded only on the back of other claims now came to represent, in more and more cases, the main bank account. Inevitably, this process was to culminate in cases where psychic injuries stood entirely alone.

As usual, the first step was wonderfully modest and reasonable. A long-standing if informal requirement under the old tort law was that claims based on fear of future disease were allowed only when the threat was truly imminent. The plaintiff could recover after a dog bite for the fear of rabies, but probably not for the fear of contracting arthritis at the point of the injury twenty years thence. There was no particularly good reason for the limit, other than that the courts of the day hated speculation.

In late 1949, however, Eleanor Ferrara was suffering from bursitis in the right shoulder. Her doctor, Anthony Galluchio, prescribed a series of X-ray treatments. After the seventh treatment, her shoulder began to itch, turned pink, then red, and then blistered. The blisters ruptured, and the skin peeled away leaving raw flesh exposed on Ferrara's shoulder. Scabs formed. About two years after submitting to Galluchio's tender care, Ferrara was referred by her lawyer to a dermatologist. Horrified at the remaining evidence of her ordeal, he advised her to have her shoulder checked every six months for signs of cancer. In 1958 Ferrara sued Galluchio for malpractice. Her psychiatrist testified that she was suffering from severe cancerphobia. The jury awarded her $25,000, of which $15,000 was for her anxiety about the possibility of future disease. Conceding that the case was "somewhat novel," New York's top court nevertheless upheld the award. "Freedom from mental disturbance is now a protected interest in this

State," the court announced. "[T]he only valid objection against recovery for mental injury is the danger of vexatious suits and fictitious claims. . . . The danger is a real one, and must be met. . . . But the difficulty is not insuperable."

The *Ferrara* ruling broke some modest new legal ground in allowing damages for a fear of disease that might materialize, if at all, only years in the future. Ferrara started with an indisputably real and immediate injury, however—a severely burned shoulder. No one would ever accuse her lawsuit of being frivolous or trumped up, and the very real risk of cancer from X-ray overdoses made her fears at least understandable, if not inevitable.

The next step down the path was to make the visible burn unnecessary as well. The Founders had some slivers of ancient precedent on which to build. In 1910, for example, the Washington Supreme Court had blocked construction of a new tuberculosis sanitarium because it frightened people. "The question is not whether the [public] fear is founded in science," the court reasoned, "but whether it exists." Few other jurisdictions accepted this logic at the time, and in any event, lawsuits of this type were limited by the contemporary cultural and scientific realities. By the 1960s, however, attitudes were changing. The legal decisions soon followed.

Vincent and Adeline Rodrigues owned a plot of land in Olowalu, on the Hawaiian island of Maui. In March 1967 they finished building a home on the lot. Before they could move in, heavy rains inundated a nearby state highway, flooding the home with six inches of water and causing extensive damage. Vincent reported that he was "heartbroken" and "couldn't stand to look at it" when he saw the mess; Adeline testified that she was "shocked" and cried because they had waited fifteen years to build their own home. They sued the state for failing to control the flood. A jury awarded $8,000 for the repairs and threw in a modest $2,500 for "mental anguish and suffering, inconvenience, disruption of home and family life, past and future, etc." With few misgivings, the Hawaii Supreme Court upheld the award. Thenceforth, the Court declared, Hawaii would allow damages for "serious" mental distress in any case, with or without accompanying physical injury, "where a reasonable man, normally constituted, would be unable to adequately cope with the mental stress."

And with that, a popular bit of contemporary doggerel was given a lucrative new legal meaning. "Don't bother me, I can't cope" was now more than just a brush-off for the unwelcome acquaintance or associate; it was a matter to bring to the attention of your lawyer. A woman who suffered no evident physical injury or pain was awarded $2,500 for drinking from a bottle that contained dirt and glass slivers. Another plaintiff, equally hardy physically, recovered for mental anguish after consuming a soft drink from a bottle found to contain a dead mouse. So did one who felt a shock wave from an explosion, though he was not evidently injured by it. So did inmates in a federal prison who claimed to have been exposed to the active tuberculosis of a fellow prisoner and suffered anxiety (or so they claimed), though none of them contracted the disease. "The nerves," a North Carolina judge alertly observed in 1981, "are as much a part of the physical system as the limbs, and in some persons are very delicately adjusted and when 'out of tune' cause excruciating agony." A right of action, he continued, could be based as much on a "wrecked nervous system" as on "lacerated limbs." Without apology or even acknowledgment, new tort practitioners thus borrowed a page from *Pride and Prejudice*. "You take delight in vexing me. You have no compassion of my poor nerves," says Mrs. Bennet. "You mistake me, my dear," her husband replies. "I have a high respect for your nerves. They are my old friends. I have heard you mention them with consideration these twenty years at least."

The most important implication of the new legal developments was the most obvious one. A host of inconveniences, fears, shocks, or irritations that could never have underwritten a lawsuit only a few years earlier were now negotiable currency and legal tender in courtrooms across the country.

The new respect for hurt feelings and the like had a second major implication. Once emotional distress alone was grounds for recovery, bystander suits were all but inevitable. These claims were first allowed by persons actually injured in an accident who also witnessed the graver injury of another. Then the circle widened to encompass all claims for distress by persons within what courts termed the "zone of danger" surrounding the accident—close enough to be at risk themselves, though not actually harmed.

A 1968 decision from California then pushed the circle out still further. Margery Dillon and one of her daughters, Cheryl, watched in horror as a car hit and killed Cheryl's infant sister, Erin Lee, at a Sacramento intersection. Both sued the driver for their distress. The California Supreme Court decided that the zone-of-danger rule that it then enforced suffered from "hopeless artificiality." "[W]e cannot draw a line between the plaintiff who is in the zone of danger of physical impact and the plaintiff who is in the zone of danger of emotional impact." From that day forward, the court announced, in language that would glaze any but a lawyer's eyes, bystanders could sue for emotional impact "from the sensory and contemporaneous observance of the accident, as contrasted with learning of the accident from others after its occurrence."

Not surprisingly, the "contemporaneous observance" breakwater that remained soon proved just as susceptible to erosion as all the old ones. In 1982 a federal court of appeals interpreting Texas law concluded that a mother who had been under total anesthesia at the time had been a sufficiently "contemporaneous witness" to recover damage for emotional distress at the birth of her injured child. (This, one must recall, was in addition to any recovery the child herself might be allowed for the injury to her person.) The mother had had, the court concluded, what was termed an "experiential perception" of the accident, and that was enough. In 1980 California revisited and expanded its own rule yet again, permitting a husband to recover for the distress he suffered upon learning from his wife of her doctor's opinion (incorrect, it later turned out) that she suffered from syphilis. By 1984, thirteen other states had adopted similar rules.

Before long, many courts were permitting emotional and bystander distress claims in ordinary consumer product cases. Mental distress from the fear of disease, as we saw in the last chapter, had become an increasingly common way to claim harm from exposure to hazardous drugs, chemicals, or pollutants where no tangible damage could be shown. A tenant sued her landlord successfully for the emotional distress caused by a badly maintained building. In 1981 the Hawaii Supreme Court, revisiting the site of its jurisprudential landmark, upheld a $1,000 award to Mr. and Mrs. Rex Campbell and three of their four children for emotional distress they suffered when their dog Princess, a nine-year-old female boxer, died in the municipal Animal Quarantine Station. The next year an Iowa court was the first to award emotional damages in a First Amendment case, giving a high school teacher $300 for the mental trauma of being exposed to prayers unconstitutionally included in two school holiday assemblies.

At least one class of emotional distress claims logically should have been shrinking during this period. The advance of women's rights and the end of child labor might have been expected to put an end to the anachronistic lawsuits for loss of consortium. Indeed, soon after legislation in the early 1900s gave women the power to own property and exercise their own legal rights, several courts ruled that the husband's vicarious interest in his wife's well-being had disappeared as a source of tort compensation. But the momentum of the new tort revolution was enough to revive these suits in all their vigor, with support from most new-school legal scholars and little objection from feminists.

For one thing, the terms were being equalized: Since the 1950s, courts have begun letting wives sue for the loss of consortium of their husbands. The old requirement that the plaintiff demonstrate a loss of spousal services was summarily dropped; today's emotional distress suits simply allege a loss of "society" as the basis for the claim. But lost services are infinitely easier to price than lost society. The result was to add yet again to the radical indeterminacy of awards.

And because society includes not only spouses and young children but also grown children and parents, the number of family members to be compensated also grew rapidly. Typical of the new genre was a 1984 Illinois decision which entitled the parents of a young driver killed in an accident "to a presumption of pecuniary injury" for his loss, to be calculated, or rather plucked from the air, as the value of "the companionship, guidance, advice, love and affection of the deceased." Faced with the unanswerable argument that in raw financial terms parents actually save money when they lose a child, the court cannily directed the jury to adjust its award downward by the estimated cost of rearing and educating a child. The latest twist is, predictably enough, an award for the loss of consortium with a "nonmarital cohabiting partner," the tort law's answer to "palimony." Courts in New Jersey and California have allowed consortium actions by unclassified "others" who can establish that their relationship with the injured party had "stability and significance."

If being deprived of a loved one can support a lawsuit for emotional injury, so can being saddled with a new and unwanted member of the family. Some courts began permitting parents to recover for the mental anguish of having a perfectly healthy but unplanned child after a faulty sterilization. Others allowed recovery for the anguish of bearing a child with a birth defect when prenatal genetic counseling was mistaken or absent. A few allowed the child to sue for its *own* wrongful life, though others modestly declined to resolve the long-moot question of whether it is worse to be born unwanted or never to be born at all. There is something profoundly ironic in this latter view, sensible though it is. In the beginning, only the immediate victim of an accident, the most central player on the scene, could sue for his emotional distress. Now, in some courtrooms at least, the right to sue is guaranteed to everyone *but* the child so unwanted that the parents are prepared to swear as much in public and create a permanent judicial record to that effect.

The much more common pattern, however, is for courts simply to add more new plaintiffs without turning away any old customers. Between bystander suits, relative suits, and the victim's own suit for emotional distress, lawsuits can now be cloned in a way that would have horrified jurists of an earlier day. A parent may some day succeed in suing for a child both coming and going, recovering both for its unintended birth and then for its unintended death hours later among ill-trained nurses. One of the great advantages of cloned suits, especially in cases where the underlying claim is weak, is that each is a separate lottery ticket in the sympathetic-jury sweepstakes. The actual and immediate victim of the accident can plead her case in one courtroom, while next door the distressed father, husband, or horrified onlooker can press an entirely independent claim against the same defendant before a different tribunal.

Open-Ended Punishment

Even as the tort system was growing more regardful and solicitous of the psyches of accident victims and their friends and families, it was growing more severe and inclement in reckoning the mental state of those who might have prevented the accident. It was as if the total amount of sympathy in the system could not change, and what was given to plaintiffs had to be taken away from defendants.

Demands for punitive damages were extremely rare until the 1960s; today they are routine when the injury is serious and a wealthy institution is numbered among the accused. Doubtless, in the cataract of all tort litigation, punitive awards remain a small tributary. But the trends in certain areas, like product liability, are remarkable. Before 1970, for example, only about 0.5 percent of all tort claims filed against the Ford Motor Company asked for punitive damages; by 1975 such demands had risen tenfold; and by 1980, punitive awards were being sought in more than a quarter of all cases. Until 1976, only three reported decisions by appellate courts had upheld punitive damages in product cases, and all the awards were under $250,000. In 1982 alone, nine such awards were upheld, and each was over $1,000,000.

Part of the growth is due to nothing more than increasingly skillful advocacy, both in general and as honed in successive stagings of the case against a given firm. The standard technique here is another "day in the life," this time focusing on the absent chief executive officer of the target company, portrayed in opulent, Olympian isolation. "Ladies and gentle-men," argued a lawyer in one 1982 asbestos case, "[y]ou can do something that I haven't been able to do in the last five years of this litigation. You can talk to the president of Johns-Manville. He is not too busy to talk to you, and you can send him a message." The rhetorical device of sending a message proved immensely effective, there and elsewhere, much as it once had in George Wallace's presidential campaign.

How loud a message? The next piece of evidence will be the target company's balance sheet. Plaintiffs in Pinto accidents pointed out that Ford had a net worth approaching $10 billion and a net annual income of about $1 billion. To whet the jurors' appetite for large numbers, plaintiffs may then offer a brief examination of the company president's own annual salary, fringe benefits, and bonuses. With numbers like these on the table, anything but a very ample sum will appear quite inadequate to catch management's attention. The jury in the asbestos case above settled on $625,000, and that was relatively modest: a 1986 study by the American Bar Association found that over half of all punitive awards exceed $1 million. One Pinto jury, as we have seen, took a wild shot at $125 million. At least one other jury on record found $100 million to be a nice round number; like the Pinto case, that decision involved a single fatality. The engineer who pleaded in vain with authorities to delay the launching of the space shuttle *Challenger* demanded a $1 billion punitive award against Morton Thiokol, the manufacturer of the solid-rocket booster responsible for the explosion. By 1985, as one observer put it, the courts' "application of the 'reckless disregard' requirement in punitive damages cases [had become] as Pickwickian as their application of the 'defect' requirement in design cases."

Demands do not always succeed, of course, but the new methods for extracting punitive damages clearly work. Manufacturers of contraceptives, for example, almost never faced punitive damage awards until the Dalkon Shield came along. The first such damages against A.H. Robins, maker of the Shield, were awarded in 1975, in the amount of $75,000. By July 1985, eleven juries had awarded a total of $24.8 million in punitive damages, with awards rising geometrically as the succession of judgments itself served to fan the flames of public outrage. Pending suits were demanding at least another $12 billion in punishment. The Dalkon Shield experience opened the floodgates for punitive attacks on its safer substitutes. There has been a $2.75 million punitive award (on top of $2 million in compensation) against the Ortho Pharmaceutical Corporation in a failure-to-warn lawsuit involving the pill and a $5.1 million punitive award against the maker of a widely used spermicidal gel. The Dalkon Shield was undoubtedly a bad contraceptive, but virtually every other major manufacturer of contraceptives today faces similar claims for punitive awards, and virtually all have paid them at least once.

As the new tort revolution has taken hold, courts and juries have developed an ever sharper, and for plaintiffs more lucrative, sense of outrage. Once invited to compensate, juries stayed on to punish. A gymnast won $14.7 million against an exercise mat manufacturer. Singer Connie Francis won $1.5 million from a motel in which she was sexually assaulted. A child injured at play won $2.5 million in a suit that pitted neighbor against neighbor and also involved the manufacturer of the play equipment. On grounds that a dilapidated downtown residential hotel violated an implied promise of habitability, a Los Angeles jury assessed the owners $1 million in punitive damages. A 1979 Alaska jury awarded almost $3 million, later overturned as excessive, to a claimant who accidentally shot himself in the leg with a gun. In 1982 yet another jury granted punitive damages even though it found no reason to award the plaintiff any ordinary damages at all. A jury awarded Jan Kemp $80,000 in lost wages, $200,000 for mental distress, and $2.3 million in punitive damages for her wrongful discharge after protesting university favoritism to athletes.

In one area after another, the expansion of the tort frontier has been followed within a decade by a triumphant march of punitive-damage awards into the formerly lawful territory. The crashworthiness theory of auto maker liability, for example, did not exist anywhere in the nation until a decision by a federal court of appeals in 1968. A short ten years later, an Orange County, California, jury handed down the $125 million punitive award in the Grimshaw-Pinto case. And that award was notable only because of its size. There was a $5 million punitive verdict in the case of the 1971 Honda accident where Honda's "reckless" act had been to use lighter-gauge materials than some other automakers. Toyota was assessed a $3 million punishment for its supposedly defective design of the 1973 Corona after the car's fuel tank ruptured in a 39 miles per hour rear-end collision. At its trial, Toyota was forbidden to show a film that compared the effect of similar rear-end collisions on a Toyota, a Chevy Vega, a Ford Pinto, a Plymouth Fury, an AMC Ambassador, and a German-built Buick Opel 1900 Series of similar model years, all of which suffered fuel tank ruptures in the test crashes.

Before long, juries were levying punitive damages, ostensibly grounded in outrageous misconduct, for acts that federal regulators had specifically contemplated and approved. One jury rendered an $8 million verdict on warning grounds against a vaccine that was wholly free of any other defect, even though the FDA had approved the product's existing warning. A jury fined a fabric maker $1 million for what it judged to be defective lack of flameproofing, though the material complied fully with the federal Flammable Fabrics Act. The astronomical punitive awards against various manufacturers of contraceptives involved attacks on chemical compositions or warnings again expressly approved by the FDA.

There then developed a sweeping new notion of vicarious punishment. As recently as 1967, the general rule, universally followed, was that an employer would never face punitive damages for the unsanctioned misconduct of an employee. It was all very well to charge the corporation for the ordinary costs of accidents caused by employees in the regular course of business. But punishment was always thought to be a much more personal issue, to be applied to individuals, not institutions. Within a few short years, however, that distinction too had crumbled.

New York City learned the lesson in 1981. On December 20, 1976, Blase Bonsignore, a twenty-three-year veteran of the New York City Police Department, shot and severely injured his wife, Virginia, and then committed suicide. Virginia sued, claiming negligence by the city in requiring her husband to carry a gun off duty. No one suggested that official policy extended to using the weapon for attempted murder and suicide. A jury nevertheless awarded her $300,000 in compensatory damages (including $124,000 for pain and suffering) and $125,000 in punitive damages. It drew the line only at her husband's suicide, refusing to let Virginia collect for his "wrongful death." The jury had reasonably concluded, a court of appeals declared, that the city's conduct in requiring off-duty police officers to carry guns was "wanton and reckless."

The tort system's mission of institutional punishment grew steadily larger. Corporations—which, of course, have no mind, reckless, callous, or otherwise—began to be held liable for "outrageous" and "reckless" misconduct, even while individual employees who had made the decisions in question were vindicated in the courts or simply left unsued. Courts and juries thus embraced new bystander rules for punishment, analogous in many ways to the bystander awards for psychic distress. It was, of course, the entities' shareholders, consumers, creditors, or taxpayers—the bystanders of the corporate and municipal worlds—who then paid the punitive bill.

This simple notion of punishing the institution for the sins of the individual opened up enormous new possibilities. Individual misconduct tends to be limited in the scope of its consequences, but institutional misconduct is not. Product liability cases can involve millions of identical objects. This then re-creates the cloning problem on an altogether new scale.

So the courts acquired, in the end, what some among the Founders had apparently wished to give them all along—unbounded power to shape the conduct of the largest economic institutions in the country. But the power was not one that any single judge could control or limit. The great jurist Henry Friendly voiced his alarm in a 1967 opinion. "The legal difficulties engendered by claims for punitive damages on the part of hundreds of plaintiffs are staggering. . . . We have the gravest difficulty in perceiving how claims for punitive damages in such a multiplicity of actions throughout the nation can be so administered as to avoid overkill."

A crowning irony is that when the accumulation of punitive damages throws a corporation, municipality, or other deep pocket into bankruptcy, other injured claimants are among those who lose out. A U.S. district court recognized the problem in 1981 when it certified a class action to resolve issues of punitive damages in the Dalkon Shield cases, observing that the potential bankruptcy of the pharmaceutical company A. H. Robins "raises the unconscionable possibility that large numbers of plaintiffs who aren't first in line at the courthouse door will be deprived of a practical means of redress." A court of appeals reversed the decision the following year. Shortly thereafter, the "unconscionable possibility" materialized as reality in a federal bankruptcy court.

In 1979, the tort system's growing obsession with institutional punishment crossed the last frontier when it spilled over into the criminal system. The Ford Pinto, a public prosecutor declared, was worse than just a blunder: It was a crime. So the Ford Motor Company—no individual associated with that company, mind you, just the company itself—was indicted on two counts of criminal homicide. The case involved the 1978 deaths of three Indiana teenagers after their Pinto was rammed from behind by a speeding van and burst into flames. (The gas tank may or may not have been misdesigned; it later turned out that the teenagers had forgotten to replace the gas cap after filling up a few miles back.) Ford, the indictment charged, "did recklessly design and manufacture the 1973 Pinto." There was no claim that Ford acted with conscious bad faith, or that any official of the company even believed that its design was unreasonably dangerous, let alone had any intent to kill or injure.

Ford was acquitted after a highly emotional two-month trial, but that case was not the last to invoke strict-liability tort standards as a new basis for criminal responsibility. The new tort law had come full circle. Strict liability was originally offered as a low-key, no-fault insurance system. Less than twenty years after its birth, these no-fault principles had been stretched to define a new class of crime.

The End of No-Fault

The distinguished Justice Roger Traynor served on the California Supreme Court for the better part of three decades. He was among the greatest of the Founders: articulate, farsighted, determined, and effective. More than any other single jurist, he crafted the strict-liability principles that were to become law in his state and most others. His was a design for an altogether new tort system, marked by simplicity and efficiency, hardly adversarial at all because the rules of responsibility for accidents would be so simple and clear-cut.

Although Traynor recognized the appropriateness of damages for both pain and punishment, he foresaw a shrinking role for both in his modern tort system. "There has been forceful criticism of the rationale for awarding damages for pain and suffering in negligence cases," Traynor wrote in a 1961 dissent. "Such damages originated under primitive law as a means of punishing wrongdoers and assuaging the feelings of those who had been wronged. . . . They become increasingly anomalous as emphasis shifts in a mechanized society from ad hoc punishment to orderly distribution of losses through insurance and the price of goods or of transportation. Ultimately such losses are borne by a public free of fault as part of the price for the benefits of mechanization."

Traynor died in 1983, having lived long enough to see a great many of his predictions come true. But not this one. Judges and legal academics may have embraced no-fault principles, drawing careful distinctions between moral blame and financial liability. But the public made no such distinction at all. Surely institutional defendants must be a callous and irresponsible lot; why else were they being admonished so often in court? Surely consumers must be helpless victims of the industrial system; why else would they so often win enormous damages for their pain and distress? In the public mind, *no-fault liability* ended up as yet another legal oxymoron, a contradiction in its own terms, an abstraction that could never fit together as real-world policy.

9

Insurance in Retreat

IN JANUARY 1976 four U.S. Army recruits at Fort Dix, New Jersey, contracted a severe new form of influenza. One died. Some months later, a mysterious disease struck American Legion conventioneers in Philadelphia. Over 200 men fell seriously ill and 34 died. A new strain of the influenza virus, later labeled *swine flu,* was identified as the source of the Fort Dix infection. Alarmed public health officials suspected (incorrectly, it later turned out) that the lethal Legionnaire's disease had also been caused by the Fort Dix virus. And there were ominous parallels between the virulence of the Fort Dix disease and the virus implicated in the great flu epidemic of 1918, which killed 675,000 in the United States alone and 20 million worldwide. The surgeon general, the secretary of health and human services, and the national Centers for Disease Control advised President Gerald Ford to launch an emergency national immunization program.

Pharmaceutical companies quickly developed a swine flu vaccine. The president requested funds from Congress for mass production and distribution. Everyone was ready to go—except the insurance companies. They had been shocked a few years earlier by a series of judgments against vaccine manufacturers, based on the tortured new theories of inadequate warning, misdesign, and reversed-proof causality. Insurers now flatly refused to touch swine flu vaccine in any way or form. And no drug manufacturer was going to bet the company store by proceeding without insurance.

Congress was outraged. From the Senate floor, Senator Ted Kennedy denounced the insurance companies' "cupidity" and "lack of social obligation." Actuaries for the Federal Insurance Administration reassuringly predicted that if 45 million Americans were immunized, 4,500 injury claims would be filed, only 90 of which would result in awards, with a total cost of under $2 million. The Congressional Budget Office confidently projected that the insurance books on any claims would be closed within five short years. But private insurers were singularly unimpressed by these cheerful government assessments. It has been noted that the prospect of being hanged in a few hours sharpens a man's mind wonderfully; insurers, having gained recent experience with some hanging judges of the vaccine liability business, resolved to trust their own pessimism in these matters over the government's optimism. When the hand-wringing was over, Congress passed a special law insulating the pharmaceutical companies from all claims and substituting the U.S. Treasury as the insurer.

Forty-five million Americans were then vaccinated. The vast majority gained effective protection against swine flu. But epidemiologists later discovered that the vaccine had occasionally promoted a rare, disabling impairment of the central nervous system, or so some of their studies suggested. As of August 1, 1986, a total of 4,169 damage claims had been filed against the government—almost exactly what the congressional studies had predicted. But cash settlements had been paid in 704 cases—eight times the earlier projection—and total payments amounted to $86.3 million—sixty times original estimates. An additional forty-one lawsuits seeking $97.8 million were still pending, ten years after the vaccination program was initiated.

Uninsurable Obligations

The Founders always took it as an article of faith that the insurance system would provide a broad financial umbrella over the expanding new tort system. Drunks, criminals, and others among the more destructive elements of society seldom have independent wealth to cover the costs of their irresponsibility. For different reasons, insurance is equally essential for cities and counties, charities, doctors, hospitals, and large corporations.

Law is not their business, and they no more care to speculate on liability futures than a baker wishes to play the commodities markets in wheat or gas.

Across the board, the Founders' cherished cost-spreading objectives thus depended on pooling resources through insurance. Their plan from the beginning was for a sort of Mutual Tort Insurance Company, underwritten somehow or other by private insurers in the background, issuing accident insurance policies to one and all. They did not aim to trap insurers in any unfair or expropriatory way, at least not over the long term. They fully expected that new liability would translate into higher insurance rates, with liability insurance remaining a profitable business like any other. But the distribution of loaves and fishes to the needy depended critically on there being fertile fields and shoals of insurance to harvest and net.

One might have expected insurers to welcome the new tort activists as highly effective cultivators of the insurance business. Tort claims, after all, are what create the appetite for what liability insurers supply. And the Founders certainly wanted more insurance, so much so that they resolved to extract it by force of law from a marketplace not otherwise disposed to provide it. But they were clumsy in their work and remarkably uninformed about how insurance markets really operate. The new rules they hastily adopted turned out to be inimical to the most basic principles of private insurance. In the end, the Founders and their successors succeeded in sharply increasing demand for liability insurance, but they devastated supply. The result was an insurance crisis eerily reminiscent of the endless gas lines during the Arab oil embargo.

A private insurance contract is built on a delicate mixture of ignorance and knowledge. Jones buys a policy because he fears (though he does not know) that some day he may need the coverage. Mammoth Insurance sells the policy because it hopes (though it does not know) that Jones will never in fact make a claim. Some degree of ignorance on both sides is essential: In a world of perfect advance knowledge of what was to befall, willing buyers and willing sellers would always refuse to deal with each other in the insurance market. But too much ignorance is as much of a problem as too little. The key to a functioning insurance market is careful selection and categorization of risk—a well-defined *risk pool.*

Suppose Mammoth is selling car insurance. Teenagers as a group can be placed in a single pool without too much trouble. But if Mammoth attempts to lump together both high-risk teenagers and low-risk middle-aged drivers, something will give. A competitor may offer older drivers more attractive terms. Or these drivers may simply recognize that Mammoth's policies are not a very good deal for them, and buy less coverage or perhaps even none at all. However it develops, this process of *adverse selection* is every insurer's nightmare. The loss of its best customers forces Mammoth to raise prices further—which encourages still more departures by the customers who least need coverage. In the worst case, Mammoth faces a progressive flight of its best customers, and consequent disintegration of its business, unleashed by seemingly small errors in its early definition of who to insure, for what, at what price.

Healthy insurance markets thus depend on defining pools of risk as narrowly as possible. But two decades of change in the tort law relentlessly pushed matters in precisely the opposite direction.

Mammoth must know, first of all, just *who* it is insuring. It will write one contract for a driver with a history of drinking at the wheel, another (at a quite different price) for a well-run municipality, and yet another for a car manufacturer. But the modern principles of a socialized defense thoroughly blurred the once-clear legal lines between drunks, municipalities, and car companies. The new long-arm liability principles swept together dozens, sometimes hundreds, of defendants into a single courtroom. Joint liability then allowed the full costs of an accident to be channeled to the wealthiest—inevitably the best insured—defendant. As the courts stretched out concepts of group responsibility, a customer's likelihood of filing a claim had less and less to do with who the customer was or how she behaved. This was a devastating blow to insurance markets; it is impossible to sell insurance when you can't really know just who you're insuring.

A second essential factor in the insurance business is accurate timing. How much risk Mammoth is covering depends not only on when the policy begins and ends—which Mammoth itself can control—but also on when legal claims are born and expire. In pricing a policy, Mammoth counts on earning some investment income during the gap between the time premiums are collected and the time claims are paid. And Mammoth also needs a reasonably quick clock on insurance claims to keep a handle on which customers are better or worse risks. It will not do to sell liability insurance to all comers for twenty years, at a flat price, and only then discover that some in the group are careful and others (as finally judged by the tort system) are grossly careless. But in the age of the new tort the courts were committed to discarding all the old timepieces. Under the new jurisprudence they put in place, lawsuits could look backward for decades—with no one knowing which of the dozens of policies a customer might purchase during that period would then be called into play. This was a second jab at the insurance business, deep enough to open a vein, and certain to prove debilitating in the longer term.

Mammoth also needs a reliable yardstick for pricing injury. A policy may talk about accidents and such, but the final accounting is always in cash, so a stable rate of exchange between injuries and dollars is essential. The conversion is not hard to make when the injury is a broken leg that must be set or lost wages that must be replaced—which is why you can easily buy first-party health or disability insurance to cover such contingencies. But the rate of exchange is quite indeterminate for pain and suffering, loss of society, or criminal fines and penalties. For precisely this reason, first-party insurance never covers such things. Liability insurers could live with the old tort rules, because medical costs and lost wages accounted for the lion's share of all awards, and intangible losses were carefully curtailed. But here again the new legal world was radically different, with vastly expanded payments for punishment, pain, suffering, cancerphobia, and loss of society. The new rules thus demanded ever-increasing amounts of coverage for losses that no insurer could ever accurately assess in advance.

A last essential ingredient of rational insurance is knowing just what risk is being covered. If Mammoth sells a policy to a vaccine manufacturer, it must plan to cover the risks of vaccines, not the general health problems faced by young children. A policy priced to cover injuries caused by a spermicide cannot also cover birth defects originating in quite independent genetic accidents or a mother's drinking habit. Here too, the old tort rules were accommodating; claims of cause and effect were usually tested skeptically, and the courts doggedly refused to speculate about causes remote in time and place. But the courts gradually came to accept ignorance about cause as a perfectly valid reason for spinning the liability wheel. That was the unkindest cut of all, so far as insurers were concerned: Deliberate, accurate risk assessment is the very heart of all intelligent insurance.

Across the board, the new tort advocates thus rewrote the law in a compulsive spirit of cost sharing, homogenization, and contempt for old limits that had kept the liability world orderly and predictable. They discarded virtually every legal rule that had previously allowed insurers to define risk pools with workable precision. In a world so relentlessly hostile to risk categorization, private insurance would inevitably decline. Only the precise timing of the retreat was ever really in doubt.

The Insurance Crisis

The retreat should have been gradual, a slow, steady reaction to the twenty-year advance of new tort principles. The pressure did indeed grow steadily over the years, like stress along a geological fault. But the reaction in fact came with the sudden violence of an earthquake. A first shock hit in the mid-1970s, a second in 1985.

Why were the adjustments so sudden? No one can say for sure, though other financial markets, the stock market in particular, have been known to react with similar abruptness to stresses built up gradually over much longer periods. The insurance industry is a prisoner of internal frictions and its huge financial inertia. The unusually high interest rates prevailing in the late 1970s and certain business cycles peculiar to the industry also helped to postpone, for a time, adjustments that would otherwise have occurred in smaller, gentler steps earlier on. And herd psychology undoubtedly plays a large role in the insurance business, just as it does on Wall Street. But the unresolvable debate about why the corrections came so abruptly is of little importance. The corrections came, as they had to sooner or later. In the end, insurers responded quite rationally, though late in the day, to hostile changes in tort law that had been accumulating for years before.

A first major retrenchment came in medical malpractice lines in the early 1970s. Insurers jacked up their rates, reduced coverage limits, and increased deductibles. A second crisis climaxed in the early 1980s. A 1985 announcement by the Chubb Insurance Corporation was typical. "Our past reports have said enough about the mistakes we made in trying to underwrite, price, and reserve medical malpractice coverages. . . . [We have] created an unwished for monument to fifteen years of . . . too optimistic belief that Chubb could somehow take the measure of the juridical inflationary engine that has been driving the cost of medical malpractice insurance. . . . During 1984 we stopped writing medical malpractice business." And that was that. "We expect this to be our last comment on the problems," Chubb tersely concluded.

Other insurers responded less drastically but no less decisively to the new legal realities. They doubled, and then doubled again, the rates charged to cities. Why cities in particular? The new principles of a socialized defense had fallen especially hard on municipalities, which—as keepers of the public streets and parks—frequently find themselves at the scene of accidents. The city of Boston went without liability insurance between

1984 and 1986 when a policy was canceled by an insurer that had decided to abandon the municipal liability business entirely. Wilmington, Delaware, dropped its liability policies in January 1986. Fort Lauderdale, Florida, could not find a general liability policy to cover accidents on the sidewalks of the Intracoastal Waterway. In early 1986, thirty California cities were operating without any insurance at all. Socialized liability likewise poisoned the insurance well for chemical companies, doctors and rescue services, generators and disposers of hazardous wastes, and the manufacturers of guns and alcohol. Insurers that had once vied to sell large policies to large clients with good accident records now discovered that insurance itself was a magnet for liability. Wherever the concepts of group guilt expanded, private insurance retreated. It was as simple as that.

Insurers also reacted sharply to the disappearance of litigation time limits. Most abandoned long-term coverage entirely. Policies had traditionally been written to cover *occurrences.* If Dr. Jones bought insurance for 1988, operated on a patient in late December, and was then sued in 1989, Jones was still covered under his 1988 policy. That made sense for both the doctor and his patient, of course; insurers were prepared to go along because they could rely on legal time limits to protect them from totally open-ended exposure. When those limits disappeared, insurers simply brought in their own limits in the form of *claims-made* policies. Now Jones received coverage only for claims actually filed in 1988, while he had a policy in effect. If he wanted coverage in 1989, he would have to buy another policy written only for that year—if he could find someone to sell it, at whatever price the 1989 market might dictate. Jones thus ended up with much less real coverage; both he and his patients faced the ever-present possibility that there would be no insurance around at all when claims might eventually materialize.

Insurers also responded cold-bloodedly to the expansive new law of psychic injuries. Insuring such things as day care centers quickly became a thing of the past. It wasn't that many serious claims had previously been filed against the centers; it was simply that past experience was no longer relevant. When all is said and done, insurance must be a forward-looking business, and lurid stories about child molestation were beginning to appear in the press. What dollar price would the courts place on a sexually abused child, and what kind of punitive award was likely on top? No insurer had the slightest idea, but the possibilities strained the imagination. Pricing a policy to cover the risk intelligently was impossible, so most prudent insurers stopped writing the policy altogether. Identical concerns dried up insurance for contraceptives, orthopedics, neurosurgery, and all sorts of other products and activities where injuries, if they materialize, are likely to have large components of pain, suffering, sorrow, or distress.

Finally, insurers fled the scene of sentenceless verdicts and merry-go-round liability in undisguised horror. There was no way at all to insure against the misdeeds of obstetricians, or drug companies, or hazardous waste companies if these actors were to be charged, at wholly unpredictable intervals, for diseases and birth defects that they had not in fact caused. It seemed painless enough for the lawyers to reverse burdens of proof, inflate conspiracy theories, and dispense with rigorous proof of cause and effect. But no insurance company could think of keeping its money on the table with rules of this character imposed by the house. So insurance rates soared or coverage dried up entirely for obstetricians; many refused new patients or even stopped practicing altogether. No insurer would provide coverage to the Searle Corporation for its IUD contraceptive, so it dropped the product entirely. In 1984, a major pharmaceutical manufacturer was likely to have about $200 million in liability coverage; by 1985 no more than $50 million was available, and by early 1986 $10 million in coverage was hard to find. By 1986, most of the country's 400 largest consulting engineering firms were unable to buy pollution liability insurance in any amount, or at any price, and were refusing to handle toxic waste sites unless their clients assumed all liability.

Nonprofit self-insured groups soon found themselves in the anomalous position of refusing to insure themselves. They were feeling all the same pressures as the for-profit public insurers, of course, and were forced to react in just the same way. Manufacturers of small aircraft, who had relied for many years on a nonprofit mutual insurance program, finally concluded that many of their own operations were uninsurable, and began to abandon both insurance and manufacturing. About one-third of doctors in private practice had joined physician-owned, nonprofit companies after the first insurance crunch in the 1970s, but they too found their rates skyrocketing even while the breadth of coverage shrank dramatically. Between 1978 and 1985, New York City's liability payments jumped from $23 million to $118 million. Other than curtailing goods and services, there was nothing the city could do about it; New York, too, was self-insured.

In one line after another, the gap between premiums paid and coverage provided began to narrow rapidly. The W.H. Brine Company, a manufacturer of sports equipment, was offered a premium of $200,000 for $1 million of coverage (a premium-to-coverage ratio of 0.2); the city of Hartford, Connecticut, was charged $1.8 million for $4 million of coverage (a premium-to-coverage ratio of 0.45); and the Specialty Systems

Company, an asbestos removal firm, paid a liability premium of $460,000 for $1,000,000 of coverage (a premium-to-coverage ratio of 0.46). In early 1987, the American Consulting Engineers Council's hazardous waste coalition was trying to set up an insurance company to carry the liability risks of waste cleanup. The expectation was that companies would pay as much as $400,000 for $1 million of insurance. Even as they lowered policy limits, insurers also sharply increased deductibles and coinsurance clauses, and broadened coverage exclusions. The insurance deductible for the city of Baton Rouge, Louisiana, was raised from $100,000 in 1985 to $500,000 in 1986. Insurers thus slashed the true level of coverage they provided, even as they raised prices. In this manner, they gradually distanced themselves from the risky business of insurance, and moved into the much calmer waters of banking.

Not surprisingly, reinsurers (who act as insurers' insurers) retreated too. In 1984, London reinsurers labeled the U.S. liability market "uninsurable" and started a mass exodus. By 1985, Lloyd's, the world's biggest reinsurer, was scrambling to get out. "The liability insurance scene in the U.S. has lost all predictability," declared one member, "and therefore has become impossible to assess in terms of premium rates." "America is now as unpredictable from an underwriter's point of view as a banana republic," another English underwriter stated. By 1985, ninety reinsurers—almost one-third of the companies that were doing business worldwide in 1983—were gone.

The U.S. liability insurance business survived in the end, of course. Indeed, it went on to prosper, a fact often noted by those convinced that the entire crisis was a fraud and a conspiracy from the beginning. But just how did insurers prevail? They learned to sell considerably less insurance at sharply higher prices. The industry's recovery, in short, was in much the same spirit as the Allies' recovery of their forces from Dunkirk in 1940.

And as was true in France, countless civilians were left behind to fend for themselves. When insurance was still available, the real level of coverage had decreased markedly and the real price—taking into account all the whys and wherefores of policy limits and exclusions—had soared. In a good number of lines, insurance had been abandoned altogether. Sometimes the insured activities had simply been discontinued. There were fewer amusement parks and small planes, fewer contraceptives, municipal services, and day care centers. Other providers chose to "go bare" instead, operating without insurance and answering the new tort jurisprudence with defiance up front, and a good bankruptcy lawyer on retainer in the back room.

Almost everyone, from ski slope operators to the largest conglomerates, did the same, in some degree, by carrying considerably less insurance than needed. But the crisis struck with peculiar force at the little guy, the nonprofit or public-service operator. Legal rules targeted at the Fortune 500 company, the large city, or the affluent, hospital-affiliated obstetrician had been quickly adapted to soak the small business, municipality, or midwife as well. And while the larger players usually found some way to cover themselves one way or another, the smaller ones often went under.

A New Attack on Contract

The new tort acolytes were aghast. The insurance collapse threatened the very foundations of their jurisprudence. For two decades they had assumed that producers could remain comfortably buffered from the ever-expanding tort law by a swaddling cocoon of insurance. It was embarrassingly obvious that without insurance in the background, the whole grand experiment in accident management and social welfare would fold in disgrace.

When the weather changes, there are always some who will blame the barometer. There began a strident campaign to condemn insurers as engaged in a wicked conspiracy against the consumer. Some of the most ardent of the new tort activists, who had spent a lifetime attacking companies like General Motors and Merrell-Dow Pharmaceuticals, suddenly became indignant defenders of these set-upon victims of the insurance industry. But the it's-all-a-conspiracy campaign was largely for public consumption. For it was a trait of the boldest new tort advocates (and in one form or other would be generally seen to pervade the depths and shallows of their new tortery) that they had never met the problem, inside the law or outside, that they did not believe might be solved with still more law and lawyering.

The challenge, as they now saw it, was to tap new wells of insurance. The first answer was to drill deeper into old holes. There was something of a tradition to work on.

Since as early as the 1930s, courts had been prone to fiddle the terms of an insurance contract to favor the widow, because no one liked to think about what she was going to live on if the insurance did not pay. Those who have seen the classic murder mystery *Double Indemnity* know that many life insurance contracts promise double payment for "accidental" death. So that term became very plastic in the courts, culminating in a ruling by the Michigan Supreme Court that a man can drink himself to an accidental death. The age of the new tort required no less creativity in such matters. The legal bits were sharpened, the paper rigs erected, and courtroom drilling for new insurance began in earnest.

In 1973, State Farm was one of the first insurers to be rebored. It had made the mistake of selling two insurance policies to one Wayne Partridge, who, it would seem, was the owner of both a small brain and a large .357 Magnum pistol. The combination proved unfortunate. In the peace of his living room, Partridge filed down the trigger mechanism on his pistol "to lighten the trigger pull so that the gun would have 'hair trigger action.'" On the evening of July 26, 1969, Wayne and two friends, Vanida Nelson and Ray Albertson, were driving around the countryside in Partridge's four-wheel-drive Bronco in search of big game, specifically jackrabbits. Vanida sat in the middle, while Wayne (who was driving, at least when he could spare the time) and Ray fired through the open windows of the moving car. Wayne spotted prey and swung off the road onto rough terrain to keep the target in the glare of his headlights. He hit a bump, the pistol in his lap discharged, and the bullet lodged in Vanida's spine, leaving her permanently paralyzed.

Wayne had little money of his own, but he did have his two State Farm policies. One provided up to $15,000 of coverage for accidents "arising out of the use of" a car. The second was a $25,000 homeowner's policy that expressly *excluded* accidents "arising out of the use of" a car. When Vanida sued Wayne, State Farm immediately offered $15,000, on the seemingly generous theory that the accident could plausibly be considered a car accident. The California Supreme Court, without apparent embarrassment, smoothly accepted the $15,000 on Vanida's behalf and declared it would take the $25,000 too. There was coverage under both policies, the court reasoned, because the accident both did—and did not—"arise out of" the use of a car. "[T]he fact that an accident has been found to 'arise out of the use of' a vehicle for purposes of an automobile policy," the court unctuously declared, "is not necessarily determinative of the question of whether that same accident falls within a similarly worded exclusionary clause" in the homeowner's policy.

And so, with a stroke of the pen the court handed Vanida an extra $25,000. Small enough compensation, to be sure, for permanent paralysis, but far more than Wayne Partridge had at his disposal and more than twice what State Farm thought it had sold in coverage to the intrepid rabbit hunter. The sums were small for a giant like State Farm, but the principle was large. An insurance contract, the *Partridge* ruling revealed, could be red-penciled after the accident to create far more coverage than the insurer ever intended beforehand.

At first, courts were rather ill at ease with such things, like a house-breaker new to the business, who can't make himself quite comfortable until he is well off the premises. But as their experience grew, so did their confidence. The first small strike in the *Partridge* case was to be followed soon enough by some real gushers. In 1970, insurers began to exclude all coverage for pollution damages from the standard *general liability* policy sold to most businesses. Insurers made the mistake, however, of continuing to promise coverage for *sudden and accidental* spills—of the type that might occur, for example, during transportation or storage. The error was understandable enough. The distinctions the insurers were trying to draw tracked legal lines between ongoing nuisances and sudden *Rylands*-style releases that had been respected by the courts for a century before. But now the courts were rewriting environmental liability law from scratch and extending liability law from sudden, sharp releases to gradual, diffuse ones. The law had conquered a new province, but the writers of insurance policies refused to follow along to service the troops. This was remarkably inconvenient. So the new tort soldiers resolved to set things right, in their usual manner, by doing it themselves.

An opportunity arose soon enough. One particular waste dump (which we have visited before), operated by Jackson Township, New Jersey, had polluted the groundwater at a steady, gradual rate over a six-year period. The township's liability policy contained the then-standard exclusion for all but "sudden and accidental" pollution. No matter, a court announced, the township was covered anyway. The pollution was "accidental," the court reasoned, because the township did not intend it to occur. And it was "sudden" because sudden is just synonymous with "accidental" and means nothing more. Coverage thus materialized once again in a place where none had existed before, and everyone but the insurance company went home happy.

There was something narcotic in all this; the courts had apparently found a way to pull money out of thin air, almost at will. Who could possibly resist repeating the trick? Not the New Jersey courts, in any event. A land development corporation called Summit bought a site that had formerly been a sewage treatment facility. It later discovered hazardous chemicals in the ground. Summit cleaned up the mess and demanded reimbursement from its liability insurer. By no stretch of the imagination could there be coverage, the insurer indignantly replied. Summit had discovered an ancient dump on newly acquired land; Summit's policy covered only "sudden and accidental" pollution incidents occurring *after* the date the policy was sold. But "the discovery of toxic waste on the property was neither 'expected or intended,' " the New Jersey Supreme Court declared in 1987. The relevant occurrence was Summit's discovery of the wastes. And in any event, "the health, safety and welfare of the people of this State must outweigh the express provisions of the insurance policy in issue." Another court got around an exclusion for pollution damage to "property which is owned by the insured" by declaring that the polluted groundwater in need of cleanup was "not capable of ownership by the above-ground legal owner of the property." Gamesmanship with words? Of course, but surely the noble ends justified the means.

The most bountiful new insurance wells were to be drilled, however, not with the gradual-is-really-sudden drillpiece but with a diamond-coated bit called the *triple trigger.* The Keene Corporation manufactured asbestos products between 1948 and 1981, during which time it bought liability policies from many different insurers. Which of Keene's insurers would be called upon to pay asbestos workers who claimed to have been injured over the years by Keene's product? All of them, was the final answer, up to the maximum limits under each and every one of the policies. Any insurer that had done business with Keene when the workers were actually exposed to the asbestos, or when the disease first manifested itself in latent form years later, or when the disease actually materialized in a harmful form, would have to pay.

The courts had thus discovered a way to stack insurance like cordwood in order to extract maximum heat value from coverage that might otherwise have escaped combustion. They had invented, in short, a new variant of joint-and-several liability, this time applied to insurers. A crowning touch also paralleled an earlier line of legal development in which the courts had brushed aside an accident victim's contributory negligence. In stacking insurance policies over the years, several courts ruled, there would not even be a discount for years during which the insured carried no insurance at all.

If compensation of the needy was to be expanded by looking far afield for coverage, it was also to be advanced by refusing to look close to home. The new tort faithful were quite prepared to search everywhere for insurance except near the victim himself. The *collateral source* rule, which they vigorously continued to enforce, had long barred a defendant from pointing out to the jury that the plaintiff had first-party health, disability, or workers' compensation insurance to draw on. And in no event was an award to be reduced simply because the victim had already been paid for medical or other expenses from other sources.

The rule was based on good logic when it was first formulated, long before the Founders arrived on the scene. In the same way that the defendant's wealth had nothing to do with her legal duty to pay, so the plaintiff's wealth shouldn't matter if he had in fact been tortiously wronged. But the Founders did not build their new jurisprudence on crabbed concepts of "legal duty" or "tortious wrong"; theirs was a utilitarian philosophy of efficient deterrence, group compensation, and risk spreading. And insurance, in whatever quarter, had everything to do with *these* objectives. It was the presumed absence of insurance on one side that argued most compellingly for an award in favor of the grievously injured child. And it was the presumed availability of insurance on the other side that made it all right to impose liability on the Mammoth Drug Company, the unique supplier of a vitally necessary vaccine, whose only fault had been to fall short of unattainable perfection.

But the courts were much too busy expanding the law on other fronts to think of cutting it back here. They were not going to dwell on the consensual insurance arrangements made by the accident victim ahead of time, any more than they were going to honor an advance contractual allocation of responsibility for the accident. The new tort mission was to father new insurance in court, by compulsion, not to rely meekly on insurance arrangements made elsewhere by consent. Relying on the victim's own insurance seemed too much like blaming him for the accident itself. An expansive new tort jurisprudence was not going to be built up on any such ungenerous error.

Insurers Retreat Again

In 1960, the death of the ordinary sales contract marked a critical victory for the Founders in their search for new insurance. Twenty years later, the insurance contract itself had become the target. Courts that had manipulated contract language to create liability now used the same tools in an increasingly desperate effort to create insurance.

This time, however, the courts had taken on opponents who knew how to fight back and had the wherewithal to do so. It was easy enough to discover contract ambiguity—and then resolve it in favor of broader coverage—the first time an issue came to court. But insurers could play the game too, and they really had no other choice. Private insurance, in the end, is nothing *but* contract. The insurance contract is a forward-looking promise built on mutual understanding and bilateral consent. These are simply not matters that can be prescribed by casual judicial order on unwilling parties after the accident has occurred. Insurers had to fight back, and they did.

Soon after the courts rewrote contracts to obliterate the distinction between sudden and accidental pollution and gradual releases, insurers turned around and began excluding *both* kinds of accident from their policies. When the courts expanded their timing rules, insurers narrowed theirs, using claims-made policies for the purpose. When the courts welcomed boundless claims for psychic and punitive damages, insurers drastically lowered their ceilings on coverage. Policy conditions and exclusions, like a no-touch provision for day care centers, became more detailed and explicit. And in one line after the next, as we have seen, insurers began exercising their final freedom, the freedom *not* to contract.

There was little the courts could do about that, but they could fight back wherever any insurance at all remained on the scene. Some courts reacted by raising the stakes. If an insurer refused to pay upon a claim that a court later declared was covered, the insurer would be assessed punitive damages on top of any direct liability under the insurance contract. In 1979, for example, in a ruling against the Royal Globe Insurance Company, the California Supreme Court created a new basis for direct suit against insurers for any deviation (always discovered after the fact, of course, by judicial decree) from state claim settlement statutes. A jury assessed $35,000 in compensatory damages and $1 million in punitive damages against an insurer for its alleged bad faith in failing to settle certain claims. Another insurer's failure to pay a $1,600 bill led to a punitive award of $3.5 million.

The supply of liability insurance continued to shrink apace, even while the demand for tort-driven compensation continued to grow. By 1984, environmental impairment insurance policies were generating premiums of under $30 million annually—a minuscule sum in the larger scheme of things, providing no more than a few hundred million dollars of total coverage. The estimate at the time, however, was that liabilities arising from environmental hazards would run into hundreds of billions of dollars.

By this point, liability insurers were in open battle with the courts on all fronts. Insurers might believe in the difference between sudden and accidental releases of pollutants and gradual ones, but the courts would refuse to countenance any such distinction. Insurers might compartmentalize their policies by type or by year of coverage, but the courts would decompartmentalize them with creative reading and the triple trigger. If an insurer had the temerity to insist on a narrow reading of a policy it had written, a punitive damage award for wrongful refusal to pay would help put the company in a more generous frame of mind. If consumers did not want to buy coverage on the terms insurers were willing to offer, the courts would require them to do so. And if insurers did not want to sell the coverage, the law would be adjusted to compel that as well. In one area after the next, private insurers wanted out from the new liability system. The courts, however, desperately wanted them in.

But despite all the powers of the courts, it was an uneven contest. *Not* writing liability insurance, or refusing to sell it at any but an exorbitant price, are skills that almost any company can master in the end.

As the courts advanced and insurers retreated, state legislatures scrambled desperately to bridge the widening gulf between them. Were companies choosing to go without any insurance at all in the face of soaring rates? *Financial responsibility* laws would decree that activities like hazardous waste management, nuclear operations, medical services, charities, or chemical enterprises could not lawfully be conducted without coverage. Did insurers continue to cancel the policies of their highest-risk customers? Thirty-eight states passed laws or regulations limiting the insurer's freedom to cancel or refuse renewal. Was coverage for particular lines entirely unavailable? Many states responded by creating joint underwriting associations, which forced all private insurers doing any business in the state to offer coverage collectively, through the pool, for the otherwise uninsurable. Did insurance prices then rise still faster? In desperation, several states turned to price controls. Did private insurers finally get out of the state altogether? A few states began trying to forbid their departure, or defiantly set about establishing their own public insurance corporations.

The federal government soon found itself in a new role of insurer and banker as well. The swine flu episode described at the beginning of this chapter required a first dose of direct underwriting by the Treasury. Then came Love Canal and the hazardous waste crisis. This launched the 1980 federal Superfund legislation, today a $9 billion program to clean up chemical dump sites not covered by other insurance. Insurance premiums were now styled as a tax of one sort or another, and the private insurance policy itself was replaced by prescribed rights to compensation from the government. In late 1986, when liability problems threatened to cut off the supply of several other vaccines, Congress enacted a National Childhood Vaccine

Injury Act. The act followed the now-familiar lines: a mandatory, broad-based tax on vaccine manufacturers, a single compensation pool, and statutory entitlements to recovery.

So in the beginning there was contract, and contract usually allocated accident costs in definite ways that kept the possibility of lawsuit to a minimum. This meant that the role of liability insurance was small, but insurance, such as it was, remained readily available and cost little. Then the Founders resolved to tap this background liability insurance to fund the Mutual Tort Insurance Company and its universal, free, accident compensation policy. This could only be accomplished at the expense of contract—so the contract between producer and consumer was stretched, rewritten, and finally discarded altogether. When insurers retreated, tort lawyers scrambled to manipulate contract once again—this time the insurance contract—and no doubt some hoped for a repetition of the earlier success. But they were to be disappointed. Take away contract and there is nothing left to insurance; either bargains of this sort are enforceable on their own mutually understood and accepted terms, or they will not be written at all. Legislative intervention was then all but inevitable, first in laws that attempted to bludgeon the private insurance contracts into submission, then through insurance directly established and funded by the government.

Perhaps that outcome was really predestined from the beginning. The tort Founders were convinced at the outset that only public prescription and mandate could provide for needy accident victims. Their philosophy of coercion in matters of compensation was inimical to private insurance all along. Liability insurance sank beneath the waves as a quietly inevitable aftermath to the torpedoing of private contract some time before.

The New Excise Tax

And how was the consumer making out on the policies issued by the Mutual Tort Insurance Company? There was no doubt at all that more money was being cycled through the courts and more claimants were being paid in larger amounts. By that simpleminded measure, the consumer was doing wonderfully well.

Often even better than well. If he had no personal insurance before the accident, the consumer now discovered he had some afterward—or at least some years afterward, once his claim had gestated to term in the courts. He made out even better if he *did* have insurance before the accident; thanks to the collateral source rule, he now discovered he had double coverage, and the second payment from the tort system was a pure windfall. What the new tort system seemed to be delivering, in short, was a free lunch.

It was just about as real. The new-style tort insurance has in fact worked out to give the consumer an unimaginably bad deal. Were it not so richly decked out in the trappings of legal process and pedantry, the tort insurance coverage we all pay for today would be universally denounced as a vicious fraud on the people it is supposed to serve.

From the perspective of those to be compensated, liability insurance is uncertain, unpredictable, and absurdly slow—tragically so when there is serious injury and urgent need. Almost half of all monetary awards in personal injury cases go to 2 percent of the claimants, who win $1 million or more. According to one major study of 9,000 jury trials, malpractice lawsuits are long-shot gambles for both plaintiffs and defendants: Plaintiffs win only about a third of the time, but when they do, they win big. The size of the award depends far more on who is being sued than on what they did. Individual defendants typically pay a third less than corporations; government defendants pay the most of all. Verdicts go against blacks more often than against whites, both as plaintiffs and as defendants. In cases of severe injury, corporations not only pay more but are significantly more likely to be found liable in the first place. It is a system "for fighting accident victims about [whether they should be paid] from accident insurance," declares Professor Jeffrey O'Connell of the University of Virginia Law School, "a system so cumbersome and tricky that the typical accident victim, even after consulting a lawyer . . . cannot know what he will be paid, when he will be paid, or if he will be paid; a system hugely wasteful . . . ; a dilatory system . . . with the outcome more dependent on luck and emotion than on need and reason."

In all of these respects, of course, tort-driven insurance is precisely the opposite of what insurance is supposed to be. The whole point of insurance is to convert the random and unexpected into the regular and predictable. But tort-backed insurance is at least as capricious as the accident itself. "It's like being in the Wheel of Fortune," rejoiced one winner of a $2.6 million award, "and winning the big prize."

If the consumer gets little real assurance of compensation out of all this, she nevertheless pays dearly for it; at the bottom line, liability insurance is unconscionably expensive. For every dollar ultimately delivered to an injured claimant, one or two dollars are paid to lawyers, insurance company administrators, judges, expert witnesses, and dozens of other camp followers whose nighttime favors are essential to the legal army's peace and contentment. Sixty cents of every dollar spent on malpractice liability insurance are absorbed by administrative and legal costs. The corresponding figures are 60 cents on the dollar for products liability and 50 cents for traffic-accident liability. And these numbers do not account for the taxpayers' direct support of judges, law clerks, secretaries, and the rest of a swelling, increasingly bureaucratic judicial system.

If a public welfare agency incurred administrative costs of this order, the taxpayer would revolt and demand reform. If a private charity skimmed off 70 percent of the take for the comfort and support of its already wealthy fund raisers and administrators, it would be prosecuted for fraud. The last charity with comparable overhead was the PTL televangelist ministry, whose success, one may recall, also depended on a high degree of uncritical faith by its supporters. The tort system routinely creams off as much, however, for its equally wealthy proselytizers, amid fervent hallelujahs to its justice, fairness, generosity, and equity.

Beyond this, tort-driven insurance is highly regressive. The car—and the insurance contract that tort law insists must be sold with it—has one price, whether the person buying it is the president of the First National Bank or its janitor. The president and the janitor thus pay exactly the same insurance premium for coverage against lost wages, disability, and death. Yet the janitor can expect to collect much less in each category after an accident. The deal may be an adequate one for the president, though he undoubtedly has comprehensive insurance elsewhere, but it is certainly a terrible one for the janitor. As George Priest of the Yale Law School has pointed out, no one today would seriously propose that everyone pay the same for life insurance if some high-income beneficiaries are to receive more coverage; or for fire insurance, regardless of the value of the home insured; or for car collision, regardless of the car's value; or for disability insurance, regardless of the income to be replaced. Yet that is exactly what modern tort law requires. Perhaps it matters little enough to affluent people that their plane ticket includes an extra $10 of liability insurance that they do not want or need, or that the stepladder is 30 percent more expensive or the vaccine ten times more costly. For those who start with much less, however, these can be real differences, especially when they add up across all goods and services.

Modern tort law thus funds insurance through an excise tax on goods and services, channels the revenue through an administrative process that skims off two-thirds of the take, and disburses the benefits in a manner that is slow, capricious, and unpredictable. The tax is uniform, but the benefits, such as they are, depend strongly on income and social status. A more inefficient and regressive scheme of social welfare could hardly be imagined. And what of all the talk of the beneficent alliance between the trial lawyer and the consumer? It can only bring to mind the day when Winston Churchill was asked by an accusing Socialist member in the House of Commons what he had to say about the Italians joining Hitler's axis. "I say it's only fair," Churchill replied. "We had the Italians in the last World War."

10

What Is Deterred?

BEFORE Columbus sailed west, Spain's standard carried the proud boast *Ne Plus Ultra*—"There Is Nothing Beyond." But the discovery of the New World proved otherwise. After some debate in the Spanish royal house, the decision was made to strike the *Ne,* leaving *Plus Ultra,* so that the standard would now declare to the world: "There Is Much Beyond." There was a certain sensible pragmatism here, for the world was what it was, and the standard had to go along. The Founders made the cardinal mistake of assuming that if they changed the standard the world would change along with it. The world, however, had ideas of its own.

With or without insurance, people do not like to be sued; there is no doubt at all about that. Litigation on the receiving end is expensive, miserably vexatious, and socially disgraceful, notwithstanding all the talk of no-fault liability. And whatever its role in the overall cost-benefit reckoning, the misery of defendants always played an indispensable role in the rationale for the new jurisprudence.

To avoid a lawsuit and all its costs, after all, corporations, doctors, municipalities, hospitals, and drug manufacturers would surely take extra care. They would pay more heed to safety in their daily routine. They would hunt around for safer products and chemicals, new drugs, superior surgical techniques and playground designs. Life would grow safer and safer. By promoting safety and spurring innovation, strict liability would more than justify its various failings and costs, even (if it came to that) a collapse on the insurance side of things. Or so the Founders and their students resolutely believed and promised for the better part of thirty years.

Even jurists of the old school assumed as much. The old negligence standard was quite direct: Carelessness resulted in liability; good care was a complete defense. A body of law so explicitly committed to promoting safety had some chances of succeeding, especially while its objectives remained modest.

But in their boundless optimism the Founders thought they could do better, and on a vastly larger scale. Negligence, they believed, was too inexact a yardstick; better to focus on the much less ambiguous fact of the accident, and its painful aftermath. If someone other than the victim was in the best position to prevent the accident in the first place, why not stop the inquiry right there? The key was to identify the *cheapest cost avoider*—the party best able to prevent similar accidents—and to send the bill to him. Discriminating between safer and more dangerous alternatives was to be accomplished through a sort of invisible hand of liability. Mammoth Drug, the manufacturer of the safest contraceptive on the market—one that caused only fifty injuries a year—would end up paying less than Colossal Drug, whose competing product caused twice as many. The reward for prudence would not be any sort of freedom from liability, but rather liability in less frequent and copious doses.

This was an impertinent piece of conceit. There was an amazing degree of hubris in the easy assumption that the doers, the makers, and the providers of this world would willingly settle into the role of perpetual prey, pursued and worried at every turn by a hound-like legal profession, with no hope of rest except in the sweet bye-and-bye where accidents cease from troubling and injuries are no more. It was a view of the world that regarded the control of evil as more essential than the creation of good. The lower passions and vices of industry would be regularly ticked off in the books, warehoused in the cells, and carted away as per accompanying invoice. But was this enough? Who would be building and fixing, developing and doing, treating, immunizing, and curing while the lawyers were busy assessing the fines and keeping the jail?

The answer, with growing frequency, was no one at all. As the tort system expanded, innovation was suppressed, not encouraged. Safety was set back, not advanced. And the consumer ended worse off, even in his personal security, than he would have been had the legal system been slower to rush to his rescue.

The Innovator Departs

Who fled most quickly for shelter from the baying new tort pack? Those quickest on their feet, of course—the person of action, the company of initiative, the mover, the shaker, and the doer. When it comes to liability problems, the bold innovators are the most fleet-footed of potential defendants. More often than not, they adjusted to the threat of liability by doing less. *Not* innovating is a remarkably easy thing to do.

The Founders had promised quite the opposite—a steady march of innovation and progress impelled by the pursuing avengers of liability. The pursuit was there all right. But the innovation did not follow. To the contrary, in the very markets where the legal pursuit was the most intense—on the trail of exotic drugs, contraceptives, pesticides, small planes and cars, hazardous waste disposal, and medical procedures—the mood among suppliers became most sullen, hostile, defensive, and then coldly stagnant. Soon tired of running, the fox retreated to its burrow and refused to come out.

Research expenditures by U.S. companies working on contraceptives peaked in 1973 and plummeted 90 percent in the next decade. Steroidal oral contraceptives in this country underwent no significant changes after 1976, and no truly new contraceptive chemical entities have been introduced since 1968. Clinical tests of a contraceptive implant system called Capronor, developed by the National Institutes of Health, were stalled for more than a year for lack of liability insurance. The implanted contraceptive Norplant, which releases a hormone for five years, was developed by the New York Population Council and as of 1986 was on the market in five other countries. But no American firm dared to market it at home. A new and effective IUD, the Copper-T 380A, won FDA approval, but no major firm was willing to market it for several years. In late 1987, one tiny company finally announced that it would sell the product, at a price vastly above the cost of manufacture, and without any liability insurance (which was, in any event, unavailable), presumably on the assumption that if a wave of lawsuits struck, bankruptcy would provide a quick and clean exit from the market. So the United States, a leader in contraceptive research and marketing well into the early 1960s, has today lost its edge and its hunger for progress. Research on other aspects of reproduction has suffered as well. "Who in his right mind," the president of a major pharmaceutical company asked in 1986, "would work on a product today that would be used by pregnant women?"

The story has been much the same in other high-tech markets favored with attention from the liability system in recent years. Between 1965 and 1985, the number of U.S. vaccine manufacturers shrank by more than half; by 1986 the nation depended on a single supplier for vaccines against polio, rubella, measles, mumps, and rabies. In the 1960s there were eight U.S. manufacturers of whooping cough vaccine; by 1986 there were only two. And only two major companies, Merck and Lederle Labs, were still investing heavily in vaccine research. America, once the world leader in this technology so vital to the public health, was quickly losing ground here too.

Consulting engineers report that they systematically favor old products over new ones in their design specifications, fearing (quite correctly) that newer design options carry a greater risk of liability, whatever real decrease in risk they might actually represent. Liability-conscious universities decline to license patents to small companies, despite the fertile environment they offer for innovation, fearing that anyone suing over a patent-related product would be sure to go for the university's deep pocket as well. Liability concerns forced a Virginia engineer to abandon his business of designing better hand controls for cars used by the handicapped, a business he had set up after his own son had been crippled in a motorcycle accident.

America, land of the Wright brothers, has lost even its appetite for innovation in small planes. Burt Rutan, the pioneering designer of the *Voyager*, didn't have the resources to compete with larger manufacturers, but he had a cheaper way of getting his products out into the marketplace. He sold construction plans for novel airplanes to do-it-yourselfers, who built the planes in their garages. But in 1985, fearful of the lawsuits that would follow if a home-built plane based on his designs crashed, he stopped selling the plans.

As the new tort soldiers marched forward, in whatever field, technologists fell back; it was that simple. The phenomenon ran so contrary to the accepted articles of the new tort faith that many in the law-and-economics priesthood doggedly refused to acknowledge the facts at all. Their theories had declared, quite emphatically, that sharper liability would spur more innovation. How could the facts dare to be otherwise? The answer was that the accepted theories were wrong.

The theories depended, first of all, on a fine-tuned and highly predictable legal process which consistently disfavored more dangerous products and favored safer ones. The success of the new liability engine thus depended on great precision in the courts. But the legal assembly line relied on unskilled workers, heavily pressed for time and with many extraneous factors—sympathy for the victim most especially—on their minds. This introduced a great uncertainty into the system. And there are limits to the total uncertainty—scientific plus regulatory—that any endeavor can tolerate. With innovative science and technology, that limit is reached much sooner than with the old and familiar.

Worse still, the new tort theoreticians penned a book of new legal rules that discouraged innovation at every turn. From the innovator's perspective, much of the damage was done at the very beginning, when the courts replaced negligence with strict liability. The negligence standard had inquired whether the technologist—the human actor on the scene—was careful, prudently trained, and properly supervised. Who is most likely to pass a negligence test? The best and the brightest—the technologists working at the leading edge of their professions. It is at the frontiers of science, after all, that the best engineers, pharmacologists, doctors, and chemists typically congregate. Under the new legal standards, however, the people themselves, and their good care, good training, and good faith, were quite irrelevant. The new inquest concerned the product itself and its alleged defects. Where once human conduct had been its focus, the tort system now placed technology itself in the dock.

This seemingly modest change sharply tilted the system against innovation. The reason lies in quite understandable human psychology. Jurors can make reasonably sensible intuitive judgments about people—even about professionals—because we are all in the people-judging business every day of our lives. But jurors are not experts about technology itself, and intuition here is a terrible guide. When a juror is asked to categorize technologies—as distinct from their inventors or managers—as good, bad, or ugly, the answers follow a quite predictable pattern. Age, familiarity, and ubiquity are the most powerful legitimizing forces known to the layperson. The inexpert juror is predisposed at every turn to identify technologies that are novel, exotic, unfamiliar, or adventuresome as unwelcome and fraught with danger—in short, defective.

It is a matter of human nature, an instinct as ancient as the species itself. Mothers who stay at home underestimate the familiar risks of their own environment—electric sockets, bottles of cleaning fluid, pediatric services, and cars, while overestimating the less familiar hazards of chemical pollution and nuclear power. Blue-collar workers see too little threat in their familiar cigarettes, alcohol, and construction-site environments, and too much threat in the less familiar hazards of air travel or high-tech medicine. People everywhere underestimate the risks they know well and face every day and overestimate those that are new and foreign. The familiar is safe, or at least bearable enough, no matter how appallingly dangerous it may be in reality. The unfamiliar is suspect, intrusive, and probably dangerous, no matter how reassuring the statistics may be.

The predisposition of juries is not by any means the end of the anti-innovation problem, however. When the search for product defects grew too convoluted, as we have seen, the courts shifted their attention to warnings. Gilt-edged safety warnings, that is, where how you pronounce it counts for everything. Exhaustive detail is the modern rule. It will not suffice to warn of a risk of death; the seller must warn specifically of the risk of stroke or serum sickness or acute encephalopathy. It will not suffice to warn the prescribing doctor of a drug's hazards; the drug company must somehow also get the information to the patient too. Grossly obvious risks must be flagged, but so must risks that arise only from the most bizarre and unexpected forms of consumer abuse.

How can any defendant learn to satisfy such requirements? Only through long perseverance in the market and in the courts. The warnings on oral contraceptives have been honed for thirty years, to the point where they run on for several pages of densely detailed text. No equivalent detail can be provided for a truly new IUD, because the risks are much less familiar—even if their general nature is known and even if the IUD is demonstrably safer, overall, than the pill it could replace. So the new law of warning further sharpens the anti-innovation bias of the new tort system.

Another blow to the innovator's peace and progress comes from the insurance side of the business. The general idea in modern tort law is that all goods must come gift-wrapped in a special-purpose insurance contract. When can such wrapping be found at any reasonable price? The availability of insurance depends largely on an accumulation of accident experience. That is something that established technologies always have and truly innovative ones never do. Insurance is easiest to find when a good has been used by many people for many years, so that the frolics and caprices of tort liability have been as far as possible washed out and the statistics of experience speak for themselves. Innovation necessarily starts without an established market, and so is often condemned to start without insurance as well. For the prudent businessperson, a start without insurance is often worse than no start at all.

Orphan drugs reveal some of these problems in particularly tragic circumstances. Only a few hundred American children suffer from cystinosis, a fatal kidney disease. About 2,000 adults suffer from Charcot-Marie-Tooth disease, a rare nerve disorder (unrelated to teeth) that severely impairs motor function. About 1,000 suffer from leprosy and experience an extremely painful allergic reaction on their skin. A tiny number suffer from a rare but incapacitating disease characterized by uncontrollable twitching of the eye muscles. There are some 5,000 other orphan diseases that shorten lives or bring agonizing disability to tiny groups. Therapies are available or under development for some 500 of them. But insurance is often all but impossible to obtain. Chemie Grunenthal, for example, a West German company that once supplied thalidomide to American leprosy victims, announced in 1986 that it planned to abandon the U.S. market to avoid the risk of liability that might arise if, for example, the drug was used in excess or fell into the wrong hands. Until recently, another West German chemical company supplied Americans with botulinum, a paralytic poison that is just right for controlling the eye-twitching disease, but the company cut off supplies in 1986 for similar reasons. Orphan drugs are condemned, in a sense, to be perennial newcomers to the commercial world and are therefore forever uninsurable under the modern rules. Business realities take care of the rest.

The law's attitude to safety improvements made after an accident has also changed for the worse. The old law strictly barred a plaintiff from offering any evidence of such conduct—the redesign or recall of a product, a postsale or postaccident change in a process, or the addition of a new safety system. The logic for the rule was simple: safety improvements must be encouraged, and so should never be used to condemn past shortcomings. But in the 1960s, this rule too came under direct attack. The courts proceeded in the usual way, fashioning one exception and then another, then yet another. Evidence of subsequent remedial measures was first admitted to impeach witnesses, then to prove that the defendant controlled the premises in question, then to show that conditions had changed since the time of the accident or that changes in design were feasible. The exceptions nibbled away at the rule until some courts were emboldened to sweep the tattered remains aside entirely. An Illinois appellate court simply declared that the rule shouldn't apply in strict liability cases because the focus was on the product itself, not on the defendant's conduct. The California Supreme Court then picked up the idea in a landmark ruling in 1974. New York and other states followed quickly.

Incredibly, the logic offered in these rulings was exactly what had been used earlier to *exclude* evidence of the plaintiff's contributory negligence before the accident. The product was on trial, the courts argued, not the people. So the plaintiff's personal conduct *before* the accident was irrelevant. But somehow the defendant's conduct *afterward* was perfectly relevant and admissible, because it would shed light on the product itself. None of this made any real sense except as a way of imposing more liability more often.

As we have seen, the courts were also resetting the clock on litigation, so that a suit could be filed years or even decades after the car gearbox, herbicide, or strip-mining machine was designed or used. Defects in technology, like negligence in human conduct, depend critically on the context of time and place. The best-designed cars of 1950 were clearly deficient by 1980 standards, as were the best medical procedures, industrial chemicals, pesticides, or home appliances. The problem is especially acute in mature industries with long-lived products. When the sun never sets on the possibility of litigation, each improvement in method, material, or design can establish a new standard against which all of your earlier undertakings, of no matter what vintage, will then be judged. Finding a way to do better today immediately invites an indictment of what you did less well yesterday or twenty years ago.

No wonder the strong temptation today is to leave well enough alone in the hope that somehow the courts then will too. The pattern is consistent: a shift in the jury's focus from negligence to design defects; a legal obsession with perfectly phrased and endlessly detailed warnings; a rigid demand for universal, special-purpose accident insurance; the use of remedial efforts in the aftermath of an accident to indict whatever came before; and no effective time limit on litigation, so that even the normal pace of technological evolution becomes legally dangerous to the technologists. No one could have brought together five elements better calculated to entrench the status quo and scare off innovators of every description.

But mightn't this slowdown be a blessing in disguise? Technological adventure is known to be dangerous. Perhaps innovation deserves that extra measure of deterrence that the new tort system provides so generously. Everything supports this conclusion, especially our most common instincts and intuitions about the safety of the familiar and the hidden danger of the novel and innovative.

But the facts are otherwise. Whatever intuition may tell us, newer is generally safer than older in the modern technological world. Slowing down the pace of innovation did not advance safety in the least; it set it back sharply. We know for sure that since the turn of the century, life has been growing steadily safer in America, and at a rapid pace. Most major diseases, including even most forms of cancer, have been on the decline, at least when one adjusts for the overall aging of the U.S. population. What accounts for these favorable trends? Innovation, technological change, and the economic growth they made possible. There is hardly a product in use today—a car, plane, boiler, municipal water system, drug, vaccine, or hypodermic syringe—that is not many times safer than its counterpart of a generation or even a decade ago.

The liability system behaves as if the opposite were true. In 1977, for example, small-plane manufacturers paid a total of $24 million in liability claims. By 1985, their payout was $210 million. Companies like Beech, Cessna, and Piper curtailed or suspended production; they quickly discovered that the new-model planes, carrying a 50 percent surcharge for liability insurance, could no longer compete with used planes already on the market. Aircraft technology, however, had been advancing steadily, so the new models kept off the market were notably safer than the old ones people went on using instead. Worse still, small-plane development has traditionally been the richest source of aerodynamic research and innovation for the aircraft industry in general, so what private pilots and hobbyists lose today, the public will likely lose a decade or two later in commercial aviation.

Small cars like Ford's Pinto, Honda's Civic, and Toyota's Corona became magnets for liability claims as well. If the new tort theories were correct, the escalating awards against manufacturers of these cars deterred sales. And what then? It is possible, of course, that those who would otherwise have bought a new Pinto took the bus instead or bought a Mercedes. But it seems likely that many of them nursed along the old family car for a few more years instead or bought a clunker from Honest Eddie's used-car lot. Did liability deter? Certainly. Did it make life safer? In all likelihood, it did just the opposite.

Counting the bodies that have fallen because of things that might have been done better but weren't will always remain an exercise in speculation—just as it is impossible to count, with any precision, the accidents that were successfully deterred by the expansion of tort law. But the difficulty of taking any exact census should not lead anyone to suppose that no one has died. One surely cannot say that every single time the tort system slows down or cuts off innovation it thereby impedes safety. But by all indications that is the result more often than not.

Risk Trade-Offs

The indiscriminate liability that characterizes modern tort law has done more than prevent the progress of safety: It has forced several great marches backward. The strategy of reducing liability by reducing effort and initiative across the board is all too common, and time and again one finds that safety itself is the largest casualty.

A drug maker can always make a product less risky by making it less potent; a vaccine manufacturer can always further weaken a weakened virus at the cost of weakening the immune response it triggers. But in case after case, the product's efficacy goes hand in hand with its risks, and less efficacy means more danger of a different sort—from the disease the medicine is supposed to cure or prevent. According to the director of the National Cancer Institute many physicians refuse to prescribe potentially curative doses of cancer chemotherapy for fear of litigation over side effects, and thousands of patients may die needlessly each year as a result of this kind of caution. The same legal forces that knocked the Dalkon Shield off the market also dispatched two other kinds of IUD. The Dalkon Shield without question deserved to go; the next two, however, were the safest effective alternatives available to many women. Leftover IUDs are still used by over 2 million Americans; when the time comes for these devices to be replaced, it has been estimated that there will be 160,000 unintended pregnancies caused by the lack of equally acceptable and effective replacements. These will result in 72,000 live births and 88,000 induced abortions—which collectively pose a far greater risk than any IUD would ever have created.

The demise of Bendectin marked progress of a similar kind. Here pregnant women lost their only certifiably safe relief from sometimes-debilitating morning sickness. Obstetricians and gynecologists have retreated too. Many of their services have become wholly unavailable in rural and less affluent communities. So women and children won their expanded right to sue, but lost services essential to their health and safety. The complication that develops in the back seat of the car heading to the delivery room at a distant hospital is not likely to yield a munificent tort award, even though it is more likely to end in a tragedy. If the child is delivered uneventfully, the tort system will continue its assault on her welfare in later years. By 1985 day care was becoming dangerous, not for the kids but for the people running the centers. More children stay at home today, as a result, where (experience abundantly confirms) they are far more likely to be abused or neglected by someone in their own family, just as before, in the good old days.

The courts won an equally pyrrhic victory in their widely applauded crusades against hazardous waste dumps and asbestos installations. Perhaps some midnight dumpers have been deterred by the thought that the tort lawyers are hot on their trail, even if experience teaches that the typical chase starts twenty years after the original dirty work was done. But just as the chemicals and materials under attack are dangerous, so is the act of cleaning them up. Wholly reputable contractors called in to clean up the old messes have been intimidated more often than anyone else because they, unlike others, are on the scene here and now, with cash in the bank and an easily identifiable corporate name on the letterhead.

If a company faced with oppressive liability problems does not abandon its business altogether, it can often adapt in subtle ways that reduce legal risk even while increasing genuine hazard. Untreated cotton fabrics used in children's sleepwear pose a fire risk, while chemically treated flame-retardant fabrics may pose some risk of cancer. But a burn is far more likely to be converted into cash through tort litigation than a cancer. So if liability is the dominant concern, it makes perfect sense to accept a comparatively large amount of chemical-exposure risk to avert a tiny risk of burns—a decision that few companies would make unless forced to by the courts. Nobody wins, but least of all the child. Hormone-based contraceptive pills are physically safer—but biologically less healthy—than IUDs, which perform their function through physical action. Once liability becomes the pivotal concern, a similar trade-off is in order, because linking a stroke to the pill is much more difficult than linking a perforated uterus to the IUD. Nobody wins, but least of all the woman.

When it comes to leaving the liability system far behind, those engaged in voluntary or quasi-charitable activities surely have the least difficulty. And the withdrawal of the Good Samaritan hardly improves the safety of the injury victim. Liability may weigh somewhat on the mind of the drunk driver, though the old tort system deterred such conduct as well. The bigger difference is that a doctor must now also pause first at his insurance agent's before stopping at the scene to help the drunk's victims. Rescue efforts are not always successful, and a common thread of the new tort experience is that when the courts cannot find a defendant who is careless, they will too often turn to one who is wealthy. The doctor driving by in his hard-won Cadillac may be wiser to keep on driving.

No doubt we want the volunteer scoutmaster who takes his troop on a hike to be careful. But just what does optimal deterrence mean for activities that are provided for free? The liability system's only effect here is to raise the cost of giving, perhaps prohibitively. Many who have little to spare but their own time, energy, and effort—and who are willing to give of them in abundance—will be much less quick to hand out gratuitous insurance contracts as well. Safety—along with a sense of caring and community—is set back yet again, because well-meaning volunteers, though not perfect in their efforts, surely succeed in doing far more good, overall, than harm.

When all is said and done, the modern rules do not deter risk: they deter behavior that gets people sued, which is not at all the same thing. A victim's consent to be left alone is much more likely to be treated as binding than his consent to accept help, so doing nothing is safer legally than doing something, even if more dangerous in all other ways. Consent aside, juries are far more prone to find fault with something that was done, and went wrong, than with something that was not done, though it might have gone right. And liability, for quite obvious reasons, gravitates toward wealthy targets. The good thing about suing the wealthy is that they can afford to pay; the bad thing is that people and corporations most often become wealthy not because they do things that are wicked and dangerous, but because they do things that are valuable and necessary.

The cautious and farsighted, those with the most safety to offer, are the ones most averse to the tort system's notorious unpredictability. The courts usually do their best, such as it is, to focus their wrath on the negligent, incompetent, or defective. But at other times the law's aim is bad by deliberate design—as when the rules of joint liability are applied. And the ever-frightening gulf between foresight and hindsight will catch many careful persons. Decisions made on the fly, in rescue situations, or amid ignorance, when truly new products are being designed, can be second-guessed in an inquest on negligence or defectiveness that will be held with the benefit of calm, eagle-eyed hindsight. The potential targets of legal indignation stirred up in such circumstances have reason to leave early. The most mobile escape first. Others take longer, but over years it is possible to leave just about any line of work.

For almost everybody, the careful and the careless, the well trained and the incompetent, the skillful and the inept, the lesson is the same. The new tort system has too much smile to be real, too much frown to be false, and too many large teeth to be visible at once without suggesting a bite. But the best and the brightest recognize this more quickly than the rest, and being more mobile in any event, they get out of the way soonest. The world is a more dangerous place as a result.

The Immobile and the Immune

And who or what is left behind at the end of the too-busy day of litigation? For the most part, the immobile and the immune—the decrepit, the infirm, and the handicapped, so to speak, of the business and legal community. But the world *they* occupy and shape is hardly one of transcendent safety, vigor, and health.

Government is the most common provider of last resort. If neither love nor money will impel the private waste contractor, drug company, or doctor on the street to clean up the dump, supply the vaccine, or attend to the roadside accident victim, the government will probably step in sooner or later, as best it can. Innovation will surely suffer again, as will the quality of the service, and safety. Experience richly confirms that government domination of medicine, hospital care, ambulance services, or environmental cleanup is usually the most ineffectual and therefore the riskiest option of all.

And government itself is not altogether immune from lawsuit, nor altogether immobile either. Government, too, is sued when things go sour, but even here, modern tort has shown an almost unerring instinct for the wrong targets, going after not the least valuable public undertakings but the most. The activities of city hall most likely to attract liability are things like police and fire protection, street and park operation, municipal hospital services, and waste disposal operations. In recent years the federal government has been sued increasingly often in connection with its initiatives in behalf of national defense and its public health measures like the swine flu vaccination program. Some will certainly applaud the political objectives that can be advanced in suing the military, or the opportunity to correct possibly erroneous public health decisions. But just who are we trying to deter in a lawsuit where the named defendant is The United States of America? The idea has an uncomfortable circularity, like the self-referencing drawing by M. C. Escher in which the right hand draws the left hand drawing the right. In suits against the government, we meet the tort system's enemy again, and see even more clearly than elsewhere that the enemy is us.

Following close on the heels of the immobile come the immune. Providers who are illegal, anonymous, or too small to bother with also gain a competitive edge over established and reputable providers every time the liability vise is tightened. A secondhand sale through the classified ads is promoted over a sale through more customary sales channels. Irregular channels of liquor distribution evade dramshop liability more easily than established taverns. These outlets bypass most liability problems; they also, of course, avoid most administrative inspections, licenses, and regulations that monitor safety in the aboveground economy.

Next in line on the slope toward less liability and less safety is the do-it-yourselfer. By 1985, the courts were levying a tax on stepladders amounting to over 30 percent of their cost. According to theory, consumers—thus efficiently alerted to the dangers of heights—promptly curtailed their use of these hazardous instruments. But there remained the vexing problem of the light bulb and the kitchen chair. Light bulbs still go out. People would still rather replace the bulb than curse the darkness. And if they cannot afford a stepladder they use a kitchen chair, which is more dangerous. Without ever quite saying so, the Founders had assumed that everything would work out in the end, because kitchen-chair makers would be sued too, presumably even more often. But even with all the excesses of the new law, light-bulb changers who fall off do not generally think to sue kitchen-chair makers, and if they do they are likely to lose.

The risks of self-help may soon be amplified once again in connection with the humble cigarette lighter, discovered by the plaintiffs' bar in late 1986. There was no doubt about it: Disposable Bic lighters had been on the scene of several dozen accidents in which the lighter fluid was accidentally ignited in a pocket or handbag. Plaintiffs' lawyers quickly got to the heart of the matter: the problem was with the whole concept of disposable lighters, which, for inevitable economic reasons, are not built of materials as durable as those of the refillable lighters they have largely replaced. But what happens when a cascade of litigation drives the disposable lighter off the market, or at least curtails its use by tripling its price? Few will quit smoking. Some will return to refillables, which will require keeping cans of lighter fluid around the home and office. Others will prefer matches. There may be fewer lawsuits. But in all likelihood, there will be many more burns, now shared indiscriminately with nonsmokers.

One arrives, finally, at a new appreciation for the existential paradoxes of being and nothingness. What remains in the end is what there was in the beginning—the risk of nothing.

The legal assault on vaccines has revealed some of the possibilities here at their most alarming. To be sure, vaccines have all but eradicated polio, whooping cough, diphtheria, tetanus, measles, mumps, and smallpox. By any measure, the vaccines are far less risky than the diseases they prevent. But in the new tort jurisprudence, "less risky" will not do. In 1986, a new claim was being filed against the manufacturers of whooping cough vaccine every week; one former manufacturer faced 100 suits demanding more than $2 billion in compensation, or 200 times the total annual sale revenues of the vaccine. And the entire industry was in panicky retreat.

The story has been told again and again. You may sue if your football helmet might have been designed differently to give you added protection, but not if helmets have become so expensive that you were playing without one. You may sue the psychiatrist and the policeman and the social worker for the might-have-been-prevented rampages of their patients or charges, but there is no one at all to sue—though more injury to contend with—when the guardians decide to take care of themselves first and stay well clear of the psychopath from the beginning. Perhaps some violence somewhere was prevented as a result of the sue-the-shrink wave of litigation set off by California's landmark *Tarasoff* decision; who knows? But therapy that starts with a reading of legal rights to the patient and notice that the most intimate of confessions may have to be passed on to the police is not likely to end in the spirit of trust necessary for successful treatment. Unwilling to grapple with the legal niceties, more than a few therapists now refuse to treat violent patients altogether.

The courts have thus slowly rediscovered, in their own tortuous way, the ancient myth of Hydra, the monster of the Lernean marshes in Argolis. Hydra had nine heads, and Hercules was sent out to kill it. But as soon as he struck off one of the heads, two shot up in its place. So it has proved to be with risk as well. It is quite possible to make life more dangerous by attacking the risky and leaving behind only the riskier. In their quixotic, undisciplined quest for safety, the courts have managed to do just that time and time again.

The Cookie-Cutter Consumer

In all they did, the tort Founders and their followers were committed to a one-size-fits-all theory of safety and product defects. A small car was either defective or it was not; it did not matter in the least that a particular buyer might not be able to afford any other car and deliberately chose the compact as best for her needs and circumstances. In its single-minded assumption of uniformity, not just among products but among consumers themselves, the new tort jurisprudence proved to be a compulsive homogenizer.

And that, in the most subtle but far-reaching way, undercut safety at every level. Safety ultimately lies in distinguishing good risks from bad ones and keeping them carefully apart in both thought and action, not across the board but in proper context. Lumping people, products, and processes together is dangerous; safety lies in tailoring choices to individual needs and circumstances, individual capabilities and responsibilities, on both the consumer's side and the supplier's.

The point is clearest on the consumer's side of the safety picture. Not all consumers are alike; the prescription that is needlessly unsafe for one may save the life of another. In all but the simplest cases, accidents originate not in defective designs but in the unwise conjunction of a particular design with a particular use and user. Take a homely but simple example, the sort of shredding machine that restaurants use to make cole slaw. The cook cuts the cabbage into manageable chunks and feeds them into the machine's intake. Too large an opening can cost a careless cook her fingers. A safe shredder, it would therefore appear, has an intake small enough to protect the most diminutive woman's hand. This means that all cooks have to do more slicing with a knife at the outset—itself a finger-threatening task and also the very job that the machine is supposed to replace. So what is the safe and functional design? It depends largely on the size and dexterity of the cook. But the cook is the one thing that may not be discussed in a modern inquest on product defects. The shredder is either defective or it is not, and there's an end to it. This is not the kind of thinking that protects real fingers.

The shredder example, real though it is, may seem frivolous. But there are many others, especially involving things medical, that are anything but. IUDs are an inappropriate form of contraception for younger women who have the self-discipline to use other forms of protection properly, but are often the safest option for older women who smoke, among others. Oral contraceptives are safer for the former group and riskier for the latter. Botulinum is a paralytic poison, except when it is a sight-saving therapy; penicillin is a miracle drug against infection, except when it is a fatal allergen; thalidomide a fearsome teratogen, except when it alleviates the misery of leprosy. An airbag-equipped car is safer, except for the driver sensible enough to wear a seat belt, for whom—because of the risk of accidental deployment—the airbag may be unnecessarily dangerous. Pure water is necessary for life but can also trigger seizures in epileptics when consumed in excess. Similar user-specific risks and benefits inhere in every power tool, food additive, transportation system, or medical therapy.

It is precisely because we are *not* all equally tough or delicate, cautious or careless, hardy or sickly, susceptible, thin-skinned, or thick-skulled, that safety lies in individuation and differentiation. Safety is not improved by treating individuals as cookie-cutter copies of each other or as interchangeable parts in a mass-production assembly line. Safety depends on treating individuals as such, not as undifferentiated members of a faceless public. But the new tort system insists otherwise.

The error was repeated in the new rules for defendants. Most accidents have a single cause, which is close to both the scene and the victim, and far more important than any others. But the courts today, for reasons by now familiar, much prefer to blame committees of strangers. The watchwords have come to be joint, several, alternative, or market-share liability, with the one-for-all principle reigning supreme. To make sure that the defendants' committee is well populated, the courts have abandoned all real limits of time or space to draw as large and nebulous a circle of responsibility as they can get away with.

At the very least, confused paternity rules of this kind, often applied long after the accident, eviscerate the liability system's deterrent value. The key to progress, on this side too, is individuation, not collectivization. If it deters crime at all, the execution of the guilty does so because the firing squad takes aim at a carefully selected target, fires at close range, does so soon after the murder, and announces to the world true facts about who should be blamed for what. Execution becomes a crime itself, not a form of deterrence, when the executioner wields a machine gun and fires at a range of 500 yards, especially when the condemned stands amid a large, panicky crowd of pickpockets, petty burglars, and more than a few outright innocents. Gilbert and Sullivan got it just right: "When everyone is somebodee / Then no one's anybody."

Just What Is Deterred?

"We are here on earth to help others," W. H. Auden once remarked, "but what the others are here for I cannot say." The Founders and their followers were of much the same mind. They were not going to spend a great deal of time worrying about just what drug manufacturers might or might not contribute to the larger scheme of public health and welfare; the lawyers' business was to see to it that people who caused accidents paid, and people who suffered accidents got paid, and that was that.

So does the new tort jurisprudence deter? Yes, certainly, it deters all sorts of things. But just what are those things? When you think about this quite different question the answer doesn't seem by any means as attractive as when you don't think about it. This much is clear: What is risky in legal terms often has little to do with what is risky in the physical world. When put to the test, the new tort system has failed to discriminate effectively among good risks and bad ones. It has been indifferent to, when not deliberately disdainful of, individual needs and individual responsibilities.

When it encourages improvement at all, the new tort system promotes the trivial and marginal change. Today's oral contraceptive manufacturer does work hard to fine-tune the warning, or microscopically adjust the hormonal balance in the pill. The drill press designer adds an extra hair guard or hand shield. The doctor administers more tests, shoots more X rays, and piles on a paper trail of his own. Large companies hire risk managers, industrial hygienists, consumer psychologists, and quality control experts in droves. The individuals and institutions all vigorously insist that they are working relentlessly to improve safety and cut their exposure to avoid liability. How could they claim otherwise? Due diligence on safety matters is still at the heart of a successful liability defense, most especially when punitive damages are at issue. No car maker, pesticide designer, or pediatrician should be eager to admit publicly to anything but the most tireless effort on safety matters.

The effort is there, but it is incremental, aimed at perfuming the violet and painting the lily. Liability-driven safety management has become a mirror image of the legal process itself—fussy, cumulative, bureaucratic, and preoccupied with paper. The risk-reduction initiatives that are encouraged by liability undoubtedly do some good some of the time. But the threat of liability also postpones or prevents the sharp break from tradition, the profound change in method or material, design or manufacture. And the sharp break, the occasional bold leap forward, is all-important in the quest for safety.

The picture is no brighter when the makers and doers are retreating rather than advancing. Yes, one can always point to some bad products driven off the market by litigation, to the overall benefit of the public health and safety. But the list of safety-enhancing products also banished is at least equally long, with safety consequences that have been even more grave. Yes, some incompetent doctors and irresponsible waste haulers have been forced out of business, as they richly deserved to be. So too have been many competent and much-needed ones. Some worthless or even danger-ous innovations have been forestalled, but only because innovation across the board has been slowed, and innovation remains the most vital, long-term promoter of safety that we know.

The Founders started their crusade under a banner of safety, prudence, and progress, but despite their best intentions they ended up fighting for the opposite side. They tackled products and services one at a time, all but ignoring the subtle trade-offs between the risks in front of them and the risks that were not in court. They engaged the risks of human creation, overlooking the still graver risks of the natural world. They ignored the ample evidence that new is generally safer than old, and set in place rules that entrench the status quo and repel all who endeavor to change it. They took the ancient parable of a man who stopped by the roadside for a stranger in need of help and rewrote it as a Kafkaesque nightmare of lawsuits, stigma, and shame. The courts' proudest and most earnestly touted objective was to make life safer. It has been their most ignominious failure.

11

Rights in Collision

STATE-SUPPORTED mass vaccination facilities were first instituted in England in 1808. A compulsory vaccination act was passed in 1853, the "guardians of the poor" being instructed to carry out the law. On February 27, 1902, the Board of Health for Cambridge, Massachusetts, adopted a new vaccination regulation. "Whereas, smallpox has been prevalent to some extent in the city of Cambridge and still continues to increase," the board declared, "be it ordered, that all the inhabitants of the city . . . be vaccinated or revaccinated." "Whoever . . . refuses or neglects to comply with such requirement," a Massachusetts law provided, "shall forfeit five dollars."

Henning Jacobson refused and neglected. He offered to prove that vaccination "quite often" caused serious and permanent injury, and that it was impossible to predict in advance what the results in any particular case might be. He maintained that as a child he had "been caused great and extreme suffering" by a disease produced by vaccination. "If injured," his lawyer further argued, "the person vaccinated is damaged without compensation. . . . Compulsion to introduce disease into a healthy system is a violation of liberty. . . . [A] compulsory vaccination law is . . . hostile to the inherent right of every free man to care for his own body and health in such way as to him seems best. . . . [T]he execution of such law against one who objects to vaccination . . . is nothing short of an assault upon his person."

The City Board had a quite different opinion. The community needed the protection that only mass vaccination could provide, and Jacobson was a perfectly normal and healthy resident.

The dispute plodded its way up to the U.S. Supreme Court. "[F]or nearly a century most of the members of the medical profession have regarded vaccination, repeated after intervals, as a preventive of smallpox," Justice John Marshall Harlan wrote for the Court. "[W]hile they have recognized the possibility of injury to an individual from carelessness in the performance of it, or even in a conceivable case without carelessness, [medical experts] generally have considered the risk of such an injury too small to be seriously weighed as against the benefits." "There are manifold restraints to which every person is necessarily subject for the common good," Harlan's opinion continued. "Real liberty for all could not exist under the operation of a principle which recognizes the right of each individual person to use his own, whether in respect of his person or his property, regardless of the injury that may be done to others. . . . Even liberty itself, the greatest of all rights, is not unrestricted license to act according to one's own will."

Seat Belts, Straitjackets, and Handcuffs

But that was then, of course, and this is now. The Founders reshaped tort law to protect against just the kind of oppressions Henning Jacobson suffered. They viewed the world as fundamentally coercive, a place where helpless consumers are constantly victimized by manufacturers, doctors, airline companies, and the organs of state. Expanded liability might not, indeed, give the little guy a chance to pull out from such coercive relations, but it would at least compensate him for the losses he sustained therein. The institutional provider would not be forced to release him from its smothering grip, but it would be given the new duties of Institutional Nanny: held responsible for any and all accidents that it might cause or fail to prevent.

There are certain vicious gangs of facts, however, that sometimes thrust themselves rudely on the scene just as one is peacefully contemplating the landscape of pure theory. One fact is that when outsiders are roped into accidents they soon realize as much and take steps to protect themselves. One of their options, as we saw in the last chapter, is to render themselves even more outsiders by staying farther away from the emergency room, the maternity room, or the pediatric ward. And people left to their own devices often face considerable dangers. A second option is to move not farther away, but closer, and try to prevent accidents by increasing control over the potential victim.

Things started modestly enough. The courts began to place a very high premium on the crashworthy car. But there is no such thing, short of a Sherman tank. The most effective protection in a car accident, by a wide margin, is a three-point seat belt that someone has taken the trouble to buckle. So insurance companies, the real financial targets of the crash-worthiness lawsuits, and in many cases automakers as well, began to work tirelessly for such things as ignition interlock systems, mandatory seat belt laws, and mandatory helmet laws for cyclists. So what? Seat belt laws are hardly the most savage impositions by which the state oppresses the individual. To be sure, a few solemn legal academics and libertarian theorists, along with certain members of the general public, protested that driving beltless or helmetless is a matter of individual freedom, possibly even constitutionally protected. But they could be dismissed as cranks and eccentrics, suspected of redneck tendencies. Perhaps the seat belt could be chalked up as a new tort victory.

At least until things were carried one step further, and the seat belt became a straitjacket or a pair of handcuffs. In 1976 a court announced that psychiatrists were expected to protect people from their own dangerous impulses. Clinical psychologists and social workers were added to the list soon afterward. And what was the best way to keep a possibly suicidal patient from self-harm, or a possibly psychotic one from harming others? The seat belt once again, this time with interlocking sleeves and buttons up the back. Or perhaps a restraint even more substantial. Police officers held liable for accidents caused by the drunk or the criminal suspect would favor preventive arrest and detention; parole officers would revoke or deny parole when in any doubt, however slight. With a careless, backhand stroke, the courts thus directed those in authority to overpredict violence or self-destructiveness, and gave a powerful impetus to involuntary commitment of the criminal, the mentally ill, and the social misfit. Civil libertarians and civil rights activists, close political cousins of the Founders, had been laboring for twenty years to encourage just the opposite presumption; no matter.

Beyond the straitjacket is the scalpel. The best way to deter the all-too-common injuries of childbirth, courts have decided, is to encourage suing the obstetrician. So, between 1965 and 1984, the frequency of Cesarean sections increased fourfold as obstetricians came to understand that when in doubt, their safest liability bet was to reach for the knife. Fail to perform a Cesarean which (with benefit of hindsight) people can later say might have helped, and you will most certainly be sued. Perform a Cesarean unnecessarily, and no one will ever be able to prove a thing against you.

In 1987, three researchers writing in the *New England Journal of Medicine* documented the "important and growing problem" of "forced obstetrical procedures"—doctors seeking court orders to force pregnant women to undergo treatment they did not want. Most of the requests were for Cesarean sections after a diagnosis of fetal distress; others involved forced hospitalization of women who were diabetic or had bleeding; others were for forced blood transfusions to fetuses with a condition that can induce potentially fatal anemia. In 1985 a pregnant sixteen-year-old girl in Wisconsin was held "in secure detention" because she lacked "the motivation or ability" to seek prenatal care. Civil libertarians loudly protested that such interference violated the mother's "autonomy" and "right to self-determination." What autonomy? The patient's wishes undoubtedly prevail in a world governed by consent and contract. But one cannot live in the past, and the new legal world was built from the beginning on assumptions of consumer helplessness, incompetence, and ignorance. How can the mother's expressed wishes possibly count beforehand if they do not count later on, when the baby, or the mother herself, or perhaps her estranged husband, files suit for the baby's injury?

Notwithstanding workers' compensation laws, the courts also found ways to insinuate themselves into the workplace, in hopes of improving employer-employee relations. Surely the employee could only benefit from an expanded right to sue the employer or its outside suppliers. What did the workers of the world have to lose, other than the chains of dangerous employment? Unfortunately, more than a few employers understood the demand to be for more chains rather than fewer. The cheapest and most effective protection, many employers discovered, was to control the employee rather than the risk.

In early 1987, a company that used asbestos in its acoustical ceiling products announced that employees in eight states would have to stop smoking, both at work and at home, or lose their jobs. Unions and employees howled in dismay: the worker's freedom and autonomy to make personal choices for himself had been violated. What freedom? There was a law of contract once, which respected personal choice, assumption of risk, and the like. But no one had paid any attention to *that* for decades, least of all in the new era when contract had been redefined as mere flypaper. An effective if heavy-handed anti-smoking campaign promised to protect employee health far more reliably than any other conceivable initiative the employer might take. And since in the new legal age the employer was the one with responsibility, it would not hesitate to exercise the power.

Asbestos companies were not the only employers to understand the point. Several trucking companies installed small computers in their vehicles to monitor the drivers' every move, rest break, and speed change. By 1987, more than 6 million workers were being monitored electronically in one way or another. Polygraph screening and testing for drug residues have also become widespread. One company successfully marketed a system said to be capable of detecting drug abuse by analyzing the electrical activity of the brain. Employers undoubtedly gained better knowledge of workers' performance and attention to safety, which was the whole idea. Workers themselves, according to several unions, suffered increased anxiety, high blood pressure, and ulcers.

The Institutional Nanny principle was based on the happy assumption that the Nannies would act unobtrusively and in a spirit of great love, like the mother who would lock up the Drano while still allowing the infant to crawl around the house at will. The car maker would just toughen the chassis and install an airbag. The employer would just reduce the chemical fumes in the factory. The psychiatrist would provide the occasional warning to police, while continuing with just the right therapy, in a professional spirit of friendly tolerance for both the patient and the Trial Lawyers of America.

But providers quite naturally sought out the cheapest and most effective ways of avoiding liability, whether those ways increased the risk (as we saw in the last chapter) or undercut the value of the service provided, or curtailed personal freedom. In nine cases out of ten, the best and cheapest protection from accidents lay very close to the victim herself. So the surest way to control the accident was to monitor and then control the person at risk. That was precisely what happened. What the world gradually discovered was that those commissioned with the responsibility of a Nanny are going to behave like one, even to the point of locking the accident-prone child in her room.

The Defective Victim

There was worse to come. The new legal system is obsessed with the exorcism of defects—defects in products, defects in warning, defects in performance. The framers of the new law assumed, correctly so far as their analysis went, that if the law made defects costly, the people who paid the bills would do their best to ferret them out and eliminate them. The mistake was to assume that defects are mostly to be found in bad technology, or inferior professional technique. No one considered the appalling possibility that the search for defects would end at the victim himself.

Birth defects, for example, were around long before obstetricians, morning sickness drugs, or contraceptives—defective or otherwise—came on the scene. And people in the baby business knew all too well that birth defects would be around long afterward, whatever the law might do to the products and the professionals. The only rational response to a tort system that stridently demanded defect-free infants was to go after defects at the source. The powerful legal incentive for the modern obstetrician, in short, was to dispose of any possibly defective infant before it could gestate into a malpractice claim. As it happened, the necessary tools are fast being perfected in amniocentesis and prenatal genetic screening. So liability law, with its customary nonchalance, quietly began to promote a program of eugenic enhancement and purification.

The impulse to remove the defect in the persons on the scene could not be confined to the accident victims themselves. If a negligent hiring suit could easily be the reward for employing a former convict, or someone with less than sterling paper credentials for a job, or perhaps even the slightly less well-qualified woman or minority applicant in a position critical to safety, the simplest protection was not to hire the defective employee in the first place. If hiring a person with a contagious disease would open the employer's door to suits by fellow employees or customers, here was yet another employee defect to test for and banish. In each case, what counts is not the employer's best assessment of actual danger, but the imponderables of appearances, perceptions, and jury sympathies. Particularly alarming for the future is the incentive the new tort system will provide in the age of AIDS. The imperative will be to root out the defective victim so as to protect him or others from his own real or argued vulnerability or inadequacy. What will this lead us to in a day when a million Americans are already thought to be infected with AIDS and studies suggest (as they now do) that the infection impairs mental acuity early on?

In a legal world obsessed with their eradication, defects could be found almost anywhere. Pregnant women and their unborn children are especially vulnerable to workplace chemicals; employers are bound to recognize that being pregnant, or possessing the capacity to become so, is another defective condition, that should also be screened out with care. One heavy-handed employer offered women employees this choice: Undergo sterilization or abandon your job on a particular assembly line. In an earlier day, a paper contract promising no pregnancy (or, in any event, no lawsuit) would have sufficed. But flypaper of this kind is valueless nowadays, so a contract signed with a scalpel is clearly to be preferred. Conventional wisdom notwithstanding, the knife again proves mightier than the pen.

Genetic screening offers similar promise of protection from workplace liability through protection from work. One person in ten has a pair of variant genes that produces an excess of a particular enzyme. The enzyme normally purges the body of toxic hydrocarbons, but when present in excess, it converts them into carcinogens, to the point where people with this genetic trait are twenty times more likely than the average person to contract lung cancer from inhaling certain industrial chemicals. Naphthalene and many other widely used compounds have no effect on most people, but 2 percent of Chinese, 11 percent of Mediterranean Jews, and 13 percent of black males are prone to develop a highly dangerous form of anemia when exposed to it. There are hundreds of other genetic traits of similar character, which make some persons less susceptible, and others more so, to chemical hazards of every description.

Just as these tools for genetic analysis were being perfected in microbiology labs across the country, the courts were creating powerful incentives to use them in the most pernicious ways. A genetically "defective" employee would hardly have had to worry so much about discrimination targeted at the health aspects of her own biological constitution in a day when she made her own binding choices about where to work and what risks to accept. But when the freedom to make contracts touching on matters of self-protection disappeared, so did the freedom to choose. At least eighteen of the country's largest companies used one or more genetic screening tests between 1970 and 1982; countless others have since begun to do so.

A neofascist hunt for defects in the fetus, the employee, or the woman in her childbearing years was not at all what the Founders or their political allies had intended. To their horror, the ever-expanding right to sue had become a spur to discrimination and worse. One escape would have been to wind back liability law and resurrect older notions of consent and contract. But eating one's own words makes for bad food, whatever one's appetite, and the new tort apostles just weren't in the habit of consuming such humble fare.

So they mentally consigned their enemies to regions more than tropical and fell to setting things right in their usual manner, which was to pile new law on top of the old. If a judicial decree inflating the right to sue was causing a decline in other rights, why not simply reaffirm those rights in turn with still more legal paper? Discrimination against smokers would be outlawed; smoking is an addiction, and so a handicap, and in any event, more blacks smoke than whites, so penalizing the smoker is racially discriminatory as well. Discrimination against pregnant women would be banned as unlawful discrimination by sex. And genetic constitution was a matter of race or ancestry or handicap, so discrimination on this basis could be outlawed too. If wary apartment owners were refusing to rent to families with children or large dogs, all that was needed was another statute.

So the first-generation tort lawsuits were designed to impel progressive action on matters affecting safety; the second-generation antidiscrimination claims attempted to block these very same incentives. Negligent hiring suits were supposed to spur employers to check out prospective employees. But an explosion of privacy and defamation suits by employees who were given bad references deterred employers from cooperating with each other in the check-out process. Malpractice suits against hospitals were intended to encourage dismissal of incompetent physicians. But any attempt to do so was routinely met by a suit claiming libel, defamation of character, breach of employment contract, and other atrocities.

There began an upward spiral of rights: new rights to sue for being hurt, matched by new rights not to suffer from one's propensity to sue or give others occasion to do so. Most lawyers loved this, of course, because they stood to collect an enforcement percentage on every new right printed. But the cycle of escalation was certain to cost everyone else dearly. The states could outlaw inquiries about arrest records, as many have in fact done, but circumventing these laws remained all too easy and attractive as the liability stakes in negligent hiring suits grew steadily higher. It was easy enough to declare genetic screening illegal, but it was all but impossible to enforce the ban, most especially when employers already test the health of employees in all sorts of ways for perfectly routine and proper purposes. In all but the most brazen and systematic cases, discrimination is insidious and very hard to detect.

Worse still, an attack on knowledge and freedom themselves, rather than on the legal environment that promotes their abuse, means that still more benefits are likely to be lost. Wisely used, information about genetic vulnerabilities saves lives without any offsetting penalty to anyone. The freedom to hire and fire is equally necessary for the public safety. How else are incompetent train drivers, pilots, and doctors or dangerous ex-convicts to be kept off the job or removed when they are identified? Do we really want to outlaw discrimination against the smoker just as the evidence is beginning to accumulate about her habit's harmful effects on company workers exposed to secondhand carcinogens?

One fact remained painfully apparent throughout: Whatever the handicap and nondiscrimination laws might declare, sex, pregnancy, race, genes, propensity to smoke, and many other highly personal habits *are* important risk factors. By making so much turn on risk and its prevention, and so little on choice, the courts had created new and quite rational incentives for discrimination, even as the old and irrational ones were finally being laid to rest. The ultimate question for the tough-minded employer was what counted more—a nondiscrimination law on the books that was easy to evade or an expensive liability judgment in the courts that was not.

The Right Not to Contract

The only thing the Founders and their followers could promote directly was the right to sue. But rights do not exist in a vacuum. At a certain point, the uncontrolled advance of one right forces the retreat of others; there is simply not enough room for them all at the crowded inn of human freedom.

The escalating right to sue, and the counterescalating right not to suffer for one's likelihood to involve others in lawsuits, squeezed the right of private contract in a tightening vise. As the courts trimmed and pruned away at the freedom of contract, what often appeared was not the healthier growth that had been planned and promised, but a barren and useless desert. The freedom *not* to contract still existed, and when all else failed, people could exercise it very aggressively. The Institutional Nanny, faced with problems she simply could not solve, often decided to pack up the umbrella and the sweets, and retire to her cottage in the country.

Since 1965, for example, the Supreme Court has recognized a constitutional right to use contraceptives. That declaration dismayed some conservatives from the beginning, but no one from the political right ever succeeded in doing much about it. Skillful proponents of the new tort, however, achieved in a few short years of litigation what the religious right utterly failed to bring about in fifteen years of political agitation and constitutional argument. In barely a decade of steady work the courts stopped research dead in its tracks, sharply raised prices, curtailed choice, and stirred up a wave of paranoia against the contraceptive industry that shows no sign of subsiding. Wealthy and sophisticated women remain able, of course, to get whatever they want, but teenagers and the poor are now dissuaded, in increasing numbers, from interfering with the Almighty's will in matters of procreation.

Contraceptives only illustrate a much larger principle. The shaky edifice of modern liability law has been built on the rubble of private contract. But contract itself, it has become apparent, is the foundation of the exercise of most other rights and freedoms. The right to sue has completely eclipsed the right to do business on terms that preclude lawsuit. Every time a plaintiff successfully disclaims responsibility for his own protection inside the courtroom, he undermines another's freedom to protect himself as he alone sees fit outside.

Not in My Back Yard

The new tort law's collision with other rights extended beyond the individual's right to be let alone or to make binding private contracts of her own choosing. We are much more than individuals; more, too, than transient pairs united through bilateral contract. At the other end of the line-up are the rights of the community, like the ones that loomed so large in the compulsory vaccination case summarized at the beginning of this chapter. But despite all their grand theories about social engineering and cost spreading, the Founders had a very atomistic and isolationist view of the world, and that frame of mind has proved to be very costly.

The communal dimension of our lives is especially apparent in the fight against contagious disease. Effective immunization must be a group endeavor. The phenomenon is called herd immunity: Each individual is protected not only by his own vaccination but by the fact that his neighbors have been immunized too. The old liability law, written in the same spirit as the *Jacobson* decision, was deferential to community ventures of this character. "We are not prepared to hold that a minority, residing or remaining in any city or town where smallpox is prevalent, and enjoying the general protection afforded by an organized local government, may . . . defy the will of its constituted authorities, acting in good faith for all," wrote Justice John Marshall Harlan. "[T]he spectacle would be presented of the welfare and safety of an entire population being subordinated to the notions of a single individual who chooses to remain a part of that population."

Just such a spectacle was presented when the new tort regime elevated the quintessentially individual right to sue above all others. The result was to undercut the social contract in much the same way as the new law had eviscerated private ones. Some things have to be done collectively, by the community for the community. If everyone else in the community is going to bear the small risk of vaccination, the safest course for the selfish individual is to be the only one *not* immunized. His effective protection from the disease will come from the immunization of his neighbors; his protection against the risks of the vaccine itself comes from not using it.

The obvious flaw in this strategy is that not everyone can play the game, and if many try then all lose. The global scourge of smallpox that precipitated Henning Jacobson's suit was finally eradicated from the face of the planet in 1979, just when new tort practitioners were seriously beginning to flex their muscles against the vaccine industry. Perhaps the thought (quite incorrect) was that vaccines had by then done all they could, and it was time to begin attacking the risks of vaccines themselves. In any event, the cases decided against the federal government in the wake of the 1976 swine flu immunization program took on a distinctly hostile tone, seeming to imply that the government had taken part in a massive and wicked conspiracy against its citizenry. It will be a while before the Surgeon General is ready to risk any repetition of that costly debacle.

Though the analogy is not exact, public transportation, public schools, even the press and organized religion, are similar, in some ways, to programs devised for the public health: All hope to create positive spillovers beyond the direct benefit that each participant gets, and all are best accomplished if participation is widespread. And in each of these areas, too, the public welfare has been subverted by an overinflated private right to sue.

For a while the tram line between Roosevelt Island and Manhattan was closed because liability insurance had become unavailable; the State of New York eventually put its credit on the line to restore the service. Diving boards were removed from New York City public schools. Public beaches were closed or hours of operation curtailed. At one point, police officers in West Orange, New Jersey, refused to answer any but emergency calls because the community lacked liability coverage.

Freedoms of religion and the press were not immune either. A California court declared that a church could be sued by the family of one of its parishioners after he committed suicide, for having exacerbated the suicide victim's "preexisting feelings of guilt, anxiety and depression." Perhaps it had. But then, the very mission of many religions is to challenge heart and conscience, so as to promote a sense of contrition leading to absolution. Lawsuits against the church for having succeeded in that mission all too well can only undercut the parishioners' unfettered right to the free, collective exercise of their religion. Outspoken voices in the press have also been bystander casualties of the new tort evolution. A court system receptive to endless and unlimited claims of damage for hurt feelings and emotional injury was bound to grow increasingly receptive to claims of libel and invasion of privacy, and so it did.

By endlessly inflating the individual's right to sue, the courts multiplied opportunities for the exercise of one of the most natural and powerful of human instincts, the NIMBY syndrome. Everybody will concede that some chemical factory, highway system, hydroelectric dam, or waste dump, somewhere or other, is probably necessary. But everyone adds the caveat, "not in my backyard"—or anywhere nearby. Henning Jacobson was a NIMBY-ist too, and a very rational one, as we saw. In case after case, the courts have promoted the individual's right to sue over the community's right to act. Increasingly, the private suit is directed against the community itself—as represented by the municipality, the state, or the federal government. The community needs jails, AIDS clinics, and waste dumps, of some description, somewhere or other. But the individual enjoys an ever-expanding right not to be exposed in any way to the incidental—perhaps statistically minute but always unavoidable—public hazards. The community needs police protection, highways, and cleanup services. But the individual again enjoys a swelling right to sue for some neglect, large or small, real or imagined, in the way any of these services might be provided.

In the end, the shrinkage of all other rights in the face of an ever-expanding right to sue was a simple and unavoidable matter of bookkeeping. It is said that our debts are forgiven even as we forgive our debtors, and the converse is equally true. Modern liability is about the ruthless enforcement of debts of every character. And a propensity to sue for every trespass means a certainty of being sued for each and every one of our own trespasses against others. As we give litigation, so shall we receive.

If large corporate sellers of products are strictly liable for failing to warn of product defects, so too may be the seller who runs a garage sale or a classified ad. A right to sue the tavern after the drunk driver's accident eventually spills over to condemn the social host as well. The right to sue the car manufacturer, hospital, police officer, or public social worker soon becomes the right to sue the bus company, volunteer scoutmaster, bake-sale organizer, or roadside rescuer. The them in all of these cases, let it not be forgotten, is us. Legal principles have a life of their own, and the rules invented for Wall Street end up being applied on Main Street too, sooner or later.

As with the proverbial tango, it always takes at least two to litigate. Certainly every taxpayer has been invited to dance, and takes a turn on the floor, willingly or otherwise. The government is being sued beyond all prior imaginings, but the ones who pay the bills are not (and cannot be) negligent officials; it is "we, the people." In 1981, the city of South Tucson, Arizona, had to pay $3 million to a police officer who was shot by a fellow officer—an award that amounted to $400 for every resident of the city. The funds were raised, in part, by a $2.1 million bond sale, the repayment of which will cost the town $305,000 a year through 1999. Residents of Bay St. Louis, Mississippi, went a step further, and declared municipal bankruptcy following a judgment won by a youth paralyzed after diving off an unfinished city pier. The price of state and federal citizenship has risen too. The number of suits filed against Washington State doubled between 1982 and 1986; the state's legal costs rose tenfold in the space of a decade.

Occasionally, of course, the government strikes back, for it is a cardinal principle of law that as we sue, so shall we be sued. In April 1987, the city of San Carlos, California, filed a $13,000 claim against seven-year-old Ryan Barber, who had ridden his bike into the street from between two parked cars, hitting a city truck. (The driver apparently wrenched his back in attempting to avoid young Ryan; how badly the truck was damaged by the bike was not reported, though the lawyers undoubtedly looked into the matter.) But claims of this character are the exception; by and large the system channels funds from the many to the few. In 1985, there were 54,000 claims pending against the federal government, demanding $149 billion. There can be no doubt about this, at least: In winning a grossly expanded right to sue, we, the people, have also won a vastly broader duty to pay.

Rights, in Particular and in General

And where was the jury system during all this? The new tort theorists placed enormous trust in juries, counting on them to redesign airplane engines and high-lift loaders, rewrite herbicide warnings, determine whether Bendectin causes birth defects, place a suitable price on sorrow and anguish, and administer an open-ended system of punitive fines. The jury is undoubtedly the common law's finest legacy, so respected that the right to a jury trial is addressed in the Seventh Amendment to the Constitution. "The right of trial by jury shall be preserved" says the Amendment, "in all suits at common law" "where the value in controversy shall exceed twenty dollars." Who could dare criticize the handiwork of such a venerated and respected institution? *Vox populi, vox dei.*

Or perhaps *vox* Mother Goose. The enormous gulf between the particular and the general is one that can never be bridged in the courtroom. Juries face accidents up close, viewing them in the lurid setting of an individual tragedy already completed. But the intelligent organization of human affairs requires a broader vision, not dominated by the individual case.

Risk ahead of time is bearable and in any event unavoidable; injury after the fact is intolerable. The death of a single named child in a car accident is a boundless, wholly unacceptable loss. Yet every person who drives a car adds to that same risk every day. Humanity compels us to say no to the individual accident when we face it up close. Common sense demands that we accept the risk of accident and misadventure whenever we step back to plan our affairs. The same problems are apparent when the subject is compensation. The only human reaction to the individual tragedy, viewed close up, is unbounded generosity, which any large corporation or insurer can surely afford to underwrite. But a compensation system that must deal with tragedy wholesale necessarily follows more precise and parsimonious rules.

Wise policy can only be based on the broader perspective. Efficient deterrence looks at risk in general for the population at large; harsh though it sounds, the circumstances of the single plaintiff now in court are all but irrelevant. A tort-driven system of deterrence takes exactly the opposite approach; its focus is on the actual accident in the particular case, and it matters little that many others may have been protected or saved by the design feature in question. A workable compensation system always looks beyond the individual tragedy to the solvency of the system as a whole. Tort-driven compensation focuses sharply on the individual victim and all too easily becomes obsessed with counting the uncountable in pain, suffering, sorrow, and punishment.

That tort law is engaged and driven by the individual case explains many of its failings. It explains why juries can declare defective a vaccine that has saved millions of lives, and how they can award $50 million for an intestinal blockage or $100 million for a single fatality, figures that no program of general compensation could match even if it had all the nation's wealth at its disposal. The jury's focus is always on private harm after the accident, not on public benefit beforehand. The concern is with the individual's lonely tragedy, not with the public's bloodless accounts.

All of these might have been concerns under the old tort law, as well. But they weren't, because judges of the day were careful to keep the tort system well in check. Judges saw it as their mission to dispense retail and retrospective justice, not to shape broad, forward-looking public policy. All of that changed, however, with the advent of the new tort, which was expressly rationalized as an instrument of public policy rather than of private justice. The Founders, unfortunately, never worked out how to merge the greatness of their mission with the smallness of the courtroom arena.

It is not that today's jurors are always irresponsible or often incompetent, or in any way less qualified than juries of yesteryear. It is simply that they do not accurately represent their own members' will on matters of public policy; what they accurately represent is individual compassion for individual tragedy, within the bounds that the law permits them to express. The layperson votes in favor of expansive liability when sitting in the jury box but votes overwhelmingly in favor of limiting liability when the legal rules are put to public referendum. Most people instinctively recognize that lawyers themselves are always the greatest beneficiaries of their quixotic efforts to improve society. "Why is there always a secret singing when a lawyer cashes in?" asks the poet Carl Sandburg. "Why does a hearse horse snicker hauling a lawyer away?" As jurors they may be greatly moved by compassion, but most people recognize full well that the system, and those who manipulate it to such great personal advantage, do more harm to society than good.

Beyond all this lies a larger conflict of objectives inherent in tort law itself. While the theoreticians have talked endlessly about deterrence, most jurors have had enough common sense to suspend critical judgment on the design of vaccines and high-lift loaders. But every decent human being will respond with compassion to the brain-damaged child or the asbestos worker slowly suffocating from shattered lungs. The Founders sold judges what was described as a police car. It ended up being driven by juries as a soup truck and ambulance. This surely helped the widow and the orphan, now and again. But it also, in the end, increased their numbers by retarding safety rather than advancing it.

Safety is not improved by imposing a huge and capricious tort tax on doctors, drug manufacturers, or even the providers of more pedestrian products like cars or appliances, though it is beyond doubt that people regularly *are* injured while receiving and using these services and products. Nor is compensation advanced by infinitely particular legal standards of negligence, inadequate warning, defectiveness, or fault, which, of course, cut off liability in many cases where people have nonetheless been gravely injured. An accident victim's need for help exists quite independently of any legal standard of liability.

Effective deterrence requires a clear point of responsibility, but generous compensation depends on a broad tax base to sweep in at least one or two deep pockets. Deterrence requires swift, well-timed justice; compensation requires looking as far forward or backward in time as may be necessary to find funds. Deterrence depends on solid proof of cause and effect; broad compensation depends on ignoring the same as much as possible. Deterrence is sharpest when liability insurance contracts are construed precisely and narrowly, so that defendants themselves shoulder the bill and are monitored effectively by insurers; compensation seems to require the unashamed stretching and rewriting of insurance contracts to broaden coverage wherever possible. Responsibility means that the buck must stop somewhere certain, definite, and predictable. Effective compensation depends on simply sending the bill somewhere or other, here or there, as may be convenient for securing funds in the particular case.

The Founders were always glad to think how wonderfully their system managed to put together deterrence of the wicked with compensation of the needy. Putting this and that together is all very well. But according to the success with which you put this and that together, you get a woman and a fish apart or a mermaid in combination, and for most purposes the combination is less functional than the sum of its parts. So the world, and then finally even most legal scholars, discovered with the quite separate objectives of compensation and deterrence.

Faced with such uncomfortable realities, the academic commentary on tort law objectives began to take the form of a verbal shell game. The insurance pea is on the table when the question is whether the Mammoth Drug Company will, under the new tort assault, continue supplying the lifesaving vaccine. But when discussion turns to deterring the next Dalkon Shield, everyone agrees that liability bites like an adder, and is supposed to. Asbestos liability is applauded because it will help drive asbestos manufacturers out of business; who cares whether the claimant really needs the money or whether the lawyers take a huge cut? But liability against charitable hospitals is required to help out the helpless victim; there must be insurance in the background, and if there isn't we'd rather not think about it at all. Pain-and-suffering damages are justified even in no-fault cases because they can easily be absorbed by the insurance system, but the cushioning effect of insurance is ignored when the discussion shifts to punitive damages. The game is played out in the legal vocabulary. Negligence or product defects are the terms of art when the discussion concerns deterrence; cost-spreading and no-fault compensation are wheeled out when the focus is on paying the victim's bills. On Mondays, Wednesdays, and Fridays, the new tort system is supposed to be sharper than a serpent's tooth; on Tuesdays, Thursdays, and weekends, it is expected to be as soft as the answer that turns away wrath. A shell game, skillfully played, can be a marvel to behold. But no one ever got rich playing it, except the man with the pea.

The Chameleon Contract

There is the sort of inescapable circularity to modern tort law that Ambrose Bierce saw with food. Edible, he said, means good to eat, and wholesome to digest, as a worm to a toad, a toad to a snake, a snake to a pig, a pig to a man, and a man to a worm. Modern tort law, where consent counts for nothing, is a system of feeding on others that invites everyone to dine at everyone else's expense. The problem with any such system, of course, is that though you may start the cycle as a consumer, you surely end it among the consumed. It is inherent in the catering system itself.

Contract, the mirror image of tort, is the law of cooperation rather than of mutual consumption. Contract is the right that supports all others, most especially in a modern technological society with highly specialized production. It is through voluntary agreement that we control our own bodies by choosing medical services, contraceptives, abortions, cigarettes, and alcohol; control our movements by choosing automobiles and other forms of locomotion; control our collective health by siting sanitation facilities and eradicating epidemic disease; control our social universe by taking part in clubs and voluntary associations of all kinds; and control our spiritual destiny by choosing counselors and guides, religious or secular. In a well-ordered world, the mutual benefits that are possible through cooperation would favor it unconditionally.

Tort law, however, sharpens every possible difference or suspicion between employer and employee, between the obstetrician and the woman being treated, between the manufacturer of a drug, or contraceptive, or vaccine and the person using it, between the community and its members. Tort law magnifies conflict to the point where it swamps the benefits of cooperation. The history of modern tort law, one editorialist has noted, is one of atomization and its handmaiden, alienation. We sue the stranger; we sue as if we were disconnected from the implications of the suit. No one feels connected to the real consequences of the action. In the short run, and for a small minority of successful litigants, conflict is a profitable business. But in the longer run, as society adjusts to a legal regime that promotes division, everyone loses but the lawyers. We are all in the soup together. Only the lawyers are here to dine.

Human nature being what it is, we all like to smile and smile before the deal, and to be villains in court afterward if things happen to go sour. But it is not possible to have things both ways, because those who find themselves too often on the losing side of the chameleon contract learn from experience and adjust accordingly. The tort Founders were intent on rewriting contract, private or public, so that no individual would ever lose. Their successors discovered, in the end, that they had created a world where there were far fewer contracts in which anyone ever won. Having allowed the lawyers to cut a great road through the right of contract to get after the devil, the citizenry had nowhere to hide when the devil then turned upon them, the contractual landscape now being entirely flat.

12

Compassion by Consent

THE MOST POWERFUL agent of change in tort law has always been sympathy. The case for the new tort jurisprudence begins and ends with a heartrending catalogue of tragedy.

This, for example, about an asbestos worker: "He went through all kinds of tests at the hospital, and then another doctor operated on him and sewed him right up, and told me that he had just two months to live. . . . Each day he ate less and lived for the hypos to kill the pain. . . . He tried to get well. He loved life and he wanted to live for me and the kids. He laid down and when his last breath went out, he called me and said, 'Honey, I'm dying.' Then he died." Or this about a user of the Dalkon Shield: "Mary was first fitted with a Shield in February 1972, when she was eighteen. She began having dangerous, extremely painful, and recurring pelvic infections within a few months. . . . After seven terrible years of misdiagnosis and illness she was finally deprived of her ability ever to bear a child." Or this about a child who fell sick after being vaccinated against whooping cough: "My husband and I both remember the agony Steven was in after his DPT shots. . . . I just held him in my arms while he was screaming. I'd call the clinic and say, 'He is really sick,' and all they would tell me was to give him more Tylenol."

Of course the Founders did not at all expect the system to run on the fuel of raw emotion. For the most part their approach was coolly analytic rather than warmly indignant, as befitted a movement that sought to steer the system in a no-fault direction. They saw the new tort law as just a form of three-party insurance, in which the drug companies, midwives, and city halls would buy insurance wholesale and distribute it in little packets along with their regular offerings, at irregular intervals and under court order to be sure, but without stigma or shame nonetheless.

What the tort Founders did *not* believe in was consent, contract, and all they imply, at least not insofar as contract might address the allocation of accident costs. Having characterized the world as a fundamentally coercive place, the Founders of course looked to coercive, nonconsensual solutions to the problems at hand. Having assumed a world without real and willing contracts, they of course based all their designs for legal solutions on the opposite of contract. So the law of tort grew and grew.

The modern rules both assume and depend on legal compulsion. The freely made agreements of the parties are legal nullities. Advance agreement, in fact, is viewed as the main problem to be overcome. Did the buyer and seller agree to limit their liability to each other? The contract is flypaper, not to be enforced. Did the defendant and the insurer fail to write a sufficiently comprehensive policy in advance? Then the courts will have to rewrite that contract too, or stack up policies, or shoot with the triple trigger, as may be necessary to create coverage that no one willingly bought or sold beforehand. Did the victim happen to have her own insurance, taken out wisely, willingly, and by her own choice before the accident? *That* policy—the only one on the scene grounded in contract—is to be assiduously ignored as an irrelevant collateral source. At every turn, payment through juridical process is to supersede payment based on—and limited by—private agreement.

The legal theories dovetailed perfectly, though not by any deliberate plan or design, with the courtroom realities. The theorists assumed coercion all around. Juries confronted tragedy up close. When presented with an individual and intensely personal tragedy, the impulse is to strike back. Who can fail to be angered by the devastating injury to a young child, or by the maiming of a woman in the prime of her life, or by the slow suffocation of a retired factory worker? Every accident was recharacterized as an assault, the victims then being invited to make a bid for our sympathy in court. A system that assumes coercion through and through, and that is driven by reflexive reaction to human tragedy, inevitably seeks out solutions that are themselves emotional, reactive, and coercive. These have become the defining characteristics of modern liability.

The workings of a truly stable accident compensation scheme—a system of insurance—are quite different. The challenge of insurance is to organize accidents, things that are momentous and unexpected, into categories that are regular and predictable. Each individual accident is a rarity. But even the most bizarre accidents become matters of humdrum statistics when the focus widens to encompass many people over extended periods. Practicable, self-financing accident insurance thus depends on pooling events and people into groups that are large and stable enough to convert the random into the routine. This means that effective insurance is a necessarily collaborative endeavor. And collaboration is possible only when the accidents and the legal rules surrounding them are reasonably stable and predictable.

Take stability first. Not all misfortunes are readily insurable. Some cannot be measured well enough. We know with great accuracy the number of house fires there were last year, and how many there will be next year, but we have no idea how much emotional distress there was or will be. Fortunately, the main accident costs we wish to insure against—death, medical costs, lost wages, major disability—are susceptible of measurement. Other mishaps are uninsurable because their underlying rate is changing at a rapid, unpredictable clip, all in the same direction. Just as tornado insurance is made possible by the underlying stability of weather patterns, so liability insurance depends on reasonable stability in legal norms. Overly rapid innovation is fatal. So too are the fluid standards of unchanneled sympathy, which make every award depend on contingencies of person and position.

The second essential is cooperation among large groups. Mutual insurance against rare accidents is one of the most sophisticated forms of human collaboration. Insurance works in private markets only if agreement is promoted and honored. Insurance under duress can ultimately take only one form, which is insurance by the state.

So here is the dilemma in a nutshell. Stable accident insurance depends on agreement among crowds. The essence of liability litigation is disputes among individuals. Stable insurance requires unemotional assessment of risk and disbursement of payments, with the temperament of an actuary and a bookkeeper, treating people as statistics. The driving force in liability law today is sympathy and emotion in the individual case. Legal rules rooted in a spirit of compulsion, and applied emotionally case by case, are profoundly inimical to insurance.

Getting to Yes

How then do we encourage broader and more reliable accident insurance coverage? The guiding principle must be to promote consent and agreement wherever possible—to prefer contract over tort whenever the choice may be presented—and to elevate direct insurance over liability-driven compensation.

The collateral source rule is the first and most vivid object lesson in how not to do things. And getting this one right is the key to all that follows. The rule could not be more wrongheaded, at least if the goal is to increase insurance all around. First-party insurance, from whatever source, is the most stable, predictable, and valuable source of first-dollar coverage. To ignore its presence is to fill the courtroom with litigants whose needs have already been satisfied, at the cost, in the end, of undercutting insurance across the board, including third-party insurance for the less common accident victims who have no other sources of funds.

Defenders of the current rule insist that it is unfair to offset the accident victim's own insurance against any prospective award. Why, after all, should she be penalized for having the good sense to buy some insurance of her own in advance? That view made real sense in an earlier day when tort rights were still tied to ancient principles of fault and duty, and the right to recover was linked closely to wrongs clearly committed by the other side. But those principles have long since been discarded; we now live, it must be recalled, in the age of no-fault. What matters in the spirit of the modern times is not where the insurance money comes from but that it's available to as many victims as possible. And the more claimants who take two ladles from the compensation punch bowl, the more will go away thirsty at the end of the queue when insurers withdraw. The best way to ensure that stable third-party insurance remains available in the background when all else fails is to save it for those who need it. At least nine states have recently taken steps to reverse the collateral source rule. New York law now requires courts to reduce awards by the sum total of all past and projected future payments from collateral sources other than life insurance and Social Security.

This simple idea can and should be carried further. Consider how we deal with airplane crashes today. Postaccident litigation is inordinately complex, and the average case takes four years to resolve. Payments, when they finally arrive, are large but highly variable. Collecting them is a struggle fraught with anxiety for everyone except the plaintiffs' lawyers, who have been known to collect thousands of dollars for every hour they work on such cases. As is not unusual elsewhere, only about 25 cents on the dollar invested in this policy of the Mutual Tort Insurance Company reaches claimants; the rest is dissipated by the legal intermediaries. And all this in cases where the victims' injury is usually a quick death, and eventual payment from the airline or airplane manufacturer is never in real doubt.

If even before the accident everything is clear but the precise dollar figure, its timing, and the size of the lawyers' inevitably huge cut, why not settle these subjects too in advance? The instrument, of course, would be a binding insurance contract, sold along with each ticket and each flight, between airline and passenger, one that cuts out the lawyers more or less entirely. If the concern is with the improvident traveler who might decline insurance altogether, the sale of some basic level of coverage ($1 million per passenger, say) could easily be made mandatory—or the courts might simply continue refusing to enforce arrangements with unconscionably low levels of coverage. Higher levels of coverage could easily be offered according to a passenger's particular needs. American Express already offers precisely this coverage free or for a modest fee (in the range of $3) to all its cardholders; many other card companies provide similar coverage free when tickets are purchased on credit. Settlement after the accident occurs in a matter of days, not years. And the numbers are beyond dispute: Airlines could provide three times as much total coverage to travelers, with no increase whatsoever in fares, if they were permitted to do so through the vehicle of a binding advance contract, rather than through tort litigation after the fact.

The airline example is only one of many possible arrangements. All it really takes is for courts to rediscover the respect they once had for contract. In most accidents, the person hurt has a preexisting relationship with those he eventually sues—or could establish one if he were allowed to. Contract was once used simply to decide whether compensation was due at all. It can easily be adapted to prescribe how reasonable compensation for well-defined contingencies could best be expedited. A *neo–no-fault* proposal to that effect has been sketched out in various forms by Jeffrey O'Connell of the University of Virginia Law School and extended by others.

A test of a related plan is already underway. In 1982, the state of Washington incorporated a variant of O'Connell's proposal into its insurance program for injured high school athletes. Through the school, each student athlete pays what amounts to a first-party accident insurance premium, which now runs about $1.40 per year. When a serious accident occurs, the injured athlete is immediately offered compensation for all medical expenses, and a modest—but at the same time certain—disability benefit, in exchange for which the student agrees not to sue the school.

The system appears to work remarkably well. Marty Wittman, for example, a sixteen-year-old sophomore at Curtis High in 1982, was left paralyzed from a football accident. He promptly received compensation for all of his medical expenses, which included six months of hospitalization and rehabilitation, the costs of a new van equipped with hand controls and a wheelchair lift, and the expenses for remodeling his house to accommodate his wheelchair. The state's insurance plan further compensates parents for wages they have lost in caring for their child and pays the injured athlete $300 a week for life if he receives less than that amount from other sources of income. The plan has now been adopted by two-thirds of all school districts. The offer has been accepted by the families of all twenty-four young athletes seriously injured since the program took effect in 1981. Sports equipment manufacturers, who have not yet joined the program, are considering doing so.

There is only one reason why neocontractual solutions are not much more common today: they do not offer a complete and truly enforceable escape from the coils of liability jurisprudence. Car rental companies routinely offer comprehensive (if overpriced) collision insurance as a direct contractual option on the rental form, and the law gives full effect to these arrangements. But what can be done for the car itself, through an enforceable contract, cannot today be done for the car's occupant, at least not in any way that is certain to operate as a legally binding limit rather than an open invitation to shoot for more. The O'Connell high-school-sports plan is an opt-in system that becomes binding, if at all, only after the accident. Other providers of goods and services, who start with less·sympathy on their side than ever-popular school athletic programs, fear that the courts will always find a way to take the guaranteed money up front—characterizing it, perhaps, as just another collateral source—and then run for more in the tort system. The history of what courts have done with contract in all other areas makes such fears more than plausible.

The enormous promise of neocontractual plans is nevertheless clear. The plans can work well because they dispense with the impenetrable legal jargon, the opportunities for histrionics, the army of overpaid middlemen. A seller establishes an express insurance policy with a buyer, with the understanding that it is to replace the implicit and vastly more speculative insurance mandated by modern tort law. The benefits are unambiguously spelled out in advance, as too are the limits, in the calm that prevails before anyone has been hurt. Compensation is severed from questions of negligence, defect, or fault, just as it is under any other first-party medical or disability insurance program. In an ordinary life insurance contract, after all, we do not wait until the insured is in the Hereafter, and the lawyers are in court, to discover after some years just how much coverage there really was; the policy amount is set out openly and in advance. There is no reason that accident insurance should be handled otherwise.

Insurance benefits offered in this way will never be exact replicas of tort awards, of course. They will not include open-ended damages for pain and suffering or other psychic losses; they will certainly rule out any possibility of punitive damages, and they are likely to prefer arbitration or expert tribunals to lay juries for resolving contested questions of cause and effect. And like all first-party insurance, they will usually rely on simple, standardized schedules to assess damages for such things as lost limbs or death itself. Those enamored of the present law may reflexively denounce changes of this character as a conspiracy against the future accident victim. But the only real conspiracy here is against a bankrupt system of justice. There is no doubt that advance insurance agreement can produce a much better deal for everyone in the picture except the lawyers. Consumers and accident victims have everything to gain. In many cases, insurance in advance is the only possible route to any insurance at all; without it, coverage will be denied, if necessary, by removing the diving board, the contraceptive, or the obstetrical service itself from the marketplace.

If neocontractual insurance solutions are likely to be somewhat thinner than the occasionally munificent tort system, they are also certain to be much broader. The beauty of first-party insurance is that it need not depend on flypaper theories of contract, fault, defect, lack of warning, shifting burdens of proof, merry-go-round liability, chameleon contracts, syncopated discovery clocks, or any of the other legal concepts, notions, or fictions needed to underwrite the Mutual Tort Insurance Company we operate today. As coverage expands, even some of the more refractory questions of cause and effect can be set aside. Many injuries today are not insured, inside the tort system or outside, and even under today's law, with all its excesses, most tort claims still end in defeat for the plaintiff. First-party insurance will not pay as much in the most lurid cases, but it will surely pay much more often and reliably.

Sensibly priced direct insurance could easily be sold with almost any good or service, either as a voluntary opt-in or opt-out policy, or as mandatory wrapping paper, depending on the will of our legislators. Vaccine manufacturers have declared themselves willing to offer a fixed-sum insurance policy, capped at $1 million per injury, with every dose of childhood vaccine they sell—provided that an advance contract of this sort would be truly binding and exclusive, with questions of cause and effect referred to outside experts, and independent tort suits entirely eliminated. Obstetricians and morning-sickness drug manufacturers might likewise be able to assemble an insurance package against the (quite high) risks of birth defects. They would, of course, be providing much more insurance than their own contributions to the birth-defect level really require, and coverage would likely be expensive, but the only thing that proves is the inordinate expense of the current system.

Similar neocontractual solutions could undoubtedly be adapted to lawn mowers, drugs, medical care, and countless other goods and services. They could even cover accidents between utter strangers, if the accidents are common enough and if the law is prepared to accommodate and enforce the agreement. One such proposal has been advanced by Stephen Sugarman and Robert Cooter, both professors at the University of California at Berkeley. Nothing so novel and sensible will soon be implemented in today's legal climate, but the idea is too provocative and promising to ignore.

Suppose a state legislature passed a simple law declaring that car drivers, say, who carry full medical and disability insurance of their own, are entitled to sell their future right to sue anyone else in the event of an accident. The sale might be transacted on a standard form, approved by appropriate regulators, on file in some central depository, and renewed periodically, with new payments made to the selling driver upon proof that she had maintained her own medical and disability insurance. Would anyone care to sell? Almost everyone should. The driver selling off her future right to sue would get a good deal—because today the value of her right is heavily depressed by the need to cash it in through very costly legal intermediaries. Stated more simply, the price the driver would receive for relinquishing her right to sue would allow her to buy much more first-party insurance than she currently gets through the three-party tort system.

But who on earth would do the buying here? Conceivably, plaintiffs' lawyers or car companies, though that might be forbidden. But the most likely buyers, and certainly those with most to gain, would be insurance companies. They would buy up these waivers in quantity and process them through a central clearinghouse not unlike the futures markets for pork bellies or artichokes. The most likely buyers, in fact, would be the sellers of the first-party insurance that would be mandatory under the plan—and they would buy not by paying cash, but by offering a discount on the first-party policies they were selling. In the aftermath of an accident, a simple exchange of paper among insurers would then replace the lawsuit, at least in cases where both drivers had opted into the program. The market would thus create its own no-fault insurance system within the efficient boundaries of private choice and individual consent. And with considerably greater success, one may safely predict, than has crowned the efforts of the state governments that have tried to implement such programs through direct legal mandate.

Everyone would win but the lawyers. Drivers would get broader accident coverage at a much lower real cost. Insurance companies would win for the same reasons that drivers win—they would be able to pay off liabilities under policies they had written without the help of legal middlemen. And for society as a whole, consensual agreement and cooperation are always more profitable than adversarial litigation. Conditioning participation in the program of advance purchase of first-party medical and disability insurance would guarantee that no one would be left destitute and a public charge after an accident. Of course, a few victims of particularly tragic accidents would lose their ticket to the $100 million liability sweepstakes. By good fortune, however, most states have now started up lotteries of a more orderly nature, with higher payoff ratios. So people who can afford to indulge a taste for gambling can still play this kind of game without going to the trouble and aggravation of dealing with the courts.

Public Risks

Private insurance will always have trouble covering risks that are too broad, diffuse, uncertain, or catastrophically widespread. The classic exclusion in an insurance policy is against the hazards of war. The problem persists even if the risks are very unlikely, as with nuclear accidents or a hypothetical into-the-Pacific California earthquake. The worst potential hazards of mass vaccination programs and broadly dispersed pollutants may fall into this category too, at least under modern tort rules. These are zero-infinity hazards, of very low probability but enormously consequential when they do materialize. The net risk—the tiny likelihood of the event multiplied by its enormous consequences—is often small. But no group of private insurers would find it worthwhile to reserve the money needed to rebuild California after its coastline drew in by twenty miles.

So the government has traditionally had to insure risks of this character if they were to be insured at all. Unlike the private insurer, government can form a single large risk pool, with mandatory participation on any scale. The key to effective insurance is still consent and contract, but a social contract now substitutes for the private one. The premium is replaced by a tax; the policy coverage is defined by a statutory entitlement. And in the broadest cases, the entire population is placed within a single risk pool.

But here again, modern tort law has at every turn shunned the more efficient contractual approach in favor of the adversary combat of courtroom gladiators. Medicare, veterans' compensation programs, and the hazardous waste Superfund are all brushed aside as irrelevant collateral sources, not to be considered or even mentioned when the tort case comes to trial. Short of an express statutory declaration that public insurance is to offset or substitute for conventional tort recovery—as was made, for example, under the swine flu vaccination program—the fact that the government has foreseen the likelihood of some injury and provided for it directly is legally irrelevant in the subsequent tort suit.

The result has been to put unbearable pressure on what little private insurance there is in these areas. Environmental claims have burst all bounds and now proceed from causal assertions impossible to prove in court or elsewhere. As a direct and inevitable result, private liability insurance for public risks has retreated precipitately in recent years. In grasping for so much more than private insurance was willing to provide, tort law has driven that insurance even out of lines it would have provided willingly. The domain of uninsurable risks therefore grows larger all the time, putting still more pressure on the limited government substitutes.

Neocontractual compensation programs are a possible answer here too. The procedures are less familiar, more complicated, and much more controversial. But the possibilities should be taken seriously, for they promise far better than the current helpless slide into universal public insurance funded by general revenues.

Consider, for example, the problem of where to site a new pesticide factory, waste incinerator, or liquefied natural gas terminal. We know that some such facilities—and their attendant risks—must go somewhere; we also know that no one wants them in *his* backyard. Under current arrangements, power politics takes over, and while everybody gains from the improvements in crop yields, trash disposal, and heating capacity, only a few unlucky communities end up shouldering the safety and environmental burdens. Despite its most expansive modern aspirations, tort law still offers the losers little real consolation, and that of the most speculative character, not related in any rational way to the risks these communities actually shoulder for the common good. It comes as no surprise to learn that communities with large concentrations of blacks, Hispanics, other minorities, and the poor end up as the hosts of choice (if not through any choosing of their own) for most such facilities.

Safety at such sites will always be the paramount concern. No one would dare suggest that liability should be the exclusive or even principal instrument for safety regulation; ongoing administrative oversight is surely needed. But given that alternative safety control systems *are* in place from the beginning, society is free to search for an alternative form of accident compensation for its omnipresent environmental risks.

Howard Kunreuther, of the Wharton School in Pennsylvania, has put forward one innovative proposal. He outlines an auction, in which each potential host community—rich or poor—submits a NIMBY (not-in-my-backyard) bid for what it would pay *not* to have the dump or the public power plant in its backyard. A host community for the facility is then selected by lot. The unlucky loser (the community selected for the site) is then immediately paid the amount of its own NIMBY bid, by all the lucky winners, in amounts proportional to *their* original NIMBY bids—with the proviso, however, that any of the winners can instead step forward and volunteer to accept the site for some lesser tribute. If the facility is to be operated privately and for profit, the bidding system can obviously be simpler and more direct. Either way, the revenues so paid go to benefit the community that ends up with the facility; the community can use the funds as it wishes, with one possibility being to provide primary health and medical care and comprehensive medical and disability insurance for the residents.

The proposal is ingenious and (one discovers on close examination) strikingly fair to rich and poor alike. But is there not something disgraceful in having money corrupting the choice of where we should locate hazardous facilities? The truth is that money already counts for everything today. First at the outset when the political arm twisting is in progress (though with no compensation paid to the losers). And then again later on, when various members of the losing community, having been issued tickets in the tort lottery in lieu of real compensation, try to find out whether they have won the unlikely bonanza or been issued a worthless ticket. The difference, then, is not that money will count but that it can count on both sides, openly, in advance, and in the fairest possible way. And without having to pay at the same time for the stretch limos and private jets of a host of lobbyists and lawyers, who, one can be quite sure, will always succeed in distancing the waste dump from *their* particular homes and summer cottages.

The idea has already proved attractive enough to begin to take root in primitive form even without serious legal accommodation. Utility companies operating major electric power plants routinely absorb a large fraction of local property taxes, and so provide indirect compensation to local residents for the risk and inconvenience they necessarily suffer from their industrial guest. Communities farther afield, which pay slightly higher electric bills as a result, do so for the privilege of getting power without getting the power plant. In a similar spirit, a 1975 Massachusetts law offers to pay a $1 per ton royalty to any city agreeing to host a regional waste dump. North Andover hosted the initial site in 1977, and by 1981 several other cities had also accepted the offer. The Gray Rocks Power Plant in Wyoming, which environmental groups at first vehemently opposed, defused its controversy by setting up a $7.5 million trust fund which preserved a section of the Platte River, the habitat of several species of migratory birds. A nuclear utility in Florida has become an environmental hero by setting up special habitats for an endangered aquatic mammal, the manatee, in the warm-water discharges from its power plant.

The nuclear industry has pioneered several similar initiatives. Under the federal Price-Anderson Act, every nuclear utility in the country commits itself to contributing about $50 million in the event of any nuclear accident anywhere in the country, in exchange for a limit on its own liability in the event of an accident at its own facility. The victims of any accident are thereby guaranteed both a much larger pool of funds from which to draw (about $7 billion in all) and an advance waiver of most legal defenses by every nuclear utility. In a similar spirit, a recent Senate proposal for the establishment of a national repository for radioactive waste offers any state agreeing to host the facility $100 million per year until its closure.

The real advance, here again, is to depend on contract—public contract this time—to move the world beyond the negative-sum brawling of tort litigation. What are the obstacles to such proposals? The most important are the obvious political ones. In a world where wealthy communities already know how to use direct political action to unload unwanted facilities on others' doorsteps, a more equitable system is not likely to arrive anytime soon. And even when the political will is there, the legal framework that is our sorry legacy from the tort Founders' frolics hardly encourages alternative systems to develop. Today such arrangements can only operate on top of the tort system, never instead of it. But the greatest possible incentive for developing them, especially among those who put up the cash, is to escape from the no-win tort lottery.

Before Rather Than After

The market can provide insurance through direct coverage, if legal rules are set up to provide the stability and certainty it requires. If the rules are otherwise, as they currently are, legislative intervention, often of the clumsiest kind, is sure to come instead.

Consider the major reform initiative that has developed under the logic of the current system: caps on awards. California, for example, recently placed a flat $250,000 cap on awards for noneconomic losses in medical malpractice cases. Maryland put a $350,000 cap on pain and suffering damages in all personal injury cases. Missouri set a similar limit in medical malpractice cases. The Kansas legislature decreed a $250,000 cap on pain and suffering and another cap on punitive damage awards. Texas passed laws authorizing punitive damage caps of $200,000 or four times actual damages. More than half of the states now cap recoveries that can be won against local governments. Still others have flatly barred punitive damages in one context or another.

One step further is a complete statutory schedule of damages, spelling out so much for the loss of a limb, so much for an eye, and so much for a fatal injury. Workers' compensation laws already do just that, and similar schedules have been proposed for compensating people who have been exposed to radiation. Insurance has already been almost entirely socialized, as we have seen, for hazardous waste cleanup and vaccines.

These are desperate responses, impelled by juridical inflation that has exceeded all bounds that private insurance can accommodate. Award caps and the like provide a stopping point of sorts, but of a very rough and arbitrary kind, and not necessarily one that the two sides would have agreed on if their wishes had been consulted before the accident. Liability caps have become necessary because they are simple and can be implemented directly by a legislature. But there are better alternatives closer at hand, if ever the courts are willing to cooperate.

The fact is that under neocontractual solutions the market itself could easily set such caps, more efficiently and less autocratically. For many rare catastrophes such as airplane crashes or allergic reactions to vaccines, the lump-sum payments specified by advance insurance contracts might very well be larger than those set out in crudely legislated caps. Private liability-cap arrangements could equally be tailored to the particular product or service.

Again, what is missing is a legal framework that honors such contracts and enforces them to the exclusion of the tort system. We once had such a body of law. But instead of encouraging it to grow with the times, the Founders cut it down trunk and branch. A rediscovered respect for contract does not require us to return to a legal world in which every provider can flatly disclaim liability and leave things at that. But an advance contractual *acceptance* of financial responsibility for accidents, under fairly delineated conditions and in reasonably specified amounts, should be enforceable—against both the person who freely offers the insurance contract *and* the person who freely accepts it. Our present impasse is between a tort system intent on insurance by compulsion, and a surrounding market that runs in terror from any offers to provide coverage, knowing full well that such offers can be held against it but never cited in its favor. It is possible to do vastly better.

If neocontractual proposals of this kind sound too radical, it is worth noting that contracts are already the dominant mode of accident resolution, but contracts of a peculiarly clumsy sort. Over 90 percent of all tort claims are settled before trial, in private agreements between plaintiff and defendant. Why? Accident victims need cash quickly and definitely, which impels them to settle for less than they might expect to win on an average spin of the tort wheel. The worse the injury and the less the victim has to start with, the stronger this imperative. For their part, insurers settle because they well understand just how much everyone can save on lawyers by staying out of court. Courts encourage after-the-accident contracts of this kind, and enforce settlement agreements to the letter. But such arrangements are respected only when they are signed after the accident.

Is there any conceivable justification for this? The standard theory is that the improvident consumer is prone to accept too little insurance coverage beforehand, as someone else defines it. But after the accident, the seriously injured and (it is assumed) underinsured victim is under even greater pressure to sign on for something definite and immediate. Is it that the consumer lacks sufficient information before the accident to make any binding insurance agreement? The uncertainties are almost equally large immediately after the accident. The injury itself is now certain, of course, but what (if anything) it is worth in dollars frequently remains an almost pure guess, given the vagaries of modern tort law. And if the real concern is with improvident consumers who won't think about insurance matters ahead of time, the direct solution is just to prescribe some minimum coverage in advance.

What it really seems to come down to in the end is the flypaper theory of contract all over again. Before-the-accident insurance contracts will almost always be standard-form agreements, certain to be denounced as meaningless contracts of adhesion. After-the-accident settlements are negotiated case by case and one on one. The consumer undoubtedly wins individual treatment, but at enormous cost. Few can afford the exorbitant luxury of custom design on anything else in life, but with accident insurance the tort system allows nothing else. It is as if the courts refused to enforce any lease or employment contract, any car purchase, deed of sale, or divorce, unless both parties were attended at all times by lawyers. This is wonderful for the custom designers, who remain in complete control throughout and charge the premium always accorded to custom work. But it is a terrible deal for everyone else.

There may be a middle ground to develop here. O'Connell's successful scheme for high-school athletes relies on a contract actually signed after the accident, but set up beforehand as a standard compensation package. (His original proposal was to make the program mandatory from the outset for any student choosing to participate in high-school athletics, but he soon recognized that no contract of that character would ever be enforced in the courts today.) More recently, O'Connell has been promoting a general statutory scheme to encourage settlement programs that are set up before accidents but that are not binding on accident victims until an express choice is made after the injury has occurred. There is much to be said in favor of these efforts. But so long as binding contracts can be made only after the accident, with recourse to the unpredictable tort system always allowed, many goods and services will not be offered at all. Some undertakings are possible only if rights and responsibilities can be set out and nailed down, in their entirety, beforehand.

Judging by their propensity to settle cases, insurers and accident victims overwhelmingly agree that certainty and stability are much more valuable than a gamble in the tort system after the accident has occurred. Those qualities are even more valuable beforehand, if only because they are often essential to permit the action that will prevent the accident altogether. The market would quickly prove as much if the legal system ever so allowed.

Compassion by Consent

Words of any kind pay no debts, and legal words, far from paying anybody, cost a great deal to write and read. The courts have it in their own power to cut through the useless verbiage. They can lead the way, if they choose, toward an orderly regime in which the two sides whose values are at stake join together in the language that best suits their needs.

When all is said and done, direct insurance through the private market works; indeed, it works extremely well. To this day, there is no crisis in first-party insurance; this kind of coverage remains readily available to cover everything from bad weather on a European vacation to the accidental fracture of Meryl Streep's valuable nose. Putting aside the problem of AIDS, where insurance is again complicated by government obstacles to risk screening, this side of the market is likely to remain perfectly healthy. Direct insurance thrives on private demand, and supply comes from a robustly competitive private market.

With cooperation from the courts, direct insurance, tailored to the specific circumstances of particular activities, can provide excellent coverage for high-school sports, airplane travel, vaccination, contraception, childbirth, employment, and medical services. Given half a legal chance, it can probably develop to provide good coverage for car accidents among strangers and even the broad-ranging community hazards of chemical wastes, factories, and power plants. As first-party insurance is encouraged to expand, third-party insurance through the wasteful process of tort law will shrink, eventually back to the core minimum needed to deal with the rare accidents between utter strangers who collide with no other insurance in the background.

This chapter began with a glance at the importance of sympathy in modern tort practice. Sympathy is indeed all-important, and in the larger scheme of things we can be proud that it has become so. The measure of a society's decency is how well it takes care of those most in need of help. It is unthinkable that our wealthy society could stand unmoved by the tragedy of a worker injured on the job, or a child suffering from birth defects, or a young woman hurt by a drug or a contraceptive—or, for that matter, anyone injured by forces inside or outside human control. But sympathy does not buy a wheelchair, a physical therapy program, special schooling, job retraining, education for the orphan, or support for the widow; those are purchased with cash, paid on the barrelhead. The tort system has tried to guarantee payment through compulsion, but its clumsy efforts have backfired. Short of complete government socialization of these matters, stable, orderly insurance, developed consensually through the private market, is the only workable alternative.

The Founders were right in their desire to expand insurance but quite wrong in their belief that such expansion could be accomplished by a pure act of legal will. Consent, contract, and mutual agreement have done far more to relieve human suffering than any judicial decree ever can or will. The challenge is to make compassion work as a system, outside the courts, as a matter of mutual benefit and willing consent. Charity by compulsion is doomed to bankruptcy.

13

Choosing Safety

FREEDOM, a popular song of the 1970s had it, is just another word for nothing left to lose. In their particular neck of the woods, the liability courts bid fair to transform this doggerel into legal dogma. The only freedom they left intact was the freedom not to innovate, not to buy or sell, not to provide playgrounds, public beaches, eye drugs, or police protection. And that freedom was exercised with ever more vigor.

The new tort system can pronounce only one word clearly—"no"—and it utters that word equivocally and late in the day. But the advancement of safety, like the promotion of insurance, requires knowing when and how to say yes, firmly, convincingly, and in time to make a difference. It depends not so much on blocking agreements as on encouraging agreements of the right kind. Consent is risky because action is risky. But the inability to reach any consensus and take any action, private or public, is more dangerous still. Legal paper does not save lives. Our accustomed safety comes from chemistry, medicine, engineering, technology, and services of every description, and it is progress in these areas that will make life safer still.

The just-say-no philosophy of safety regulation has become too familiar. Up to a point, it is wise and necessary as well. The consumer spurns the compact car, rejects the discount lawn mower, avoids the rural hospital, and takes specialty medical problems out of the hands of the general practitioner. The government regulator refuses to license the unduly hazardous pesticide or power plant and shuts down the excessively dirty factory. But the positive dimension of safety choice, though less obvious, is more crucial still. The consumer chooses the useful appliance from the reputable manufacturer, seeks out the specialized services of the large urban hospital, and finds and buys the car, cosmetic, or child's toy that is not perfectly safe but better than what came before. The government regulator licenses the new and cleaner power plant, the more effective drug, the safer pesticide; the medical association approves the new surgical breakthrough. Across the board, progress in safety depends ultimately on affirmative changes in method, technology, or material.

Trying to live only by negative safety rules means living in a very spare world, devoid of countless goods and services that make life safer, healthier, and more comfortable. It has been called the Howard Hughes syndrome, after the man whose paranoid fear of contagious infection led him, in the last years of his life, to live in almost complete isolation, much of the time stark naked. It was a miserable and expensive way to exist, and Hughes ended up dead anyway, quite possibly of self-inflicted malnutrition.

Until the courts took charge, the law evenly accommodated the two-sided demands of intelligent safety regulation. Tort law existed, of course, to send out negative signals about several kinds of risk. But contract was there too, as a vehicle for doing what is positive. And most safety choices in the individual's private domain were the subject of contract. Getting to no was easy enough: The consumer could always refuse the proffered good or service, and tort law provided a shield against serious nonconsensual hazards from the outside. Getting to yes was equally straightforward. Every private contract is an affirmation. The core of contract is consent—a "meeting of the minds," as law books put it back in the days when minds still mattered. Contract law is engaged when two parties say yes to a service, yes to a sale, yes to a mutual venture or adventure, risky or otherwise.

With undertakings that implicated community risks and benefits, government regulators performed a similar role through administrative agencies. Of course the agencies had the power to reject bad risk choices. But a license is a formal yes, the agency's equivalent of a contract, the official assent by which the acceptably safe is distinguished from the unacceptably dangerous. For licensing agencies, the core of the regulatory function is to say yes—selectively, of course—on the basis of a critical comparison of the full range of options available.

What the liability revolution changed was not the need for choice, positive or negative, but the way choice would be made. By the time the Founders had finished their work, the courts were firmly in control. But the courts are singularly ill-suited to their ambitious new job; under their confused direction we are now traveling a certain path to a more dangerous, disorderly, and autocratic world.

Judges, as a group, do not constitute a coordinated management team. There are thousands of lower state courts, fifty state supreme courts, and several hundred federal district courts. Each is an individual fiefdom, and each jury is a new authority. This makes systematic, affirmative choice impossible. No positive safety judgment is ever really final in the courts; there is no such thing as a definitive bill of health. Today's plaintiff may win or lose, but tomorrow's will file a new lawsuit and will be entitled to a new decision. The results, as we have seen, are like the progress of a bus steered by a fractious committee of its passengers.

Is Bendectin a safe and valuable morning sickness drug, as the FDA has concluded, or a teratogenic poison responsible for countless birth defects? The mainstream scientific community has agreed with the FDA. So have most juries. But not all, and the courthouse door is always open for the issue to be litigated anew. Bendectin is gone as a result, and no woman today can buy it no matter how vigorously she and her doctor may affirm her need for it. The story has been repeated time and again with contraceptives, chemical disposal facilities, compact cars, and pesticides. There is no way a producer can win an effective go-ahead on a new product before—or even after—committing itself to actual production and marketing. Instead it must stake huge sums on what might be called liability futures—a highly speculative venture even in the best of circumstances. And the producer will have to realize that it may well win most of its liability battles and still lose the war; the torturous litigation process itself may become punishment enough.

If the judicial process is one of fragmentation, it is also one of polarization. Decision making in the courts is inescapably bilateral; what one side wins the other necessarily loses. All the bystanders whose interests may be strongly, though indirectly, affected do not appear at all. But bilateral decision making is exactly what cannot work in managing matters that touch public (as opposed to purely private) safety and welfare. Such matters, by their very nature, require public management. They are lifted out of the world of private contract, precisely *because* one-on-one decision making is unworkable for one reason or another. No matter how good their intentions, no matter how sober their individual judgments, an uncoordinated multitude of judges and juries cannot provide wise management of the most far-reaching issues of public safety. Handing over these issues for ultimate resolution by the courts undoes all that was originally accomplished in transferring them from the individual to government management in the first place.

No invisible hand gives order to the legal bazaar. Whether the courts decide private safety matters through the endless repetition of identical lawsuits, or public matters through the polarizing process of bilateral litigation, they are condemned to offer bad guidance on matters of safety. They can never show green to signal full speed ahead; the best they can do is a flashing yellow of brooding equivocation.

Getting to Yes, Again

What are the alternatives? How do we get to a prudent yes on important questions of safety? The only way is to promote positive, consensual safety choices outside the courts wherever possible, and so downplay the role of negative, adversarial mismanagement inside. The instrument to embody such informed choice and deliberate consent must again be contract, though we can afford, today, to insist on contract with a modern face.

We must categorically reject, at the outset, the notion of contract as flypaper, the idea that to offer one's goods and services to others is to entrap them in an attractive nuisance, like a disused coalpit that entices children to danger. Whatever lawyers may tell us, we each do have it in our power to say no to the cigarette, the cut-rate lawn mower, the contraceptive, and the ride in the propeller aircraft. The theory of adhesive contracts notwithstanding, consumers in a free society are not flies. Of course, we cannot bargain one on one with United Airlines or General Motors. But we can do what amounts to the same thing by choosing among different companies, different modes of transportation, and different insurance packages that may be willingly offered as part of the plan. And who is to say, anyway, what is adhesive and what is not? When Sugar Ray Leonard demands $10 million for his next fight, or Luciano Pavarotti declines to sing at the Met for anything less than the same, the promoters are surely facing take-it-or-leave-it choices too. But are we therefore prepared to say that the Metropolitan Opera is another hapless victim of an adhesive contract, and so relieved of any duty to abide by what it agrees to? The model of consumer ignorance and flypaper contracts is dangerous. By dismissing the consumer as one with the intelligence and free will of a fly, the modern law ultimately leaves her with no greater freedom to shape her own environment. Flies do not help themselves very wisely, nor each other very often, but people can and will, if they are only allowed to.

Today, what keeps the patient with the orphan disease from the pharmaceutical company capable of providing the orphan drug he needs is their joint inability to write a contract that will be treated as binding in the courts. The missing power of contract likewise separates the pregnant mother from the supplier of Bendectin, the municipality saddled with an orphan dump from the waste cleanup contractor, the private pilot from the maker of small planes. Time and again, deals that could protect health, cure disease, or improve safety—not to mention increase the stock of human happiness in other ways—go unconsummated because the law will not allow them to be settled on terms both sides would gladly accept.

The old tort law perhaps erred in the other extreme, elevating freedom of contract to the point of enforcing deals that were grounded on blind ignorance all around. There can be a middle ground; the courts showed as much in recent years, if only by blithely zipping past it. Getting to an effective yes, in modern times, depends on giving people a fair clue as to why they might want to say no. The doctor or drug manufacturer often knows of risks that the consumer does not. Full disclosure should be an ordinary and essential part of fair dealing. When it is—as it most commonly already is today—a deal should be treated, once again, as a deal.

Detailed warnings have long been the commercial norm for such things as therapeutic drugs, vaccines, medical care, consumer appliances, pesticides, and cigarettes, in part because of commendably persistent pressure from the tort system. Recent congressional initiatives have extended warning requirements to other areas where warning has historically been underemphasized. The 1986 amendments to the federal Superfund included a community "right-to-know" clause, which requires industries that produce, store, or use hazardous chemicals to report the presence of such substances to community authorities and to report routine or unauthorized releases of hazardous substances to the EPA. Congress and OSHA have also begun to develop plans to require fuller disclosure of workplace health hazards to affected employees.

These are, for the most part, welcome developments, especially at a time when our understanding of risk improves daily. Accurate information, sensibly conveyed and intelligently used, is an unconditional good. A law of accidents built on fair warning can serve society far better than one built on an unending judicial hunt for elusive defects or even negligence in products or people. The consumer's contemplation of what he is doing and why *should* count; in fact, it should count for everything.

That having been said, the actual warning rules of the liability system today are badly out of balance. With risks that are indisputably real and unavoidable, the legal demand is for endless, unachievable detail and outright overstatement of warnings, even to the point of undercutting the effectiveness of the warning itself. With risks that are diffuse and uncertain, the warning itself can become a ticket to a lawsuit based on cancerphobia or other fears of disease. All courts today pay lip service to the idea that a full, coherent warning provides protection against liability for known and unavoidable risks. But "unavoidable" is good for a week's litigation, at least, and there is an entirely separate body of law to condemn both negligence and design defects, whatever the warning given. Across the board, the literary deconstruction of warning is too often a sword to condemn but almost never a shield to exonerate. The warning not given counts for everything, while the warning given hardly counts at all. In warning, as elsewhere in liability law, we have, in short, a jurisprudence that knows a hundred words for no but can never give a convincing and wholly reliable yes.

Few would suggest returning to the day when a warning had to be particularly sought out and paid for, and the unwary were simply out of luck. The answer is to reanchor the law of warning to its contractual roots by applying the modern rules symmetrically, with a firm sense of balance that is missing from today's how-you-pronounce-it warning jurisprudence. The courts may have to sort out the wreckage that results from uninformed choice. But informed choice, deliberately made outside the courtroom and before the accident, should count for everything. Not because the choices will always be wise—they surely won't—but because respecting the right to choose, with the responsibility that necessarily goes with it, will advance overall safety more often than it retards it. A law of warning that demands omniscience up front and the eloquence of Cato in committing the warning to paper is a law that guarantees dangerous paralysis. Contract, informed or otherwise, cannot be the engine of safety unless it is binding for better and for worse, for richer and for poorer. If the informed consumer is not free to make foolish choices, on his own, he can never be free to make wise, lifesaving ones either.

The most urgently needed correction here concerns warnings prescribed by regulatory agencies like the FDA and the EPA. With drugs, vaccines, medical devices, food additives, pesticides, and toxic chemicals, the agency-prescribed warning is mandatory. No substitutions or elaborations are allowed. The objective, of course, is to provide just the right amount of warning—not too little certainly, but not too much either, for the risk on that side is to frighten users into less safe alternatives. So here, at the very least, we should have one inviolable safe harbor from liability. If the agency has weighed the question of warning, and spelled out the language to be used in detail, that should be a certain end to the matter for tort purposes.

Would this cut off some tort claims by accident victims? Yes, of course, many of them. That would be the whole idea. Because in so doing it would also clear the way for many others to *get* the exotic drug, the specialty medical service, the new and improved small plane, the needed employment, without which these others will become victims of a different sort, more numerous and more grievously hurt.

Honestly applied, the law of warning is the law of modern contract. Not the old-style contract law, where silence was encouraged and the gullible could be sold anything under the sun with impunity, but the new, where reasonably full disclosure of safety-related information is a required part of fair dealing. Warning and disclosure enhance individual autonomy, control, and free choice. A balanced law of warning, one that firmly accepts the no-tort implication of a reasonable warning fairly given, is the surest path to a safer world.

Shelter Under the Law

Some safety matters will always remain too complex or far-reaching to be collapsed into the world of private agreement, with or without full warning. Informed consent by the individual is never going to take care of such things as waste disposal or central power generation. The right to sue, in those cases, is both too little and too much. Even if everyone starts with a legal right not to be exposed to a factory's smoke, each individual may lack the motivation to sue the polluter, and needless harm may continue. By the same token, when it is in the communal interest to *agree* to a publicly risky activity—the construction, say, of a needed power plant—the selfish individual may be tempted to overstate her aversion to the smoke, in the hope of being bought off by the community at a price reflecting the huge collective benefit at stake. Such matters, by their very nature, must be delegated to a central authority charged with making choices for the collective good. And sometimes it makes sense to delegate safety choices to experts purely for convenience and peace of mind, as we routinely do, for example, with drugs and aircraft.

A legal prescription that is good for the individual, facing private risks, is equally appropriate for the collective, facing public ones. A government agency is, as its name implies, an agent, acting on behalf of a principal. The agent negotiates, chooses, and consents, and when backed by properly delegated authority its decisions are fully binding on those for whom it acts. But to represent the principal effectively an agent must be able to buy as well as sell. In safety matters, that means not just rejecting the bad safety choices but also embracing the good.

Since 1962 the FDA has had to pass not only on safety but also on efficacy, which requires the agency to reach an affirmative conclusion that a drug it approves is actually beneficial, not merely harmless. Other agencies regulating such things as power plants, aircraft, pesticides, and toxic chemicals have similar mandates, not just to protect safety but to pick and choose to advance the public good. Perhaps, as some defenders of today's liability system will contend, these agencies are uninformed, incompetent, and captured by outsiders, though if that is true, it is hard to see why the violation of an agency's regulations should count for anything in the tort system either. But if we accept that professionally staffed agencies, imperfect though they are, provide the best, reasonably unbiased, source of balanced expertise available in these matters, their positive judgments must count as much as their negative ones.

So here again the answer is not radical change in the law, but a new moderation and balance. The licensing of a nuclear plant, for example, reflects a conscious decision that the risks are worth bearing compared with those of alternative energy sources, in accidents, pollution, and in security of supply, just as the denial of a license reflects the contrary judgments. We would certainly be appalled if tort law invited a jury to approve operation of a nuclear power plant after the NRC had denied a license on safety grounds. But the reverse pattern is considered quite proper. Twelve jurors from off the street can today veto the positive safety choices of a regulatory agency at will. This asymmetry makes no sense, except to those unalterably opposed to nuclear power regardless of how it really measures up against alternative technologies. No one doubts that if a nuclear utility's violation of federal regulations results in an accident, a court will immediately label this negligence, with hefty damages to follow. So it should be. But by the same token it is absurd to call an act negligent that the regulators have carefully contemplated and approved.

Regulators, quite simply, are better equipped than any jury to make the systematic risk comparisons on which all progressive choice is based. The point may sound modest to the nonlawyer, especially when made with reference to drugs and airplanes rather than endlessly controversial nuclear matters. But it is considered unpardonably bold in today's legal circles. All the more reason to press it audaciously. The formal federal licensing of a new drug, medical device, vaccine, aircraft, or nuclear power plant should be viewed as the momentous matter it really is—not as a routine and irrelevant pleasantry, to be forgotten as soon as the first tort plaintiff walks into the courthouse. At a very minimum, complete compliance with a comprehensive licensing order should provide liability protection against punitive damages. It has always been true that ignorance of the law is no excuse. Today, knowledge of the law is no excuse either. It should be.

Safety in the Singular

Choice and consent are all-important precisely because circumstances change and people are different. Neither safety nor freedom are served by a one-size-fits-all attitude toward consumer needs and supplier responsibilities. Much is made in the legal literature about the courts' aptitude for doing individualized justice that fits the case at hand. But the way to fit law to particular circumstances is to lay out a set of clear rules by which any two parties can reach any agreement they wish, however nuanced. Individualized justice is the victim, not the beneficiary, when we promulgate a myriad of hazy tort standards that, whatever their seeming indeterminacy before the event, boil down afterward to a persistent attempt to collectivize risk and second-guess private choice.

Under the old contract law on the one hand, and negligence on the other, accidents were analyzed discretely, in a narrow context of person, action, time, and place. But those days are long gone. Modern jurisprudence demands global assessments of risk and utility, safety and defectiveness, benefits and burdens, social cost and collective insurability. Modern liability theories, built around far-flung objectives of general deterrence and social insurance, always shift the focus away from individual need or want, individual consent or acquiescence, individual responsibility or control. And this, in the end, is dangerous.

Over the years, other bodies that regulate safety have slowly learned the advantages of flexibility and individuation. Regulators still ban some products outright, of course, and apply some standards rigidly to all. But much more commonly today, regulation accommodates user and supplier differences through more supple oversight. Even if the medicine has side effects that are quite dangerous, the FDA can try to oblige the rare individual who should use it, under careful labeling and dosage limits, prescription conditions, and the like. The FAA has long succeeded in steering light aircraft design in generally progressive directions without crushing the industry altogether, as modern tort law has more recently managed to do. Other agencies rely on the flexible tools of periodic inspection, exposure limits, and operating guidelines, on the sensible view that the safest course is to keep things moving rather than to freeze them in place. But none of these pliant regulatory tools are available to jury or judge. Even if one jury tries to issue a considered go-ahead—hinging its no-liability verdict on the fact that precaution X or Y was taken in the case at hand—its decision can always be undone by the next's. In practical terms, this means that products like morning sickness drugs, small planes, and vaccines end up being judged—and often condemned—across the board, for all users and all circumstances.

A return to contract, built on open warning and informed consent, would permit once again infinite calibration to the varying needs of individual consumers. Sometimes consent will be sought and given privately, in the purchase of a family car or kitchen knife. Sometimes it will be channeled in part through an expert intermediary, like the doctor who prescribes a complex medicine and the federal agency that approves it. Sometimes consent will come from a public agency for a public enterprise—a smokestack, a dump, or a cleanup effort. Contract, in its very essence, is a meeting of minds, and in the most private cases only two minds need meet for there to be a deal. No liability system, and no system of broader regulation, can ever do better; rarely can they do anywhere near as well. And the individuality and flexibility that contract allows is the ultimate key to the consumer's safety.

Individuation is equally important on the supplier side. The private individuals or institutions that make most safety decisions, good or bad, do so either alone or in pairs—not in larger crowds. The automaker assigns ultimate engineering responsibility to one point within the company, if it is smart. It negotiates one on one with the safety agency, with its liability insurer, with each dealer, and ultimately with each buyer. Delegating safety authority to some free-floating committee made up of representatives of all sides would be a recipe for disaster. Tort liability should be imposed accordingly. Joint-and-several liability, the socialized defense, should be reserved for the rare case of concerted action where the separate defendants are truly indistinguishable in their degree of culpability. In all other cases, individual liability should be sharply tailored to individual responsibility.

It is rarely recognized just how corrosive a doctrine of joint liability, carelessly imposed, really is. Most understand that focusing responsibility is the best way to deter individual misconduct. The house stays cleaner when each child is responsible for picking up his own room. When everyone is legally responsible, no one really is for sure. Less often understood, but even more important, is that the threat of unfocused liability makes getting to yes all but impossible. Contract, whether private or public, works only when the parties to the deal are known, both to themselves and to others, both before the accident and after it. Risk choices, like most other agreements, are not that hard to make when the decision maker acts alone or one on one with the actual parties concerned. Simplicity is the key to making a deal; trying to move a whole crowd at once leads either to stasis or stampede. Contract and agreement depend on clear lines, clear rights, clear responsibilities, definite agreements, and consequences that are as predictable as Nature will permit. Joint liability inflicts precisely the opposite set of conditions.

Here again, if the courts refuse to set their own houses in order, legislatures will sooner or later intervene to do it for them. A reasonably certain, if clumsy, way of getting to yes when tort law says only no or maybe is to lift certain activities out of the system entirely. The old tort law conferred immunity on a few selected groups—government entities and charities in particular. Another major immunity came along when the tort system's handling of workplace accidents grew too confused and workers' compensation programs were put in as a substitute. In recent years, as tort law has whittled away at these exceptions and advanced in a hundred other areas, legislatures have begun to react as is their wont—by scattering around immunities like purple hearts after a bloody battle. The objective, of course, is to rally troops who might otherwise be inclined to retreat in the face of the implacable legal opposition. So we now have immunities for Good Samaritans and nuclear bomb contractors, for the military and those who clean up hazardous wastes, for contractors who assist in nuclear defense programs and for injuries from the space shuttle program, for offshore oil operations and the trans-Alaska pipeline. At least nine states enacted legislation in 1986 providing immunity for directors, officers, or volunteers of charitable enterprises. Pennsylvania and New Jersey have granted immunity to volunteer athletic coaches, managers, and officials in Little League programs. The list could be extended, and doubtless will be if we do not change course.

Like the damage caps we examined in the last chapter, these immunity initiatives, necessary though they have become, are sadly clumsy solutions, the equivalent of a congressional pardon granted long before a crime is committed. They are born of nothing more than desperation. Pushing a special exemption of this type through Congress or a state legislature requires a brush with disaster first, or something very close to it. It is a measure of the excesses of the tort system that such legislation has become so often necessary in recent years.

In the long run, a more systematic approach to reform is needed; the corrections cannot all be made by legislative proclamation. To make life safer, faster, we must gradually uncouple compensation from deterrence. The child who suffers permanent brain injury from a vaccination must be helped; the worst possible way to secure that help is to assault the vaccine manufacturer whose product has saved a thousand other children from similar injury. New forms of direct insurance can provide reasonable assistance to accident victims, whose plight accounts for so much of today's bad tort law. With direct consensual insurance in the background, the principles of on-the-scene, long-arm, and joint liability—the brutish recruiting sergeants sent out to entrap and conscript insurance after an accident—can surely be dismissed. And when a safety net of direct insurance hangs below, it will be much easier to accept choice, by the individual or by the collective, as the principal instrument for managing safety—to abandon coercion as our principal safety management tool and rediscover the subtle power of consent. Freedom should become, once again, a word for something yet to gain.

A Bonfire of Vanities

It is all too easy to declare, as the modern tort system repeatedly does, that this option or that one is not as safe as we might wish it to be. The postmortem, brilliant or otherwise, is undoubtedly a valuable tool in law as it is in medicine. But good therapy depends even more on doing something, as best one can, beforehand, while the patient is still alive. When we cut off the freedom to choose, out of fear that it would be exercised badly, we also lost the freedom to choose wisely. The loss far outweighs the gain. Zechariah Chafee, Jr., made the point in 1948; he spoke about freedom of the press, but what he said applies equally well to other human endeavor. "Freedom from something is not enough. It should also be freedom for something. Freedom is not safety but opportunity."

The greatest vanity of the legal profession—a profession with more than a few vanities—is its conviction that there are no limits to the contributions that law and lawyers can make to the public safety. The natural, self-aggrandizing instinct of the profession, especially the most activist among us, is to suggest that our services are needed when any aspect of life seems less than perfect. But sometimes, especially in the most difficult times, a lawyer needs the wisdom to do nothing. Life has grown safer not because of the legal system but despite it. The technologists that the courts are trying to rein in may create some new terrors, but on the whole they have built an extraordinarily safe society. And the most feared of their creations—infernal engines and motors, synthetic chemicals and vaccines—save the most lives, on balance. Not every scientific advance ushers in full enlightenment. But the alternative to lighting more candles is to curse the darkness of starvation and disease.

The path to a safer existence lies as much in beatifying good risks as in exorcising bad ones. It lies in the replacement of risks that are old and grave with risks that are new and less grave. The answer lies in choice, in the affirmative needed to counterbalance every negative. Conceiving of safety without risk, or progress without change, or freedom without choice, is like seeking love without courting the danger of rejection. Hotspur was right. It is out of the nettle, danger, that we pluck the flower, safety.

14

Consent and Coercion

So in the fullness of time, the liability courts worked their way through the Mock Turtle's four branches of arithmetic: ambition, distraction, uglification, and derision. There was ambition aplenty at the beginning: to make life safer and more generous quickly, without the mess or fuss of working through markets or elections. Distraction followed soon enough, as the reformers found themselves hacking through a dense underbrush of ancient legal principle: the inviolability of contracts, the need for a determinate party on both sides of the case, the requirement that litigation be ripe but not stale, the requirements that genuine fault be found and genuine proof of causation be nailed down. Uglification was then inevitable: a collapse of private insurance, a decline in innovation, alarming reverses in safety itself, and a gradual contraction of other rights under pressure from the endless expansion of the right to sue. Finally, they arrived at derision. There are the have-you-heard-the-latest stories. A jury awards $986,000 to a woman who claims she lost her psychic powers after a CAT scan, a contestant in a refrigerator-carrying footrace recovers for injury to his back, two men who stuffed a hot-air balloon into a commercial laundry dryer (which then exploded) recover from the manufacturer of the machine, the occupant of a telephone booth demolished by a drunk driver collects from the booth manufacturer. And there are the cartoons.

"A jellyfish, eh?" says the thoughtful lawyer, eyeing his client. "That's a tough one. But maybe we can sue Jacques Cousteau."

What the legal pioneers invented in the 1960s came to be called *strict liability,* a once-narrow legal term that emerged as a generic label for the new tort jurisprudence. A more accurate name would have been *more liability.* All that the new system could promise, and all it ever delivered, was more lawyers and more litigation. That was not a good place to start in a program aimed at bettering the human condition. The intentions were undoubtedly good. But when we take stock thirty years later, we can confidently declare that the results were very bad—though not so bad that they cannot still get worse, if we let them.

By delivering only an endless stream of negatives, modern tort law undercuts insurance and safety, both of which demand an affirmative. Stable insurance against accidents requires the willing aggregation of similar risks in a common pool large enough to regularize what is random. It requires, in other words, contract, private or public. But in its penchant for coercion over consent, the modern law dismisses first-party insurance and demands third-party coverage on terms that no functioning market can accommodate. Promoting safety requires an affirmative, too—this drug *will* be prescribed, that vaccine *will* be adopted, that new car, appliance, aircraft, or pesticide *will* be used—not because it is absolutely safe but because it promises something better than what we now have. But litigation is like the neighborhood grouch: It knows how to shoo but not how to beckon.

The law has always deprived children and those of unsound mind of the power to bind themselves fully in contracts. But at least it acknowledges that it is imposing a disability on them, on the assumption that they will be cared for by others who are not so disabled. And it holds out hope that they can graduate at some point to self-sufficiency. Modern tort law, by contrast, is unchangeably pessimistic about the consumer's competence, and unduly optimistic about the prospects for universal institutional care. Courts and juries, the law assumes, must operate for the consumer *in loco parentis,* now and forevermore. This attitude robs us of our most important economic freedom, the freedom to plan in advance, to make commitments, and to arrange deals on terms mutually agreeable to the parties involved. Modern tort law abrogates our freedom to cooperate.

Applied as it has been in recent years, open-ended tort law serves only as an engine of social destruction. Sometimes the effect is to alienate individuals from each other. The freedom of contract is undermined, private bilateral deals are curtailed. Sometimes the effect is to alienate the individual from community and state. Each individual is issued his own quiver of claims against the state and the publicly risky activities it has sanctioned; the state strikes back with more and more paternalistic legislation to protect citizens willy-nilly from injury. The unchecked inflation of the nonnegotiable right to sue eventually undercuts a panoply of other freedoms.

Americans have always taken for granted a structure of private legal rights that protects individual freedom and consensual economic relations. In Peru there is no functioning market for real estate, because the authorities refuse to administer a law of property that allows for most concepts of ownership or sale, at least not in terms penetrable by the average citizen. In some socialist and third-world countries, a similar paralysis, with similar roots in the repudiation of private law, grips the markets for consumer goods of every description. Anyone who cares to make the trip can see the results: squalid shanty towns with great numbers of people permanently frozen out of the market economy, black-market trading of desperately needed antibiotics that cannot be provided under the terms prescribed by law, starvation on a mass scale when the right of farmers to sell their produce as they wish is abolished. It is not that the individual citizens in these countries are less wise or industrious or compassionate than we are; they are prisoners of legal structures and social systems that systematically foil progressive self-help and generosity. Good law brings out the best in people, communities, and economies; bad law brings out the very worst.

In its law of safety and accident insurance today—or rather in its lack of sound and coherent law—America must count itself among the primitive, the backward, and the underdeveloped. We no longer have a functioning law to encourage and enforce the settlement of accidents beforehand, through deliberate choice, private insurance, and specified compensation or assumption of risk. We have, instead, an open-ended struggle of all against all, after the fact and in court, a struggle in which preexisting treaties and nonaggression pacts are viewed as irrelevant slips of paper. Strife has become so familiar that courts forget that risk was once handled through voluntary cooperation, and could be again if the law permitted. They grow impatient with any lingering remnants they find of the old order, any surviving contract terms that touch on matters of health, safety, and personal insurance. The courts' power to force a peace has been subverted into a destructive weapon for making war.

How did things come to such a pass? We were led here, quite deliberately, by a professional community that should have known better. And once their good intentions had set the system on its path, the self-interest of practitioners created a powerful lobby that prevented any corrective change of course. The story is told of a small-town lawyer who was starving for lack of work. A second lawyer then moved into the same town, and from that day on both thrived. From the day tort was retained to serve as Institutional Nanny and Mutual Insurance Company, it was bound to develop in just this way, with the lawyers who ran the system generating an ever-increasing demand for what they themselves supplied. "The one great principle of the English law," Charles Dickens explained in *Bleak House,* "is to make business for itself. There is no other principle distinctly, certainly, and consistently maintained through all its narrow turnings. Viewed by this light it becomes a coherent scheme, and not the monstrous maze the laity are apt to think it."

The one great principle took longer to gain hold in America, but when it came to full flower in the new tort jurisprudence it outdid even the famous excesses of the British Chancery law. Has the defendant improved the product to a point of unprecedented safety? Then sue him for the failings of what he made forty years ago, comparing them unfavorably with what came after. Does he plaster the product with ever more detailed and lurid warnings in hopes of avoiding suit? Then sue him for fear itself, for cancerphobia and psychic distress. Does he adamantly deny having caused any harm? Then you can't possibly be charged with early discovery of your injury, so wait as long as you like to sue. Does he offer a clear and fixed guarantee of compensation in case of injury? Then take this collateral-source money as tendered, and run to court for more. Is it unclear whether the product hurt anyone? Argue you weren't warned of its precise qualities, dangerous or otherwise. Were you warned? Say you didn't pay attention but the product was defective anyway. Every imaginable argument gives you one more chance to get to the jury.

Once lawyers take charge of an area of life, the person of low cunning acquires mastery over the person of high simplicity. With lawyers in charge, the mean person gets the better of the generous one. How long such conquests last is another matter; that they are regularly achieved in the courts is an everyday experience. Tort law may be a necessary evil, not because it solves problems, but because in the best of circumstances it can palliate them. In the worst it feeds on its own acrimony. One player's gain is always another's larger loss. As a group, litigants are always certain to lose for the same reason that as a group Las Vegas gamblers always lose.

When the final accounts are drawn up, tort law always operates in the red. Human progress, however, depends on positive creation, on operating in the black. Tort law is conflict, and in a better world we would have less of it, not more.

Choosing Better

So what might have been is not what is. With this commentary on human life, indicating an experience of it not exclusively my own, I propose that we take a better way to the end of our journey.

The path we have been traveling is not inevitable, and there is yet time for a serious change in course. Not to abandon generosity or compassion for the victims of accidents, or return to the nineteenth-century notion of contract in all its harsh logic. We strive to be a humane society, and we can now afford to be. There are ways of achieving the aims of the new tort jurisprudence, through a reliance not on less but on better choice by the individual, the private insurer, and the expert agency.

The alternatives, at least, are fairly clear. Do we want real compensation for real victims, or is the objective to go on paying half the accident insurance dollar to the lawyers? Business as usual achieves only the latter objective. Are the disposal of chemical or nuclear wastes or the siting of factories and power plants to provide only endless opportunities for litigation, or do we want to get some real cash quickly into the pockets of the communities, wherever they are, that end up hosting these facilities, for whatever reasons? Sober agreements, made in advance, can provide more generous and equitable payment, to more people, than endless lawsuits built on fear, suspicion, and pervasive ignorance of the risks themselves. How are we to set out standards of confidentiality for the psychiatrist who treats a potentially violent patient, or the doctor ministering to one with AIDS? One strong current of tort law presses for broad disclosure; a second, contradicting the first, provides that we can sue professionals if they *do* disclose our circumstances to others. Does anyone really believe that this welter of incoherent case law is the best way to tell professionals what they can or should disclose, and tell all the rest of us what we may expect to have kept private? The issues here should not align liberal against conservative. Our present arrangement is liberal only in the pejorative sense of being generous with others' money, and conservative only in the pejorative sense of being hostile to innovation and change on every front. The only real political line is between lawyers and the rest. Who among us, liberal or conservative, benefits when the provision of day care services remains utterly dependent, as it is today, on a conservative insurance industry caught up in an endless guessing game with the courts? The Trial Lawyers of America, that's who.

The expense of after-the-fact tort law is especially inappropriate when we know, long in advance, roughly how many accidents of a given sort will occur. The approximate number of air crash deaths over a span of several years is highly predictable, especially if one controls for a few simple variables like the volume of passenger traffic. Yet tort lawyers continue to charge full contingency fees in crash cases, and the legal system continues to capture an appallingly high share of the total money changing hands. In a way, the law is serving as an anti-insurance system in such cases. Instead of transforming the capricious into the reliable and predictable, it does the reverse. It can take two essentially similar crashes and make them come out with vastly different compensation totals depending on locale, jury composition, and advocacy technique.

Cutting out the legal middlemen could more than double the pool of funds available for compensation at a single stroke. That would leave a lot of room for reductions in the supplier's costs or the consumer's price, on the one hand, and improvements in the breadth and certainty of coverage, on the other. Direct insurance, through general health and disability policies or arrangements specific to particular goods and services, is in every way superior to court-mediated coverage. As direct insurance is promoted across the board, we will quickly find coverage being extended to all sorts of accidents that today are not covered at all.

Contract solutions—unlike tort law, however packaged—are consistent with the ideal of true no-fault compensation. Tort law is intrinsically retributive and admonitory, which guarantees that its compensatory efforts are endlessly resisted by people on the paying side. Contract carries no such moral baggage. It can make liability absolute, not because morality so requires, but because the parties so agree. When we file a claim on a health, disability, life, or other direct insurance policy, no one has to waste much time over how the injury was caused, or just who was warned, or whether negligence or defect figured in the accident. Advance agreement is also what keeps contract remedies in control, sensibly limited, and on a sustainable budget. In the end, compensation clothed in the working garb of contract is far more beautiful than tort dressed up in China silks, cashmere shawls, and Golconda diamonds, because the attire of contract is affordable, earned, and paid for, not just seized from others by the compulsion of misguided law.

Whether in the form of simple, bilateral insurance of the familiar risks of airline travel or high-school sports, or as an answer to the vastly more complicated and higher-stakes problems of nuclear-accident coverage, contract-based compensation programs can preserve all the best from the old law and offer all the best of the new. Neocontract holds out the promise of compensation that is flexible but predictable, compassionate but nonadversarial, simple but nuanced—everything that a compensation system should be, and that the modern tort system is not. At the same time, neocontractual solutions can coax real, substantial compensation for badly injured people out of institutions that could organize such help—an objective in which the old law of contract took no interest, and that modern liability law at least attempts to advance.

As the increase in direct insurance dispels the specter of penniless accident victims abandoned to the public charge, we will win the freedom to advance boldly toward greater safety as well. Most people, most of the time, know their individual needs better than any jury ever can. Do we really wish to continue shaping our legal world, in the name of safety, so that the victim of a rare disease cannot freely do business, on mutually agreeable terms, with the one drug company that might be able to help? Some safety choices, of course, will always belong to experts. But those experts are not to be found in court. If government is at all competent, they will be found in the regulatory agencies. Virtually every public health expert who has looked at the question knows that the vaccines on the American market today are vital to the public health; it is only in court that there has ever been any real doubt on the point.

Freedom of choice, private or public, exercised under an umbrella of direct insurance, is the only certain path to a safer and healthier world, with more financial security for all. Contract and contract alone allows us to anticipate problems and to cover contingencies sensibly in advance, whether our objective is insurance or safety. It allows us to weigh the risks and benefits of our actions in the objective coolness of the beforehand rather than in the emotional heat of the aftermath. It allows us to separate the sometimes contradictory objectives of physical and financial protection, and so advance both goals more effectively. Contract reinvented, with a more human face, will advance autonomy as well, giving the individual the freedom of positive choice, with responsibility to go with it. Tort offers only negatives imposed by outsiders.

But isn't it unwise—some will ask—to tamper at all with a body of common law that has operated smoothly for centuries? The short answer is that tampering is what brought us to where we are. Centuries-old tort law has been rewritten from first word to last in the past thirty years. The question is not whether we should tamper with a venerable body of law. It is whether we should return to one.

No glib answer can be entirely right, and reform of the considerable muddle we are now in should not be confused with unthinking reaction. We do not have to reembrace a jurisprudence in which every blanket disclaimer of liability is mechanically enforced, in which sellers are utterly free to put any product on the market no matter how shoddy or dangerous. Nor would our modern society be tempted to embrace any such plan of reform. "As we look back on the nineteenth century theories," Grant Gilmore once observed, "we are struck most of all . . . by the narrow scope of social duty which they implicitly assumed. No man is his brother's keeper; the race is to the swift; let the devil take the hindmost." We have changed all that, and for the better. One need not insist on following the logic of contract wherever it leads to realize that consensual private exchanges make enormous benefits possible. All we really need to insist on are stable, predictable rules that systematically favor deliberate choice and deliberate agreement, and that can be understood and followed consistently by all sides.

Cooperation works better than conflict for both doctor and patient, both employer and employee, both vaccine seller and buyer, for both producer and consumer of a car, contraceptive, appliance, airplane ticket, or insurance policy. Cooperative agreements are likelier to bring about safety, and likelier to bring reliable compensation when accidents nevertheless occur. Overwhelmingly, both buyers and sellers recognize as much, at least when they examine the question dispassionately, beforehand. Outside the jury box, the public recognizes as much. So do most legislatures.

The only real reason we continue to put up with the tort system as it now operates is a humane conviction that we surely can afford to help out people who have been badly hurt. The conviction is a generous one, and accurate too. We can afford to help. But we can do vastly better than we are doing now if we can persuade those who make the law to let us.

The Challenge of Tomorrow

The need for reform is as urgent today as it ever has been. We still have many accidents, and many people who need help of some sort in the aftermath. And we are still an underinsured society, at least by the standards set in many other industrialized countries. It is precisely because the opportunities for progress today are so great that our obstructionist tort system is such great cause for concern.

The right to an abortion, for example, said to be guaranteed by the Constitution itself, obviously depends on the right to get help from others in the mainstream economy, at least if the right is to mean anything more than a coat-hanger or a back-alley butchery. French women today can buy a once-a-month pill—a chemical abortifacient—which is cheaper, much less traumatizing, and possibly safer than mechanical procedures. But the once-a-month pill will not easily be brought to market in America in the current tort climate, for it would immediately become a magnet for lawsuits, a prime on-the-scene suspect in virtually any case of subsequent sterility, pelvic disease, or birth defect.

Another great opportunity comes from our evolving power to unravel the human genetic signature, a power that promises the greatest advances in public health since Jenner discovered vaccination in 1798. Genetic analysis is frightening because it tells us so much about our individual weaknesses and differences. But like all other tools it is not itself good or evil; it is merely powerful, and can be used for better or for worse. The main incentive created by today's tort system is for sly abuse. The doctor has reason to use genetic screening as a matter of self-defense, for it allows him to locate defects outside his own performance and steer well clear of them one way or another. The employer faces similar incentives with her employees.

The answer surely cannot be to banish the technology itself, for that would prevent us from saving many lives and much suffering. So here again, we urgently need law that promotes the consensual search for mutual benefit. With lawyers not so prominent in the picture, doctor and patient can find ways to recognize their common interests, as can employer and employee. On the basis of advance discussion and agreement, the doctor and the expectant mother can make an informed choice about whether to use a genetic test at all and how to act on the information it may yield. Bargaining, discussion, and agreement can allow the employer and the employee or his union to settle how, if at all, such tests are to improve workplace safety, while simultaneously protecting both the health and the economic interests of more susceptible employees. If we do not establish a framework of law that allows such arrangements to be made openly and bilaterally, they will surely be made in secret and on one side alone. The tests are too easy to conduct, the information is too easy to conceal and abuse. If the law will not permit good faith and advance agreement all around, it will surely produce bad faith and exploitation in abundance.

Other important opportunities of the information age are equally at risk. Researchers are holding back from marketing certain kinds of computer technology, frightened off by the tort exposure of computer software that diagnoses patients, runs factories, and performs other complex tasks. Tort lawyers are also eyeing with interest the video display terminal, standard equipment on most computers, hoping to find actionable hazard in the minuscule levels of radiation these systems emit. Any half-competent lawyer can launch a credible paper assault on any of these technologies at any time. Victory is not always guaranteed, but each such effort is good for a spin of the lucrative tort wheel in today's wide-open legal casino. Yet here again, the system threatens technologies that hold enormous promise for improving safety and welfare. It is the technology of robotics—not the paper shuffling of those who come up with novel tort claims—that will someday lower a final curtain on the sordid hazards of the nineteenth-century factory and assembly line.

One thing is certain: Whether or not we stand paralyzed in the grip of tort liability, other countries around the world will not. Legal structures that promote friction and conflict among Americans most certainly also undermine our ability to compete against others.

Made in America generally means you can sue in America. A U.S. firm selling an American-made drug, car, chemical factory, or aircraft to India is forced today to sell expensive accident insurance along with it; a German firm competing for the same sale is not. Of course, the Indian consumer will get something extra along with the American product—the right to sue in U.S. courts if an accident should occur. But how much is it worth to him? The tort-mandated accident insurance that is a bad deal for the American bank janitor (because it is priced to compensate the lost earnings of the American bank president) is a horrendous deal for the impoverished Indian farmer.

The American competitive position is disadvantaged even within the U.S. market. Manufacturers remain liable for their products as long as they are in use. When an established U.S. company goes shopping every year to renew its insurance policy, it is therefore likely to be paying in part for its commercial history. More-recent business arrivals on our shores do not carry the excess insurance baggage of their own past. In industries as diverse as light aircraft, truck wheel rims, machine tools, sporting goods, and industrial machinery—all long-lived products—U.S. tort law has given foreign manufacturers an important competitive edge, not just in overseas markets but in the United States as well. Simple diseconomies of scale play their part. American companies have their commercial base in the United States, and thus shoulder U.S. liability costs on all their start-up development and production. Foreign competitors can build up a large base of operations without this element of overhead—which tends to be especially large with young and innovative technology—and then move into the U.S. market at the margin, when the product is mature enough to make exact warnings possible and insurance affordable. Finally, many foreign companies can effectively limit their total liability on U.S. operations by the cold-blooded expedient of keeping few of their assets in this country. No U.S. concern can get away with such a strategy.

Whether at home or abroad, the question, in the end, is whether we have control over our own choices, our own affairs, and our own tort lawyers. The question could not loom any larger than it does as we confront the most serious pandemic in modern history, the scourge of AIDS. Sooner or later, an AIDS vaccine will be developed; as of early 1988, several prototypes were already being tested. Producing vaccines correctly, in quantity, is a difficult and expensive art, and most vaccines have side effects of one sort or another. FDA tests will be carried to the point where everyone is sure that the vaccine prevents far more disease than it causes. But there is simply no way to discover the one-in-a-million problem without actually vaccinating huge numbers of people first. No private drug company would be foolish enough to go ahead with such a program without comprehensive liability insurance, and no insurance company would be foolish enough to write the policy. In today's legal climate, any mass vaccination program against AIDS will therefore have to be conducted entirely under public auspices, just like the swine flu program in 1976. This means that tort law has made vaccination at best a profitless activity, and at worst an undertaking suitable only for public charity. Those who disdain the profit motive in any circumstances may take quiet satisfaction in knowing that no private company will profit from development of an AIDS vaccine. But those threatened with the disease, who understand that profit is a remarkably powerful incentive for innovation, must view the situation as an all but criminal disaster.

State and Utopia

The new tort Founders were traditional utopians. Their vision was a shining one, grand enough to stir the mind, thrill the heart, and inspire the young lawyer. Theirs was a promise of society made more just, generous, and compassionate through the ministrations of activist litigators. Where the private buyer and seller lacked the incentive or the knowledge to make wise judgments about safety, the courts would intervene to substitute their own greater insight. Where the individual lacked the prudence, the foresight, or perhaps merely the wherewithal to secure insurance against misadventure, the courts would intervene once again to correct the error. The objectives were grand, the intentions were good, the promises were wonderfully beneficent. Utopian promises always are.

But utopia, at least along the lines traditionally described, is unattainable, and when the utopians succeed politically, they deliver only tyranny in practice. A less overweening state is better, not because it promises more than the traditional utopia, but because it delivers the closest approximation to it in an imperfect world.

Tort law in some measure will always be needed, so that we may not be used in certain ways by others merely as means or tools or material resources. But a boundary to tort liability is needed, too, if we are to accept ourselves as persons having individual rights with the dignity this constitutes and the responsibilities it implies. A firmly limited law of tort treats us with respect by respecting our rights. It allows us, individually or with whom we wish, to choose our life and to realize our ends and our conception of ourselves, insofar as we can, aided by the voluntary cooperation of other individuals possessing the same dignity. How dare the law do more? Or less?

And what of the lawyers? It is remarkably easy for members of my contentious profession to denounce what is wrong with doctors and drug companies, car makers and waste dumps, to condemn all that is imperfect, to stir up the flames of conflict and let slip the dogs of war. Identifying the good, building a consensus around it, and getting to a constructive yes is vastly more difficult, and it is something too many lawyers prefer to leave to others. Lawyers have great power in America, and the best of lawyers use it for great good. Collectively, we would do well to heed the advice offered by Abraham Lincoln in a law lecture: "Discourage litigation. Persuade your neighbors to compromise whenever you can. . . . As a peacemaker, the lawyer has a superior opportunity of being a good man. There will still be business enough."

I shall conclude by paraphrasing Grant Gilmore, whose words have rich meaning for those sincerely dismayed, as I am, by the recent, hasty, and ill-considered transformation of tort law. Law reflects but in no sense determines the moral worth of a society. The better the society, the less law there will be. In heaven there will be no law, and the lion will lie down with the lamb. The worse the society, the more law there will be. In hell there will be nothing but law, and due process will be meticulously observed.

NOTES

Chapter 1. *Uncommon Law*

Page 3 Long Island tour bus: R. Hanley, "Insurance Costs Imperil Recreation Industry," *New York Times,* 12 May 1980, p. A1.

Page 3 price of a small airplane: "General Aviation Tort Reform Considered," *The Executive Letter,* Insurance Information Institute (18 August 1986); see also "Business Struggling to Adapt as Insurance Crisis Spreads," *Wall Street Journal,* 21 January 1986.

Page 3 hyperemesis pill: T. R. Reid, "Insurance Famine Plagues Nation," *Washington Post,* 23 February 1986, pp. A1, A6.

Page 4 $300 per birth: Lester Thurow, "In Suit-Happy Society, the Economy Ends Up Suffering the Damages," *Los Angeles Times,* 15 December 1985, Part IV, p. 3.

Page 4 $85,000 a year: "Business Struggling to Adapt as Insurance Crisis Spreads," *Wall Street Journal,* 21 January 1986, p. 31.

Page 4 New York City schools: "Sorry, Your Policy is Canceled," *Time,* 24 March 1986, p. 16; Advisory Commission on Liability Insurance, *Insuring Our Future, Scope of the Problem* (Report of the Governor's Advisory Commission on Liability Insurance to Governor Cuomo, State of New York, 7 April 1986).

Page 4 "CJ" Jeep: "Insurance Famine Plagues the Nation," *Washington Post,* 23 February 1986, p. A6.

Page 4 *Voyager* plans: P. Huber, "Who Will Protect Us from Our Protectors?" *Forbes,* 13 July 1987, p. 56.

Page 4 St. Joseph, Missouri: R. Lindsey, "Soaring Liability Premiums Threaten Some Bus Lines," *New York Times,* 29 December 1985, p. A16.

Page 4 Lafayette County: "Business Struggling to Adapt as Insurance Crisis Spreads"; see also "Liability Insurance in Crisis" (editorial), *New York Times,* 4 March 1986, p. A26.

Page 4 Miami railbus: "Business Struggling to Adapt as Insurance Crisis Spreads."

Page 4 ice-skating rinks: "Insurance Famine Plagues Nation," *Washington Post,* 23 February 1986, p. A1; *New York Times,* 12 May 1980, p. A1.

Page 4 top 200 corporations: *Chief Executive,* Summer 1986, p. 32.

Page 4 $1 of direct tax they pay: "Defensive Medicine: It Costs, But Does It Work?" 257 *J.A.M.A.* 2801 (May 1987).

Page 9 average award has grown more rapidly still: D. Hensler, M. Vaiana, J. Kakalik, M. Peterson, *Trends in Tort Litigation: The Story Behind the Statistics* (Santa Monica, Calif.: Rand Institute for Civil Justice, Special Report R-3583-ICJ, 1987).

Page 9 fourfold increase between 1976 and 1986: David Kelley, "Editorial Commentary: When Atlas Shrugs," *Barron's,* 21 April 1986, p. 11; *Annual Reports of the Director* (Washington, D.C.: Administrative Office of the United States Courts, 1974–85) cited in J. Fried, "U. S. Courts Are Jammed by Caseload," *New York Times,* 9 July 1987, p. A15.

Page 9 claims against cities between 1982 and 1986: *The Need for Legislative Reform of the Tort System, A Report on the Liability Crisis from Affected Organizations* (Washington, D.C.: Sidley & Austin, May 1986), citing Haas, "U.S. Towns and Cities Paying More for Less," *Credit Markets,* November 1985, p. 47.

Page 10 claims against the federal government: L. McGinley, "Explosive Growth of Lawsuits Against the U.S. Creates Concern Over Potential Budget Impact," *Wall Street Journal,* 14 January 1985, p. 38.

Page 10 fivefold increase in average judgment: R. Hunter, "Taming the Latest Insurance 'Crisis'," *New York Times,* Letter, 13 April 1986, p. F3; Mary Zavada, "Brushing Up on Basic

Arithmetic" (Letter to the Editor), *New York Times,* 20 April 1986; David Kelley, "Editorial Commentary"; *Annual Reports of the Director.*

Page 10 jury verdict exceeding $1 million: S. Taylor, "Product Liability: The New Morass," *New York Times,* 10 March 1985, Section 3, p. 1; *Chief Executive,* Summer 1986, p. 38; "Courting Disaster: Is America's Civil Liability System Totally Out Of Control?" *World,* April 1986, p. 30.

Page 10 medical malpractice awards doubled every seven years: Impact of the Liability Crisis on Health Care in America: Hearings on S. 1804 Before the Senate Comm. on Labor and Human Resources, 99th Cong., 2d Sess. (1986) (Statement of St. Paul Fire and Marine Insurance Company at 4); see Gordon Crovitz, *Curbing the Medical Liability Crisis: The English Rule on Costs As an Alternative to the Contingency Fee* (Washington, D.C.: Washington Legal Foundation, Working Paper Series, No. 11, Feb. 1987).

Chapter 2. *The Death of Contract*

Page 19 Vandermark case: *Vandermark v. Ford Motor Co.,* 37 Cal. Rptr. 896, 391 P.2d 168 (1963).

Page 22 ". . . [it becomes for the court] a matter in fact": Y. B. 14 Hy. VI p. 18 pl. 58 (1436), quoted in Holdsworth, *History of English Law,* Vol. 3 (London: Methuen & Company Ltd, 1909) p. 330.

Page 22 which the law will then enforce: E. Farnsworth, *Contracts,* Section 1.1 (Boston: Little, Brown & Company, 1982) pp. 3–5.

Page 22 Hawkins case: *Hawkins v. McGee,* 84 N.H. 114 (1929).

Page 23 to bear the costs of any accident: W. Keeton, "The Meaning of Defect in Products Liability Law—A Review of Basic Principles," 45 *Mo. L. Rev.* 579 (1980).

Page 23 "impairing the obligation of contracts": Art. 1, Sec. 10, Para. 1.

Page 24 Joseph Lochner case: *Lochner v. New York,* 198 U.S. 45 (1905).

Page 24 sulfanilamide: This account is summarized from Crout, "The Nature of Regulatory Choices," paper published by the Center for the Study of Drug Development, 1977.

Page 25 could not be more different: See generally G. Priest, "The Invention of Enterprise Liability: A Critical History of the Intellectual Foundations of Modern Tort Law," 14 *J. Leg. Stud.* 461 (1985).

Page 28 Helen Henningsen case: *Henningsen v. Bloomfield Motors,* 32 N.J. 358, 161 A.2d 69 (1960).

Page 29 building contractor rather than the homeowner: W. Prosser, "The Assault upon the Citadel: Strict Liability to the Consumer," 69 *Yale L. J.* 1099, n.153 (1960); see also Prosser's follow-up article, "The Fall of the Citadel: Strict Liability to the Consumer," 50 *Minn L. Rev.* 791 (1966).

Page 29 chimpanzees welcoming a python: I am indebted for this metaphor to Peter Lewis, of the *New York Times,* though he used it in a quite different context.

Page 30 "And set yourself free": Friedrich Kessler laid the intellectual groundwork two decades earlier in his seminal article, "Contracts of Adhesion—Some Thoughts About Freedom of Contract," 43 *Colum. L. Rev.* 629 (1943); see also T. D. Rakoff, "Contracts of Adhesion: An Essay in Reconstruction," 96 *Harv. L. Rev.* 1174 (April 1983).

Page 30 among the most skilled of lawyers: The *Henningsen* court itself had found it necessary to dispose of a sweeping disclaimer that read: "It is expressly agreed that there are no warranties, express or implied, made by either the dealer or the manufacturer on the motor vehicle, chassis or parts furnished hereunder." *Henningsen v. Bloomfield Motors, Inc.,* 161 A.2d 69, 74 (N.J. 1960).

Page 30 even if it did appear on the contract: *Zabriskie Chevrolet, Inc. v. Smith,* 99 N.J. Super. 441, 240 A. 2d 195 (1968); *DeCoria v. Red's Trailer Mart, Inc.,* 5 Wash. App. 892, 491 P. 2d 241 (1971).

Page 30 nullify the document in its entirety: Cf. *Walsh v. Ford Motor Co.,* 59 Misc. 2d 241, 298 N.Y.S. 2d 538 (Sup. Ct. 1969).

Page 30 ". . . exiting with a check in his pocket": B. Clark and M. Davis, "Beefing Up

Notes

Product Liability Warranties: A New Dimension in Consumer Protection," 23 *U. Kan. L. Rev.* 567, 581–82 (1975).

Page 30 should be dismissed out of hand: See F. Kessler, "Contracts of Adhesion—Some Thoughts About Freedom of Contract," 43 *Col. L. Rev.* 629 (1943); G. Priest, "A Theory of the Consumer Product Warranty," 90 *Yale L. J.* 1297 (1981).

Page 31 would not be contemplated in the new legal order: See Uniform Commercial Code, §2–719(3); Clark and Davis, "Beefing Up Product Liability Warranties"; W. Prosser, "The Assault upon the Citadel"; DeChaine, "Products Liability and the Disclaimer," 4 *Will. L. J.* 364 (1967).

Page 32 contract had been absorbed back into tort: Grant Gilmore, *The Death of Contract*, Law Forum Series, College of Law (Columbus: Ohio State University Press, 1974).

Chapter 3. *A Search for New Rules*

Page 34 "Contorts:" the term apparently first appears in print in J. Feinman and M. Feldman, "Pedagogy and Politics," 73 *Geo. L. J.* 875, n. 16 (1985).

Page 34 very limited notions about liability: P. Winfield, "The Myth of Absolute Liability," 42 *L. Q. Rev.* 37, 38 (1926).

Page 34 Carl Brown case: *Texas & Pac. R. Co. v. Brown*, 33 S.W. 146 (1895).

Page 35 MacPherson case: *MacPherson v. Buick Motor Co.*, 138 N.Y.S. 224 (1912); see also 217 N.Y. 382, 111 N.E. 1050 (1916).

Page 35 ". . . under a duty to make it carefully": 111 N.E. 1050, 1053.

Page 36 ". . . among all its members": Oliver Wendell Holmes, *The Common Law* (Boston: Little, Brown and Co., 1923) p. 96.

Page 37 William Greenman case: *Greenman v. Yuba Power Products, Inc.*, 59 Cal. 2d 57, 27 Cal. Rptr. 697, 377 P.2d 897 (1963).

Page 38 Barbara Evans case: *Evans v. General Motors Corp.*, 359 F.2d 822 (7th Cir. 1966), *cert. denied*, 385 U.S. 836 (1966).

Page 38 David Larsen case: *Larsen v. General Motors Corp.*, 391 F.2d 495 (8th Cir. 1968).

Page 38 defects in design as well as manufacture: The *Larsen* court decided to file its conclusion under a "negligence" theory, but soon thereafter the crashworthiness of a car's design became just another issue of strict liability. When the case went back for trial, GM won again.

Page 39 paydozer without rearview mirrors: *Pike v. Frank O. Hough Co.*, 2 Cal. 3d 465; 85 Cal. Rptr. 629, 467 P.2d 229 (1970).

Page 39 car roof unable to withstand a rollover: *Turner v. General Motors Corp.*, 584 S.W.2d 844 (Tex. 1979).

Page 39 car roof unable to withstand runaway horse: "The Hanging Judges of Business," *Forbes*, 7 April 1986. (Ford Motor lost a $1.5 million jury decision to the estate of a woman who was killed when her car hit a horse, causing it to jump through the roof of her 1980 Ford Pinto.)

Page 39 single-control shower faucet: "Drawing the Limits on Liability," *Wall Street Journal*, 4 April 1984.

Page 39 lawn mower pull rope: *Share v. Sears, Roebuck & Co.*, No. 2984 (Pa. C. 27 April 1984), noted in S. Taylor, "Product Liability: The New Morass," *New York Times*, 10 March 1985, Section 3, p. 1.

Page 39 second base: *David Smith v. Bolko Athletic Co.*, cited in Schwartz, "New Products, Old Products, Evolving Law, Retroactive Law," 58 *N.Y.U. L. Rev.* 796 (1983).

Page 40 Goodyear tire: Marisa L. Manley, "Controlling Product Liability," *Inc.*, February 1987, pp. 103, 104.

Page 40 skid loader: *Hammond v. International Harvester Co.*, 691 F.2d 646 (3rd Cir. 1982); see also "Drawing the Limits on Liability."

Page 40 Tylenol capsules: James Feron, "A Year Later, Few Clues in Tylenol Poisoning," *New York Times*, 8 February 1987, p. 35; see also Desmond Barry and Edward DeVivo, "The

Evolution of Warnings: The Liberal Trend Toward Absolute Product Liability," 20 *Forum* 38 (1984).

Page 40 Puerto Rico hotel: J. Nordheimer, "First Steps Taken in Expected Suits Over Fatal Blaze at Dupont Plaza," *New York Times*, 6 January 1987, p. B5.

Page 42 Ford Pinto: Richard Epstein, "Is Pinto a Criminal?" *Regulation*, Mar./April 1980, p. 15.

Page 42 1971-model Honda: *Dorsey v. Honda Motor Co.*, 655 F.2d 650 (5th Cir. 1981) ($5,000,000 punitive verdict).

Page 42 Toyota $3 million judgment: *Toyota Motor Co. v. Moll*, 438 So.2d 192 (Fla. 5th Dist. Ct. App. 1983); see also *American Motors Corporation v. Ellis*, 403 So.2d 459, 6 Fla. Law Weekly, 1808 (Fla. Ct. of App., 5th District, 14 August 1981); *Leichtamer v. American Motors Corp.*, 67 Ohio St.2d 456, 424 N.E.2d 568 (5 Aug. 1981).

Page 43 "... the first best never gets built": S. Rubin, "Engineering Realities" (letter to the editor), *New York Times*, dated Feb. 25, 1986, responding to "The Seal on NASA's Fate" (editorial), *New York Times*, 22 February 1986.

Page 43 jury instructions and appellate decisions: J. Wade, "On the Nature of Strict Tort Liability for Products," 44 *Miss. L. J.* 825 (1973); D. Owen, "Rethinking the Policies of Strict Products Liability," 33 *Vand. L. Rev.* 681 (1980); W. Keeton, "The Meaning of Defect in Products Liability Law—A Review of Basic Principles," 45 *Mo. L. Rev.* 579 (1980).

Page 43 "... or carrying liability insurance": J. Wade, "On the Nature of Strict Tort Liability for Products."

Page 44 growth rate of about 15 percent: "Expert Witnesses: Booming Business for the Specialists," *New York Times*, 5 July 1987, p. 1.

Chapter 4.   *Knowledge of the Law Is No Excuse*

Page 45 Wilson case: *Wilson v. Piper Aircraft*, 282 Ore. 61; 577 P.2d 1322 (1978).

Page 46 Boiler explosions are extremely rare: See generally, John G. Burke, "Bursting Boilers and the Federal Power," in M. Kranzberg and W. Davenport, *Technology and Culture: An Anthology* (Society for the History of Technology, 1973) p. 93.

Page 47 at least in a negative context: C. Morris, "The Role of Administrative Safety Measures in Negligence Actions," 28 *Tex. L. Rev.* 143 (1949).

Page 47 "... those who live in organized society are under a duty to conform": *Martin v. Herzog*, 228 N.Y. 164, 126 N.E. 814 (1920); *Restatement 2d of Torts* (St. Paul: American Law Institute Publishers, 1965) §288B(1), Comment a.

Page 47 Ray Mitchell case: *Mitchell v. Hotel Berry Co.*, 34 Ohio App. 259, 171 N.E. 39 (1929).

Page 49 glaucoma test: *Helling v. Carey*, 83 Wash. 2d 514, 419 P.2d 981 (1974).

Page 49 cotton flannelette pajamas: *Gryc v. Dayton-Hudson Corp. et al.*, 297 N.W. 2d 727, 741 (Minn. 1980); *cert. denied*, 101 S. Ct. 320 (1980).

Page 49 Karen Silkwood case: *Silkwood v. Kerr-McGee Corp.*, 464 U.S. 238 (1984).

Page 49 birth control pill: *Ortho Pharmaceutical Corp. v. Wooderson*, 235 Kan. 387, 681 P.2d 1038 (1984), *cert. denied*, 105 S. Ct. 365 (1984).

Page 50 Other contraceptive cases: *Ortho v. Wooderson*, 235 Kan 387, 681 P.2d 1038 (1984); *MacDonald, et al. v. Ortho Pharmaceutical Corp.*, 394 Mass. 131, 475 N.E. 2d 65 (1985); *Brochu v. Ortho Pharmaceutical Corp.*, 642 F.2d 652, 656 (1st Cir. 1981); *Wells v. Ortho Pharmaceutical Corp.*, 788 F.2d 741 (11th Cir. 1986); *Nat'l. L. J.*, 11 February 1985, p. 11.

Page 51 Apperson case: *Lewis v. Terry*, 111 Cal. 39, 43 P. 398 (1896).

Page 52 Mrs. Robbins case: *Robbins v. Georgia Power Co.*, 171 S.E. 218 (Ga. Ct. App. 1933).

Page 52 warn against tampering and improper repair: W. Keeton, "The Meaning of Defect in Products Liability Law—A Review of Basic Principles," 45 *Mo. L. Rev.* 579 (1980).

Page 54 Eli Trujillo case: *Trujillo v. Uniroyal*, 608 F.2d 815 (10th Cir. 1979).

Page 55 cologne flammability: Cf. *Moran v. Williams*, 19 Md. App. 546, 313 A.2d 527 (1974); Keeton, "The Meaning of Defect in Products Liability Law."

Page 55 aboveground pool: R. L. Miller, "Drawing Limits on Liability" (op-ed), *Wall Street*

Notes

Journal, 4 April 1984; see also *Burton v. Montgomery Ward* (No. 389886, Maricopa County Sup. Ct. Ariz, 12 October 1984) cited in 4 P.L.L.R. 29 (February 1985).

Page 55 peanut butter: *Fraust v. Swift & Co.* (D.C. Pa., No. 84-1344, 23 May 1985) cited in " 'Dangerous' Peanut Butter?" *Product Liability Newsletter,* July 1985, p. 5.

Page 55 playground slide: Rather than risking a jury's finding of liability under the broad duty to warn doctrine, the City settled the case. "Sorry, Your Policy is Canceled," *Time,* 24 March 1986, p. 16.

Page 55 champagne corks: Marisa L. Manley, "Controlling Product Liability," *Inc.,* February 1987, pp. 103, 104.

Page 55 telescope sun filter: *Midgley v. S. S. Kresge Co.,* 55 Cal. App. 3d 67, 127 Cal. Rptr. 217 (1976).

Page 55 Richard Ferebee case: *Ferebee v. Chevron Chemical Co.,* 736 F.2d 1529 (1984).

Page 56 helmet manufacturer: *Rawlings Sporting Goods Co. v. Daniels,* 619 S.W.2d 435 (Tex. Civ. App. 1981).

Page 56 birth control pill and stroke: *MacDonald, et al. v. Ortho Pharmaceutical Corp.,* 394 Mass. 131, 475 N.E. 2d 65 (Mass. 1985).

Page 56 Kut-Koat furniture stripper: Manley, "Controlling Product Liability."

Page 57 ". . . not mitigated by the invitation to ask questions": *Unthank v. United States,* 732 F.2d 1517 (10th Cir. 1984).

Page 57 Anita Reyes case: *Reyes v. Wyeth Laboratories,* 498 F.2d 1264 (5th Cir. 1974), *cert. denied,* 419 U.S. 1096.

Page 57 warning the patient: *MacDonald, et al. v. Ortho Pharmaceutical Corp.,* 394 Mass. 131, 475 N.E. 2d 65 (1985).

Page 58 those who might not read the manual: Manley, "Controlling Product Liability."

Page 58 warning on the tires: Miller, "Drawing the Limits on Liability."

Page 58 "contemplated by the ordinary consumer": Cf. *Restatement 2d of Torts* Section 402A; J. Wade, "On Product 'Design Defects' and Their Actionability," 33 *Vand. L. Rev.* 551 (1980).

Page 59 "A. . . . what they are going to put next": 498 F.2d 1264, 1282 n.30.

Page 60 videotape of patient: F. James, "Videotaping Doctor Visits: Rx for Lawsuits?" *Wall Street Journal,* 25 November 1987, p. 17.

Page 60 could not be wished away by the courts: E.g., *Johnson v. Niagara Machine & Tool Works,* 666 F.2d 1223 (8th Cir. 1981).

Chapter 5.   *The New Town Meeting*

Page 62 vets settled for $180 million: See P. Schuck, *Agent Orange on Trial* (Cambridge, Mass.: Belknap Press, 1986).

Page 63 Rylands case: *Rylands v. Fletcher,* 1865, 3 H. & C. 774, 159 Eng. Rep. 737, *reversed, Fletcher v. Rylands,* 1866 L.R. 1 Ex. 265, *affirmed, Rylands v. Fletcher,* 1868, L.R. 3 H.L. 330.

Page 65 American culture was irreversibly changed: R. Carson, *The Silent Spring* (Greenwich, Conn.: Fawcett, 1962).

Page 65 microscopic assaults on the body: Compare S. Epstein, *The Politics of Cancer* rev. ed. (San Francisco: Sierra Club Books, 1979), and E. Efron, *The Apocalyptics: Cancer and the Big Lie* (New York: Simon & Schuster, 1984).

Page 68 settled with Hooker for $20 million: Lindsey Gruson, "Ex-Love Canal Families Get Checks," *New York Times,* 20 February 1985, p. B1; *BNA Reporter,* 4 January 1985, p. 1445.

Page 69 Jackson Township, New Jersey: *Ayers v. Township of Jackson,* 189 N.J. Super. 561, 461 A.2d 184 (1983); *Nat'l L. J.,* 9 January 1984, p. 7; *New York Times,* 8 June 1986, Section NJ, p. 32.

Page 69 Triana, Alabama: *Wall Street Journal,* 22 April 1983, p. 4; *Nat'l L. J.,* 23 November 1981, p. 10.

Page 69 Times Beach, Missouri: "Attorneys Announce $19 Million Settlement To Conclude Times Beach, Mo., Damage Suits," *BNA Environment Reporter,* 28 November 1986, p. 1266;

BNA Environment Reporter, 25 February 1983, p. 1886; "Settlement Is Reached for 128 Dioxin Victims," *New York Times,* 20 November 1986, p. A22.

Page 69 Toone, Tennessee: *The Executive Letter,* Insurance Information Institute, 18 August 1986.

Page 69 "far more significant" than Love Canal: "Toxic-Water Suit Is Settled," *New York Times,* 5 July 1986.

Page 69 "far higher" than Woburn: Philip Shabecoff, "Uncertainties of a Chemical-Filled World Bring Fear to a Suburb of Denver," *New York Times,* 19 April 1987, p. 26.

Page 70 demanding billions of dollars in compensation: See *Allen v. United States,* 588 F. Supp. 247 (D. Utah 1984), *reversed,* 21 April 1987; *Mondelli v. United States,* 711 F.2d 567, 568 (3d Cir. 1983), *cert. denied,* 104 S. Ct. 1272 (1984); S. Taylor, "New Act Restricts Atomic Test Suits," *New York Times,* 4 November 1985, p. 26; L. McGinley, "Explosive Growth of Lawsuits Against the U.S. Creates Concern Over Potential Budget Impact," *Wall Street Journal,* 14 January 1985, p. 38. See also *In re Three Mile Island Litig.,* 87 F.R.D. 433, 442 (M.D. Pa. 1980); *In re Three Mile Island Litig.,* 557 F. Supp. 96 (M.D. Pa. 1982).

Page 70 1,500 claims by other nearby residents: "Settlement Is Reached for 128 Dioxin Victims."

Page 71 Helen Palsgraf case: *Palsgraf v. Long Island R. Co.,* 248 N.Y. 339, 162 N.E. 99 (1928).

Page 72 A hundred contained ten tithings: Cf. 1 Blackstone's Commentaries (1871) 115; 4 Blackstone's Commentaries (1871) 411; Black's Law Dictionary (4th ed. 1968), pp. 874–75.

Page 73 ". . . in the entire history of the law of torts": W. Prosser & W. Keeton, *Prosser and Keeton on Torts,* 5th ed. (St. Paul: West Pub. Company, 1984) p. 690.

Page 75 Saturday night special: *Kelley v. R.G. Industries,* 304 Md. 124, 497 A.2d 1143 (M.D. Apps. 1985).

Page 75 bomb paraphernalia: *Stencel Aero Eng'g Corp. v. United States,* 431 U.S. 666, 667–68 (1977).

Page 75 pawnshop pistol: "$1.9 Settlement in Killing," *New York Times,* 8 May 1987, p. A19.

Page 75 escaped convict: *Johnson v. State,* 69 Cal. 2d 782, 73 Cal Reptr. 240, 447 P.2d 352 (1968); *State v. Silva,* 86 Nev. 911, 478 P.2d 591 (1970).

Page 76 suspected wife beater: D. Johnson, *New York Times,* 25 June 1986, p. E8.

Page 76 negligent security: F. Zacharias, "The Politics of Torts," 95 *Yale L. J.* 698, 699 (1985).

Page 76 AIDS exposure: See, e.g., M. Engel, "Short, Joy-Giving Life Comes to an End for AIDS Victim," *Washington Post,* 15 February 1986, p. B1; *New York Times,* 19 June 1987, p. 10.

Page 76 manager who raped tenant: L. Reibstein, "Firms Face Lawsuits for Hiring People Who Then Commit Crimes," *Wall Street Journal,* 30 April 1987, Section 2, p. 1.

Page 76 traditional rule for alcohol: H. Weinert, "Social Hosts and Drunken Drivers: A Duty to Intervene?" 133 *U. Penn. L. Rev.* 867 (1985).

Page 76 social guest's drunken driving: *Kelly v. Gwinnell,* 96 N.J. 538, 476 A.2d 1219 (1984).

Page 76 overruled by statute: *Wiener v. Gamma Phi Chapter of Alpha Tau Omega Fraternity,* 258 Or. 632, 485 P.2d 18 (1971); *Williams v. Klemesrud,* 197 N.W.2d 614 (Iowa 1972); *Ross v. Ross,* 294 Minn. 115, 200 N.W.2d 149 (1972); *Coulter v. Superior Court of San Mateo County,* 21 Cal. 3d 144, 577 P. 2d 669, 145 Cal. Rptr. 534 (1978); see Weinert, "Social Hosts and Drunken Drivers."

Page 76 failing to diagnose promptly enough: "Researchers Note Rise in Complaints Charging Late Diagnoses of Cancer," *American Medical News,* 20 March 1987, p. 39; D. Rubsamen, "Medical Malpractice," *Scientific American,* August 1976, p. 18.

Page 77 "wrongful life": Cheryl Frank, "Wrongful Life?" 71 *A.B.A.J.* 26 (February 1985); Alan Otten, "Wrongful Life? Parents and Newborns Win New Legal Rights to Sue for Malpractice," *Wall Street Journal,* 7 June 1985, p. 1. See, e.g., *Curlender v. Bio-Science Laboratories,* 165 Cal. Rptr. 477, 106 Cal. App. 3d 811 (1980); *Harbeson v. Parke-Davis, Inc.,* 98 Wash. 2d 460, 656 P.2d 483 (1983); *Procanik v. Cillo,* 97 N.J. 339, 478 A.2d 755 (1984).

Page 77 Tatiana Tarasoff case: *Tarasoff v. Regents of University of California,* 17 Cal.3d 425, 131 Cal. Reptr. 14, 551 P. 2d 334 (1976); see also *People v. Poddar,* 518 P.2d 342 (1974).

Page 77 encouraged suicide: *Nally v. Grace Community Church of the Valley,* 204 Cal. Rptr. 303

Notes

(Cal. App. 1984); see also J. Cummings, "Suit Against Clergy in a Suicide Case is Reinstated," *New York Times,* 20 September 1987.

Page 77 dial-a-porn services: K. Bishop, "Access of Young to 'Dial-a-Porn' Faces Key Challenge in West," *New York Times,* 22 November 1987.

Page 78 most other states followed suit: Leo Winstead and Paul Cottrell, "Negligence: Doctrine in a State of Flux," *Risk Management,* October 1984, p. 30.

Page 78 jumped in front of a subway train: Michael Kinsley, "Craziness in the Courtroom," *Reader's Digest,* May 1986, p. 39.

Page 78 thirteen-year-old who committed suicide: D. Johnson, "Father Sues School in Son's Suicide at Home," *New York Times,* 8 February 1987, p. 44.

Page 79 Inadequate trimming of bushes: *Sills v. City of Los Angeles,* No. C-333504 (San Fernando Super. Ct. 4 March 1984).

Page 79 San Diego paid for speeding drunk driver: *Duggan v. City of San Diego, et al.,* Civ. 484152 (San Diego Superior Court, filed 2 April 1982, dismissed 10 February 1984).

Page 79 Michigan driver collected $240,000: *Bacon v. Michigan Department of Transportation,* discussed in James R. Granelli, "The Attack on Joint and Several Liability," 71 *A.B.A.J.* 61, 63 (July 1985).

Page 80 money-first principle of liability: *American Motorcycle Association v. Superior Court,* 20 Cal. 3d 578, 146 Cal. Rptr. 182, 578 P.2d 899 (1978).

Page 80 Summers, Tice, and Simonson case: *Summers v. Tice,* 33 Cal. 2d 80, 199 P.2d 1 (1948).

Page 81 blasting caps case: *Hall v. E.I. Du Pont De Nemours & Co.,* 345 F. Supp. 353 (E.D.N.Y. 1972).

Page 81 DES case: *Sindell v. Abbott Laboratories,* 26 Cal. 3d 588, 607 P.2d 924, 163 Cal. Rptr. 132, *cert. denied,* 449 U.S. 912 (1980).

Page 81 400 parties will end up defending the case: Cf. *United States v. Wade,* 577 F. Supp. 1326 (E.D. Pa. 1983).

Page 82 air and water pollution: See, e.g., Note, "Pollution Share Liability: A New Remedy for Plaintiffs Injured by Air Pollutants," 9 *Colum. J. Envtl. L.* 297, 312–319 (1984) (market-share liability for polluters).

Chapter 6. *Resetting the Clock*

Page 84 Raul Martinez-Ferrer case: *Martinez-Ferrer v. Richardson-Merrell, Inc.,* 105 Cal. App. 3d 316, 164 Cal. Rptr. 591 (1980).

Page 85 Bealey case: *Fletcher v. Bealey,* 28 Ch. 688 (1885).

Page 86 ". . . judicial remedy is available to the plaintiff": *Dincher v. Marlin Firearms Co.,* 198 F. 2d 821, 823 (2d Cir. 1952) (Frank, J. dissenting) (footnotes omitted).

Page 88 should obviously be swept aside: Comment, "Statutes of Limitations and the Discovery Rule in Latent Injury Claims: An Exception or the Law?" 43 *U. Pitt. L. Rev.* 501 (1982); Dworkin, "Product Liability of the 1980s: 'Repose Is Not the Destiny' of Manufacturers," 61 *N.C.L. Rev.* 33 (1982); Comment, "Statutes of Limitations in Product Liability Actions: the Discovery Rule of Franzen v. Deere & Co.," 69 *Iowa L. Rev.* 1127 (1984); see also *Urie v. Thompson,* 337 U.S. 163, 170 (1949).

Page 90 military bomb tests: *Allen v. United States,* 527 F. Supp. 476, 489–91 (D. Utah 1981); *Allen v. United States,* 588 F. Supp. 247 (D. Utah 1986). In April 1987 a court of appeals overturned the verdict in the A-bomb case on grounds unrelated to the timing issue.

Page 94 Laxton case: *Laxton v. Orkin Exterminating Co.,* 639 S.W.2d 431 (Tenn. 1982).

Page 94 Jackson Township, New Jersey: *Ayers v. Township of Jackson,* 189 N.J. Super. 561, 564–65, 461 A.2d 184, 186 (Law Div. 1983); *Laxton v. Orkin Exterminating Co.,* 639 S.W.2d 431, 434 (Tenn. 1982); *Nat'l L. J.,* 9 January 1984, p. 7.

Page 96 "enhanced risk": Cf. *BNA Environment Reporter,* 10 August 1984, p. 576. A worker suffering from asbestosis was not permitted to claim damages for the risk that he might some day contract lung cancer, but could claim compensation for future medical examinations to check for the disease. *Jackson v. Johns-Manville Sales Corp.,* 727 F.2d 506, 522 (5th Cir. 1984); see

David Rosenberg, "The Causal Connection in Mass Exposure Cases: A 'Public Law' Vision of the Tort System," 97 *Harv. L. Rev.* 851 (1984); see also G. Robinson, "Probabilistic Causation and Compensation for Tortious Risk," 14 *J. Legal Studies* 779 (1985); Note, "Increased Risk of Cancer as an Actionable Injury," 18 *Ga. L. R.* 563 (1984).

Page 96 urgent candidate for still more lawyering: Cf. G. Schwartz, "New Products, Old Products, Evolving Law, Retroactive Law," 58 *N.Y.U. L. Rev.* 796 (1983).

Chapter 7. *Sentence Without Verdict*

Page 98 new search for traumatically induced cancer: Ewing, "Modern Attitudes Toward Traumatic Cancer," 19 *Arch. Path.* 690 (1935).

Page 98 skin cancer at the site of the original injury: Wainwright, "Single Trauma, Carcinoma and Workman's Compensation," 5 *Am. J. Surg.* 433 (1928).

Page 99 ". . . or cupidity": Stewart, "Occupational and Post-Traumatic Cancer," 23 *Bull N.Y. Acad. Med.* 145 (1947).

Page 99 ". . . medical testimony concerning trauma": Ibid.

Page 99 ". . . slightest injury may result in cancer": Crane, "The Relationship of a Single Act of Trauma to Subsequent Malignancy," reprinted in Alan R. Moritz and David S. Helberg, *Trauma and Disease: Selections from the Recent Literature* (New York: Central Book Co., Inc., 1959) pp. 147, 148; see also Comment, "Sufficiency of Proof in Traumatic Cancer: A Medico-Legal Quandary," 16 *Ark L. Rev.* 243 (1962).

Page 99 ". . . litigation which keeps it alive": Auster, "The Role of Trauma in Oncogenesis: A Juridical Consideration," 11 *J.A.M.A.* 98 (1961).

Page 99 ". . . cancer cannot result from trauma": Comment, "Sufficiency of Proof in Traumatic Cancer: A Medico-Legal Quandary."

Page 99 ". . . upon the victims of industrial accidents": Dyke, "Traumatic Cancer?" 15 *Clev-Mar. L. Rev.* 313 (Sept. 1966).

Page 99 ". . . so strong as to establish a causal connection": *White v. Valley Land Co.,* 64 N.M. 9, 15, 322 P.2d 707, 711 (1958); see also Comment, "Sufficiency of Proof in Traumatic Cancer Cases," 46 *Cornell L. Q.* 581 (1961).

Page 100 to enforce their wishes: I believe it was Judge Robert Bork who first pointed out how fortunate we all are that the Joint Chiefs choose not to be activists in advancing their views of sound law or government.

Page 101 mystics of every description rushed in: See, e.g., E. Imwinkelried, "Science Takes the Stand: The Growing Misuse of Expert Testimony," *The Sciences,* November/December 1986, p. 20.

Page 102 33 million pregnancies: Tamar Lewin, "Pharmaceutical Companies Are the Hardest Hit," *New York Times,* 10 March 1985, p. D1.

Page 102 a jury awarded Mary $750,000: The trial judge struck down the award on the ground that Oxendine had made no adequate showing of cause and effect, but a court of appeals reinstated the jury's verdict. *Oxendine v. Merrell Dow Pharmaceuticals, Inc.,* No. 83-1055 (D.C. Ct. App., filed 7 September 1983).

Page 102 $20,000 for medical expenses anyway: "The Cause and Defect of Orangemail" (editorial), *New York Times,* 24 March 1985, p. 22E; "Morning Sickness, Legal Miscarriage" (editorial), *New York Times,* 30 July 1984, p. A20.

Page 102 a flood of new claims: See, e.g., *Koller v. Richardson-Merrell, Inc.,* No. 80-1258 (D.D.C., filed 25 February 1983).

Page 102 six-year-old boy born with club feet: See Lewin, "Pharmaceutical Companies Are the Hardest Hit."

Page 102 $95 million for another birth defect: Fred Strasser, "Bendectin Award: $95 Million," *Nat'l L. J.,* 27 July 1987, p. 29. In October 1987, the trial judge upheld $20 million awarded in compensation but struck down the $75 million punitive damage component.

Page 102 Bendectin–birth defect link: F. Strasser, "Bendectin Award: $95 Million."

Page 102 ". . . made a devastation and called it a settlement": *New York Times,* 30 July 1984, p. A20.

Page 102 the drug was pulled from the market: "Bendectin Production Ends," *New York Times*, 14 March 1985.

Page 102 Katie Wells case: *Wells v. Ortho Pharmaceutical Co.*, 788 F.2d 741 (11th Cir. 1986).

Page 103 ". . . an intellectual embarrassment": *New York Times*, 27 December 1986, Section 1, p. 22.

Page 103 the vaccine or the wild virus: *Reyes v. Wyeth Laboratories*, 498 F.2d 1264 (5th Cir. 1974), *cert. denied*, 419 U.S. 1096.

Page 103 "serum sickness": *Petty v. United States*, 740 F.2d 1428 (8th Cir. 1984).

Page 104 vaccinated three times against whooping cough: See C. DeMuth, Should Product-Liability Law be Nationalized? (unpublished manuscript, September 1985).

Page 106 Ray Barker case: *Barker v. Lull Engineering Co.*, 20 Cal. 3d 413, 143 Cal. Rptr. 225, 573 P.2d 443 (1978).

Page 107 earlier diagnosis would not have produced a cure: *Fosgate v. Corona*, 66 N.J. 268, 330 A.2d 335 (1974); *Anderson v. Somber*, 67 N.J. 291, 338 A.2d 35 (1975). See also Gordon Crovitz, *Curbing the Medical Liability Crisis: The English Rule on Costs as an Alternative to the Contingency Fee* (Washington, D.C.: Washington Legal Foundation Working Paper Series, No. 11, February 1987).

Page 107 fallout from the nuclear tests: S. Taylor, "Product Liability: The New Morass," *New York Times*, 10 March 1985, Section 3, p. 1.

Page 110 crane manufacturer: John Carson-Parker, "The Liability Crisis: Who's At Risk?" *Chief Executive*, Summer 1986, p. 29.

Page 110 cases against MER/29: R. Seltzer, "Punitive Damages in Mass Tort Litigation: Addressing the Problems of Fairness, Efficiency and Control," 52 Ford. L. Rev. 37 (1983).

Page 110 hooking up to an uncontaminated water supply: *Nat'l L. J.*, 9 January 1984, p. 7.

Page 110 Down's syndrome: "No Cancer Increase Found in Three Mile Island Study," *Wall Street Journal*, 6 September 1985.

Page 110 Toone, Tennessee: Wolff, "Love Canal Revisited," 251 *J.A.M.A.* 1464 (1984); Bruce N. Ames, "Six Common Errors Relating to Environmental Pollution," testimony for California Assembly on Water, Parks and Wildlife, 1 October 1986.

Page 111 $20,000 per claim to do so: S. Johnson, "Malpractice Costs vs. Health Care for Women," *New York Times*, 14 July 1985, p. A14.

Page 111 annual profit on the device: E. Connell, "The Crisis in Contraception," *Technology Review*, May-June 1987, p. 47; "Birth Control: Vanishing Options," *Time*, 1 September 1986, p. 78.

Page 112 ". . . apt to put compassion ahead of dispassion": "Orangemail: Why It Got Paid" (editorial), *New York Times*, 8 March 85, p. A34; see also "Agent Orange—Let It Lie" (editorial), *New York Times*, 4 September 1986, p. A26.

Page 112 Jewel Companies: Deirdre Fanning, "Enough Is Enough," *Forbes*, 20 April 1987, p. 56; see also *New York Times*, 22 November 1987, p. 35.

Page 113 ". . . continuing basic cancer research": Stoll and Crissey, "Epithelioma from Single Trauma," 1962 *N.Y. State J. Med.* 496 (1962).

Page 114 ". . . 'cause' of tuberculosis": G. Calabresi, "Concerning Cause and the Law of Torts: An Essay for Harry Kalven, Jr.," 43 *U. Chi. L. Rev.* 69, 105–6 (1975).

Chapter 8. *Pain and Punishment*

Page 115 Richard Grimshaw case: *Grimshaw v. Ford Motor Co.*, 119 Cal. App. 3d 757, 174 Cal. Rptr. 348 (1981).

Page 116 some claims for hurt feelings: O'Connell and Bailey, "Appendix V: The History of Payment for Pain & Suffering," 1972 *U. Ill. Law Forum* 83 (1972).

Page 116 little harm but large offense: J. O'Connell and K. Carpenter, "Payment for Pain and Suffering through History," *Ins. Counsel J.*, July 1983, p. 411.

Page 116 a fortune at the time: *Ash v. Lady Ash*, 90 Eng. Rep. 526 (K.B. 1696).

Page 116 case from the year 1348: Y.B. 22 Edw. iii, f. 99, pl. 60 (1348).

Page 117 no grounds for a suit: *Lunch v. Knight,* 11 Eng. Rep. 854, 9 H.L. Cas. 577, 578 (1861); *Spade v. Lynn & Boston R.R. Co.,* 172 Mass. 488, 52 N.E. 747 (1899).

Page 117 an essential predicate: Comment, "Loss of Consortium: Paradise Lost, Paradise Regained," 15 *Cum. L. Rev.* 179 (1984).

Page 118 Susie Waube case: *Waube v. Warrington,* 216 Wis. 603, 258 N.W. 497 (1935).

Page 118 imprisonment pursuant to "a nameless warrant": *Huckle v. Money,* 2 Wils. K.B. 205, 95 Eng. Rep. 768 (1763).

Page 121 painfully struggling through daily chores: J. O'Connell and K. Carpenter, "Payment for Pain and Suffering through History."

Page 121 awards attributable to psychic distress: George Priest, "Modern Tort Law and the Current Insurance Crisis," Yale Law School, Program in Civil Liability, Working Paper 44, May 1986, at 32; J. O'Connell & K. Carpenter, "Payment for Pain and Suffering through History."

Page 122 received $2.5 million: Ibid.

Page 122 $6 million for pain and suffering: *Nichole Fortman v. Hemco, Inc.* (Los Angeles Superior Court, NWC 86375); "Record Award in California," *The Executive Letter,* Insurance Information Institute, 27 October 1986.

Page 122 $58 million for pain and suffering: "New York Court Awards $65 million in Malpractice Case," *The Executive Letter,* Insurance Information Institute, 28 July 1986.

Page 122 Eleanor Ferrara case: *Ferrara v. Galluchio,* 5 N.Y.2d 16, 152 N.E.2d 249, 176 N.Y.S.2d 996 (1958).

Page 123 burn unnecessary as well: T. Dworkin, "Fear of Disease and Delayed Manifestation Injuries: A Solution or a Pandora's Box?" 53 *Fordham L. Rev.* 527 (1984).

Page 123 tuberculosis sanitarium: *Everett v. Paschall,* 111 P. 879, 61 Wash. 47 (1910).

Page 124 dirt and glass slivers: *Greer v. Ouachita Coca-Cola Bottling Co.,* 420 So.2d 540 (La. Ct. App., 1982).

Page 124 dead mouse: *Coca-Cola Bottling Co. v. White,* 545 S.W.2d 279, 280 (Tex. Civ. App., 1976).

Page 124 shock wave from an explosion: *Kasey v. Suburban Gas Heat, Inc.,* 60 Wash. 2d 468, 476, 374 P.2d 549, 553–54 (1962).

Page 124 exposed to tuberculosis: *Plummer v. United States,* 580 F.2d 72, 76 (3d Cir. 1978).

Page 124 ". . . cause excruciating agony": *Dickens v. Puryear,* 302 N.C. 437, 448–49, 276 S.E.2d 325, 332–33 (1981), clarifying dicta in *Stanback v. Stanback,* 297 N.C. 181, 254 S.E.2d 611 (1979).

Page 124 "lacerated limbs": 302 N.C. 437; see also Robert A. Bohrer, "Fear and Trembling in the Twentieth Century: Technological Risk, Uncertainty, and Emotional Distress," 1984 *Wis. L. Rev.* 83 (1984).

Page 124 graver injury of another: W. Winter, "A Tort in Transition: Negligent Infliction of Mental Distress," 70 *A.B.A.J.* 62 (1984).

Page 124 Margery Dillon case: *Dillon v. Legg,* 68 Cal. 2d 728, 441 P.2d 912 (1968); see also *Amaya v. Home Ice, Fuel & Supply Co.,* 59 Cal. 2d 295, 29 Cal. Rptr. 33, 379 P.2d 513 (1963).

Page 125 birth of her injured child: *Haught v. Maceluch,* 681 F.2d 291 (5th Cir. 1982).

Page 125 "experiential perception": See T. Dworkin, "Fear of Disease and Delayed Manifestation Injuries."

Page 125 suffered from syphilis: *Molien v. Kaiser Foundation Hospitals,* 27 Cal. 3d 916, 616 P.2d 813, 167 Cal. Rptr. 831 (1980). See also J. Langhenry, "Personal Injury Law and Emotional Distress," 9 *J. Psych. L.* 91 (1981).

Page 125 adopted similar rules: W. Winter, "A Tort in Transition: Negligent Infliction of Mental Distress; T. Dworkin, "Fear of Disease and Delayed Manifestation Injuries."

Page 125 ordinary consumer product cases: *Shepard v. Superior Court of Alameda County,* 76 Cal. App. 3d 16, 142 Cal. Rptr. 612 (1977); J. Silverman, "Recovery for Emotional Distress in Strict Products Liability," 61 *Chi-Kent L. Rev.* 545 (1985); *Gnirk v. Ford Motor Co.,* 572 F. Supp. 1201 (D.S.D. 1983).

Page 125 badly maintained building: *Simon v. Solomon,* 385 Mass. 91, 431 N.E.2d 556 (1982).

Page 125 nine-year-old female boxer: *Campbell v. Animal Quarantine Station,* 63 Hawaii 557, 632 P.2d 1066 (1981).

Page 125 school holiday assemblies: *Abramson v. Anderson,* No. 81-26-W (S.D. Iowa 1982).

Page 125 disappeared as a source of tort compensation: *Marri v. Stamford St. R. Co.,* 84

Notes

Conn. 9, 78 A. 582 (1911), *overruled; Hopson v. Saint Mary's Hosp.,* 176 Conn. 485, 408 A. 2d 260 (1979).

Page 125 little objection from feminists: Comment, "Loss of Consortium: Paradise Lost, Paradise Regained," 15 *Cum. L. Rev.* 179 (1984).

Page 126 loss of consortium of husbands: E.g. *Hitaffer v. Argonne Co.,* 87 U.S. App. D.C. 57, 183 F. 2d 811 (1950) *cert. denied* 340 U.S. 852 (1950) *rev'd on other grounds; Smither & Co. v. Coles,* 242 F. 2d 220 (D.C. Cir. 1957), *cert. denied,* 354 U.S. 914 (1957); *Dini v. Naiditch,* 20 Ill. 2d 406, 170 N.E. 2d 881 (1960).

Page 126 loss of "society": Comment, "Loss of Consortium."

Page 126 family members to be compensated also grew rapidly: J. Love, "Tortious Interference with the Parent-Child Relationship: Loss of an Injured Person's Society and Companionship," 51 *Ind. L. J.* 590 (1976); J. Bainbridge, "Loss of Consortium Between Parent and Child," 71 *A.B.A.J.* 47 (October 1985); Comment, "Recovery for Loss of Parental Consortium: An Undue Extension of Liability," 43 *U. Pitt. L. Rev.* 285 (1981).

Page 126 ". . . love and affection of the deceased": *Bullard v. Barnes,* 102 Ill. 2d 505, 82 Ill. Dec. 448, 468 N.E.2d 1228 (1984).

Page 126 "stability and significance": *Butcher v. Superior Court of Orange County,* 139 Cal. App. 3d 58, 188 Cal. Rptr. 503 (1983); *Bulloch v. United States,* 487 F. Supp. 1078 (D.N.J. 1980) (applying New Jersey law).

Page 126 faulty sterilization: See, e.g., *University of Ariz. Health Sciences Center v. Superior Court,* 136 Ariz. 579, 667 P.2d 1294, 1296 (1983); *Berger v. Weber,* 411 Mich. 1, 3, 303 N.W.2d 424, 425 (1981); *Speck v. Finegold,* 497 Pa. 77, 80, 439 A.2d 110, 112 (1981).

Page 126 genetic counseling was mistaken or absent: See, e.g., *Strohmaier v. Associates in Obstetrics and Gynecology, P.C.,* 122 Mich. App. 116, 332 N.W.2d 432 (1982); *Berman v. Allan,* 80 N.J. 421, 425, 404 A.2d 8 (1979).

Page 126 child allowed to sue for its *own* wrongful life: See, e.g., *Tirpin v. Sortini,* 31 Cal. 3d 220, 226, 643 P.2d 954, 958, 182 Cal. Rptr. 337, 343 (1982); *Harberson v. Parke Davis, Inc.,* 98 Wash. 2d 460, 466, 656 P.2d 438, 442 (1983).

Page 127 more than a quarter of all cases: Note, "The Punitive Damage Class Action: A Solution to the Problem of Multiple Punishment," 1984 *U. Ill. L. Rev.* 153 (1984).

Page 127 each was over $1,000,000: "Punitive Damages," 69 *A.B.A.J.* 727 (1983); Note, "Palmer v. A. H. Robins Co.: Problems with Punitive Damages in Products Liability Actions," 57 *U. Colo. L. Rev.* 135 (1985); D. Owen, "Problems in Assessing Punitive Damages Against Manufacturers of Defective Products," 49 *U. Chi. L. Rev.* 1, 2–7 (1982).

Page 128 ". . . you can send him a message": P. Brodeur, *Outrageous Misconduct* (New York: Pantheon, 1985) p. 243.

Page 128 half of all punitive awards exceed $1 million: "ABA Study Shows Punitive Awards Surprisingly Rare," *Los Angeles Daily L. J.,* 11 February 1986, p. 1.

Page 128 involved a single fatality: "Judge Orders New Trial in $108 Million Award," *New York Times,* 28 June 1986.

Page 128 space shuttle *Challenger:* P. Boffey, "Engineer Who Opposed Launching Sues Thiokol for $1 Billion," *New York Times,* 29 January 1986.

Page 128 ". . . the 'defect' requirement in design cases": C. DeMuth, Should Product-Liability Law be Nationalized? (unpublished manuscript, September 1985).

Page 128 another $12 billion in punishment: "Robins Sets $615 Million Pool to Cover Dalkon Shield Claims, Halts Dividend," *Wall Street Journal,* 3 April 1985, p. 2; see "Robins is Rebuffed in Bid to Combine Dalkon Shield Punitive-Damage Claims," *Wall Street Journal,* 24 July 1985, p. 4; M. Mintz, *At Any Cost: Corporate Greed, Women, and the Dalkon Shield* (New York: Pantheon Books, 1985), pp. 238–39.

Page 128 failure-to-warn lawsuit involving the pill: "Damage Award," *New York Times,* 30 October 1984, p. D11.

Page 128 spermicidal gel: See *Wells v. Ortho Pharmaceutical Co.,* 788 F.2d 741 (11th Cir. 1986); *Nat'l. L. J.,* 11 February 1985, p. 11.

Page 129 exercise mat manufacturer: "Sky-High Damage Suits: The Impact on Consumers, Business and Professions," *U.S. News & World Report,* 27 January 1986, p. 35.

Page 129 in which she was sexually assaulted: Ibid.

Page 129 manufacturer of the play equipment: Ibid.

Page 129 shot himself in the leg with a gun: *Sturm, Ruger & Co. v. Day,* 594 P.2d 38, 47 (Alaska 1978).

Page 129 any ordinary damages at all: *Wells v. Smith,* 297 S.E.2d 872, 880 (W. Va. 1982).

Page 129 university favoritism to athletes: M. Goodwin, "Protester of Georgia Grades Policy Wins Suit," *New York Times,* 13 February 1986, p. B23.

Page 129 federal court of appeals in 1968: G. Schwartz, "Deterrence and Punishment in the Common Law of Punitive Damages: A Comment," 56 *So. Cal. L. Rev.* 133 (1982).

Page 129 lighter-gauge materials than some other automakers: *Dorsey v. Honda Motor Co.,* 655 F. 2d 650 (5th Cir. 1981).

Page 129 39 miles per hour rear-end collision: *Toyota Motor Co. v. Moll,* 438 So.2d 192 (Fla. Dist. Ct. App. 1983) ($3,000,000).

Page 130 federal Flammable Fabrics Act: *Gryc v. Dayton-Hudson Corp.,* 297 N.W.2d 727, 741 (Minn., 1980), *cert. denied,* 449 U.S. 921 (1981).

Page 130 unsanctioned misconduct of an employee: The *Restatement of Torts* so provided. See also Note, "Palmer v. A.H. Robins Company."

Page 130 Blase Bonsignore case: *Bonsignore v. City of New York,* 521 F. Supp. 394 (1981).

Page 131 ". . . can be so administered as to avoid overkill": *Roginsky v. Richardson-Merrell, Inc.,* 254 F. Supp. 430 (S.D.N.Y. 1966), *rev'd in part on other grounds,* 378 F.2d 832 (2d Cir. 1967).

Page 131 ". . . a practical means of redress": See "Robins Rebuffed in Bid to Combine Dalkon Shield Punitive-Damage Claims."

Page 131 "did recklessly design and manufacture the 1973 Pinto": Richard Epstein, "Is Pinto a Criminal?" *Regulation,* Mar./April 1980, p. 15.

Page 132 ". . . the price for the benefits of mechanization": *Seffert v. Los Angeles Transit Lines,* 56 Cal. 2d 498; 364 P.2d 337; 15 Cal. Rptr. 161 (1961).

Chapter 9. *Insurance in Retreat*

Page 134 ten years after the vaccination program was initiated: "Vaccine Compensation Update and Review," *The Executive Letter,* Insurance Information Institute, 8 September 1986.

Page 136 how she behaved: Fred L. Smith, Jr., *Managing Risk in a Modern Society: Barriers to Private Insurance,* Risk and Insurance Policy Report No. 1 (unpublished manuscript, 12 November 1986).

Page 137 cancerphobia, and loss of society: Some states bar insurance for the insured's own deliberate wrongdoing, but most permit coverage for unintentional misconduct and for punitive damages assessed vicariously against an institution for the misconduct of its employees. John W. Morrison, "Punitive Damages and Why the Reinsurer Cares," 20 *Forum* 73 (1984), cited in S. Daniels, *Punitive Damages: Storm on the Horizon?* preliminary report of the Punitive Damages Project (Chicago: American Bar Foundation, 1986) n.19.

Page 137 kept the liability world orderly and predictable: Kenneth Abraham, "Making Sense of the Liability Insurance Crisis," 48 *Ohio State L. J.* 399 (1987).

Page 138 Chubb tersely concluded: The Chubb Corporation, *Annual Report,* 1985, pp. 5, 10.

Page 138 find themselves at the scene of accidents: T. Lewin, "The Liability Insurance Spiral," *New York Times,* 8 March 1986, Section 1, p. 35; K. Sawyer, "How a Good Town Became a Bad Risk," *Washington Post,* 25 February 1986, p. A1; Lindsey, "Increase In Suits Strains Budgets Of Many Cities," *New York Times,* 12 May 1985, Section 1, p. 1.

Page 139 abandon the municipal liability business entirely: "Businesses Struggling to Adapt as Insurance Crisis Spreads," *Wall Street Journal,* 21 January 1986, p. 31.

Page 139 Most abandoned long-term coverage entirely: See *BNA Environment Reporter,* 30 March 1984, pp. 2198, 2200.

Page 139 in the form of claims-made policies: D. Hilder, "Changes in Liability Insurance Spur Confusion Among Business Clients," *Wall Street Journal,* 20 November 1985, p. 33.

Page 139 the 1989 market might dictate: Lawrence C. Parberry, "A Contractor's View of Risk Management," in Albert Dib, *Legal Handbook for Architects, Engineers and Contractors,* Vol. 2 (N.Y.: Clark Boardman Company, Ltd., 1986) p. 75.

Notes

Page 139 child molestation stories in the press: Dorothy Wickenden, "Good-bye Day Care: The Insurance Crisis Hits Preschool," *The New Republic*, 9 December 1985, p. 14.

Page 139 or even stopped practicing altogether: Daniel Ein, *Washington Post*, 24 February 1986.

Page 140 Searle dropped the product entirely: John Carson-Parker, "The Liability Crisis: Who's at Risk?" *Chief Executive*, Summer 1986, p. 29.

Page 140 $10 million in coverage was hard to find: J. Williams, "Rising Product-Liability Costs Threaten New Products," *Chief Executive* (Summer 1986); "Businesses Struggling to Adapt as Insurance Crisis Spreads."

Page 140 their clients assumed all liability: "New Snag in Toxic Cleanups: Insurers End Liability Role," *New York Times*, 8 September 1986, p. D6; "Insurance Problems Hinder Asbestos Removal at Schools," *New York Times*, 22 April 1985; M. Abramowitz, "Liability Insurance Seeping Away for Managers of Toxic Waste: Cleanup Firms Increasingly Reluctant to Bid for Jobs," *Washington Post*, October 1985, p. G4; cf. United States Department of Justice, *Report of the Tort Policy Working Group on the Causes, Extent and Policy Implications of the Current Crisis in Insurance Availability and Affordability* (Washington, D.C.: Government Printing Office, February 1986) p. 6; Robert Lindsey, "Increase In Suits Strains Budgets Of Many Cities," *New York Times*, 12 May 1985, Section 1, p. 1.

Page 140 small aircraft had relied on mutual insurance: "General Aviation Tort Reform Considered," *The Executive Letter*, Insurance Information Institute, 18 August 1986.

Page 140 the breadth of coverage shrank dramatically: Daniel Ein, "Malpractice Insurance: A Search for Solutions," *Washington Post*, 24 February 1986; American Medical Association, Special Task Force on Professional Liability and Insurance, *Professional Liability in the 1980's*, Report I, October 1984.

Page 140 New York City's liability payments: Editorial, *New York Times*, 9 April 1986; see also Advisory Commission on Liability Insurance, *Insuring Our Future* (Report of the Governor's Advisory Commission on Liability Insurance to Governor Cuomo, State of New York, 7 April 1986).

Page 140 Sample premium-to-coverage ratios: George L. Priest, "Modern Tort Law and the Current Insurance Crisis," Working Paper No. 44, Yale Law School, Program in Civil Liability, May 1986, pp. 48–49.

Page 141 $400,000 for $1 million of insurance: L. Poggemeyer, Letter to the Editor, *New York Times*, 4 March 1987, p. A30.

Page 141 $100,000 in 1985 to $500,000 in 1986: See George Priest, "Modern Tort Law and the Current Insurance Crisis," pp. 40–41; *Time*, 24 March 1986, p. 18.

Page 141 reinsurers started a mass exodus: "London Mart Shrinkage Adds to Insurance Woes," *Journal of Commerce*, 30 April 1986.

Page 141 ". . . to assess in terms of premium rates": Ibid.

Page 141 "banana republic": Quoted in George Clemon Freeman, "Tort Law Reform: Superfund/RCRA Liability as a Major Cause of the Insurance Crisis," 21 *Tort & Ins. L. J.* 517, 528 (Summer 1986).

Page 141 ninety reinsurers were gone: John Carson-Parker, "The Liability Crisis," p. 19.

Page 141 fewer day care centers: William Glaberson, "Liability Rates Flattening Out as Crisis Eases," *New York Times*, 9 February 1987, p. 1, D5.

Page 142 less insurance than needed: Ibid.

Page 142 nonprofit or public-service operator: See W. Olson, "A Naderite Backflip on Liability," *Wall Street Journal*, 11 March 1986, p. 30.

Page 142 if the insurance did not pay: H. G. Sparrow III, "Hazardous Waste Insurance Coverage: Unexpected Past, Uncertain Future," *Mich. Bar J.*, February 1985.

Page 143 a man can drink himself to an accidental death: Ibid.

Page 143 Wayne Partridge case: *State Farm Mutual Automobile Ins. Co. v. Partridge*, 10 Cal. 3d 94, 109 Cal Rptr. 811, 514 P.2d 123 (1973).

Page 144 general liability policy sold to most businesses: *BNA Environment Reporter*, 30 March 1984, p. 2198.

Page 144 the township was covered anyway: *Jackson Township Municipal Authority v. Hartford Accident and Indemnity Co.*, 186 N.J. Super. 156, 451 A.2d 990 (1982); see generally B. Rich,

"Environmental Litigation and the Insurance Dilemma," *Risk Management,* December 1985, p. 34.

Page 144 went home happy: See Dennis R. Connolly, "Insurer Perspectives on Causation and Financial Compensation," 6 *Regulatory Toxicology and Pharmacology* 80 (1986).

Page 144 Summit case: *Summit Associates, Inc. v. Liberty Mutual Fire Insurance Company,* Superior Court of New Jersey, Docket No. L-47287-84 (25 February 1987).

Page 145 ". . . legal owner of the property": *U.S. Aviex, Inc. v. Travelers Insurance Company,* 125 Mich. App. 579, 336 N.W.2d 838 (1983).

Page 145 liability policies from many different insurers: *Keene Corp. v. Insurance Co. of North America,* 513 F. Supp. 470, 215 U.S. App. D.C. 156, 667 F.2d 1034 (D.C. Cir. 1981), *cert. denied,* 455 U.S. 1007, 102 S. Ct. 1644 (1982).

Page 147 state claim settlement statutes: *Royal Globe Insurance Company v. Superior Court of Butte County,* 23 Cal. 3d 880, 153 Cal. Rptr. 842, 592 P. 2d 329 (1979); *Tibbs v. Great American Insurance Company,* 755 F.2d 1370, 1375 (9th Cir. 1985).

Page 147 bad faith in failing to settle certain claims: *Garvey v. State Farm Fire and Casualty Co.* (A017878, certified for publication 19 March 1986) cited in D. Hauser and C. Kent, "Concurrent Causation in First-Party Insurance Claims," 21 *Tort & Ins. L. Q.* 573 (1986). See generally Bob G. Freemon, Jr., "Reasonable and Foreseeable Damages for Breach of an Insurance Contract," 21 *Tort & Ins. L. J.* 108 (Fall 1985).

Page 147 punitive award of $3.5 million: *Lavoie v. Aetna Life & Casualty Co.,* 470 So.2d 1060 (Ala. 1984), *rev'd* 54 USLW (1986). The U.S. Supreme Court reversed the award, not for its size but because of bias by the judge.

Page 147 under $30 million annually: *BNA Environment Reporter,* 30 March 1984, p. 2198.

Page 147 liabilities into hundreds of billions of dollars: Ibid.

Page 148 insurer's freedom to cancel or refuse renewal: David J. Brummond, "Searching for Balance in the Liability Insurance Triangle: Tort Reform, Court Reform and Insurance Reform," *Forces Restricting the Insurance Industry,* Monograph (Malvern, Pennsylvania: Society of Chartered Property/Casualty Underwriters, 1987).

Page 148 price controls: E.g. Florida S-465, Chapter 86-160, 1986 Florida Laws (approved 26 June 1986); Hawaii S-1X, Act 2, 1986 Hawaii Laws (approved 4 August 1986). New York established limits on rate increases or decreases, New York regulation No. 129, 11 NYCRR 161 (9 September 1986). California and Oregon tried to do the same. See California Insurance Bulletin #86-4 (October 22, 1986); Oregon Administrative Rules 836-42-501 (10 November 1986).

Page 148 public insurance corporations: W. K. Stevens, "Malpractice Insurers Stir Wrath of West Virginia," *New York Times,* 3 May 1986; see also "West Virginia Court Blocks 5 Insurers Trying to Leave," *Wall Street Journal,* 12 May 1986, p. 14.

Page 148 the hazardous waste crisis: See *BNA Environment Reporter,* 4 January 1985, p. 1445.

Page 150 who win $1 million or more: Cheryl Frank, "Trends in Million-Dollar Verdicts," 70 *A.B.A.J.* 52 (September 1984).

Page 150 they win big: Audrey Chin and Mark A. Peterson, *Deep Pockets, Empty Pockets: Who Wins in Cook County Jury Trials?* (Santa Monica, Calif.: Rand Institute for Civil Justice, R-3249-ICJ, 1985).

Page 150 ". . . than on need and reason": J. O'Connell, *Ending Insult To Injury: No-Fault Insurance For Products And Services* (Urbana: University of Illinois Press, 1975) p. 54.

Page 150 "and winning the big prize": M. Goodwin, "Protester of Georgia Grades Policy Wins Suit," *New York Times,* 13 February 1986, p. B23.

Page 151 absorbed by administrative and legal costs: P. Danzon, *Medical Malpractice* (Santa Monica, Calif.: Rand Institute for Civil Justice, 1985) p. 31.

Page 151 60 cents on the dollar for products liability: Interagency Task Force on Product Liability, U.S. Dept. of Commerce, *Final Report* (Washington, D.C.: Government Printing Office, 1977) pp. 24–26; see also J. Kakalik, *Variation in Asbestos Litigation Compensation and Expenses* (Santa Monica, Calif.: Rand Institute for Civil Justice, 1984) pp. xvii–xix; P. Munch, *Costs and Benefits of the Tort System if Viewed as a Compensation System* (Santa Monica, Calif.: Rand Institute for Civil Justice, June 1977) p. ix.

Page 151 exactly what modern tort law requires: George Priest, "Modern Tort Law and the Current Insurance Crisis," pp. 61–62.

Chapter 10.   *What Is Deterred?*

Page 154 more essential than the creation of good: Cf. S. Florman, "Engineering: An Ideal Profession for Idealists," *Technology Review,* October 1987, p. 18.

Page 155 Capronor stalled for lack of liability insurance: Cf. "Birth Control: Vanishing Options," *Time,* 1 September 1986, p. 78.

Page 155 Copper-T 380A: E. Connell, "The Crisis in Contraception," *Technology Review,* May–June 1987, p. 47. As one observer has noted, "a pharmaceutical company would have to be altruistic to the point of suicidal to market an IUD today." Quoted in "Birth Control: Vanishing Options."

Page 155 quick and clean exit from the market: T. Lewin, "Birth Control Device Returning for Sale in U.S.," *New York Times,* 18 October 1987, p. 30.

Page 155 ". . . that would be used by pregnant women?": John Carson-Parker, "The Liability Crisis: Who's At Risk," *Chief Executive,* Summer 1986, p. 19.

Page 156 investing heavily in vaccine research: "Business Struggling to Adapt as Insurance Crisis Spreads," *Wall Street Journal,* 21 January 1986, p. 31.

Page 156 decrease in risk they might actually represent: D. Dimond, "Know-How or No Way?" *Insurance Rev.,* October 1987, p. 34.

Page 156 university's deep pocket as well: Ibid.

Page 156 cars used by the handicapped: Michael Brody, "When Products Turn Into Liabilities," *Fortune,* 3 March 1986, p. 20.

Page 159 uncontrollable twitching of the eye muscles: P. Boffey, "Loss of Drug Relegates Many to Blindness Again," *New York Times,* 14 October 1986, p. C1.

Page 159 under development for some 500 of them: N. R. Kleinfield, " 'Orphan' Drugs: Caught in Limbo," *New York Times,* 20 July 1986, Section F, pp. 1, 27.

Page 159 fell into the wrong hands: Ibid.

Page 159 cut off supplies in 1986 for similar reasons: Ibid.

Page 159 or the addition of a new safety system: E.g., *Columbia & P.S. Railroad Company v. Hawthorne,* 144 U.S. 202 (1892).

Page 159 this rule too came under direct attack: See J. Hoffman and G. Zuckerman, "Tort Reform and the Rules of Evidence: Saving the Rule Excluding Evidence of Subsequent Remedial Actions," 22 *Tort & Ins. L. J.* 497 (Summer 1987).

Page 159 focus was on the product itself, not on the defendant's conduct: *Sutkowski v. Universal Marion Corporation,* 5 Ill. App. 2d 313, 281 N.E.2d 749 (1972).

Page 159 California landmark ruling in 1974: *Ault v. International Harvester Company,* 13 Cal. 3d 113, 117 Cal. Rptr. 812, 528 P.2d 1148 (1974).

Page 160 somehow the courts then will too: T. Lewin, "Insurance a Liability for Some: Costs Rise Prohibitively," *New York Times,* 8 March 1986, p. 35; S. Johnson, "Malpractice Costs vs. Health Care for Women," *New York Times,* 14 July 1985, p. A14; V. Schwartz, "The Post-Sale Duty to Warn: Two Unfortunate Forks in the Road to a Reasonable Doctrine," 58 *N.Y.U. L. Rev.* 892 (1983).

Page 160 life has been growing steadily safer: See E. Crouch and R. Wilson, *Risk/Benefit Analysis* (New York: Ballinger, 1982) p. 3; *New York Times,* 9 July 1984, p. A15.

Page 161 a generation or even a decade ago: Bruce N. Ames, "Six Common Errors Relating to Environmental Pollution," testimony for California Assembly on Water, Parks and Wildlife (1 October 1986).

Page 161 later in commercial aviation: D. Dimond, "Know-How or No Way?"

Page 162 as a result of this kind of caution: Ronald Kotulak, "Cancer May Feed on Malpractice Fear," *Chicago Tribune,* 26 March 1986, Section 1, p. 3, quoted in Walter Olson, "Overdeterrence and the Problem of Comparative Risk," paper for APS-Manhattan Institute Conference, "New Directions in Liability Law," Columbia University, 10 November 1987.

Page 162 greater risk than any IUD would ever have created: E. Connell, "The Crisis in Contraception."

Page 162 sometimes-debilitating morning sickness: D. Dimond, "Know-How or No Way?"

Page 162 unavailable in rural and less affluent communities: S. Johnson, "Malpractice

Costs vs. Health Care for Women"; T. R. Reid, "Insurance Famine Plagues Nation," *Washington Post*, 23 February 1986, pp. A1, A6.

Page 162 dangerous, not for the kids but for the people running the centers: Dorothy Wickenden, "Good-Bye Day Care, The Insurance Crisis Hits Preschool," *The New Republic*, 9 December 1985, p. 14.

Page 163 identifiable corporate name on the letterhead: "New Snag in Toxic Cleanups; Insurers End Liability Role," *New York Times*, 8 September 1986, p. D6.

Page 164 gravitates toward wealthy targets: I discuss these factors at greater length in P. Huber, "Safety and the Second Best: The Hazards of Public Risk Management in the Courts," 85 *Colum. L. Rev.* 277, 317–20 (1985).

Page 165 the immobile and the immune: See W. Olson, "Overdeterrence and the Problem of Comparative Risk," Paper presented at the APS-Manhattan Institute Conference, "New Directions in Liability Law," Columbia University, 10 November 1987.

Page 166 in a pocket or handbag: "Lawsuits, and Worry, Mount Over Bic Lighter," *New York Times*, 10 April 1987; Tamar Lewin, "Bic is Facing a Rising Tide of Injury Lawsuits," *New York Times*, 10 April 1987, p. 1.

Page 166 refillable lighters they have largely replaced: Walter Olson, "Comparative Risk," Civil Justice Memo (New York: Manhattan Institute for Policy Research, 13 June 1987). I have borrowed freely from Olson's analysis of the problem.

Page 167 annual sale revenues of the vaccine: Tamar Lewin, "Pharmaceutical Companies Are the Hardest Hit," *New York Times*, 10 March 1985, Business Section, p. 1; T. R. Reid, "Litigation Loosens the Stiff Upper Lip," *Washington Post*, 24 February 1986, pp. A1, A7.

Page 167 so expensive that you were playing without one: W. Olson, "Overdeterrence and the Problem of Comparative Risk."

Page 167 necessary for successful treatment: Alan L. Otten, "More Psychotherapists Held Liable for the Actions of Violent Patients," *Wall Street Journal*, 2 March 1987, Section 2, p. 1.

Page 168 except when it alleviates the misery of leprosy: N. R. Kleinfield, " 'Orphan' Drugs: Caught in Limbo," *New York Times*, 20 July 1986, Section F, pp. 1, 27.

Chapter 11. *Rights in Collision*

Page 172 Henning Jacobson case: *Jacobson v. Massachusetts*, 197 U.S. 11, 17–18 (1905).

Page 174 possibly even constitutionally protected: Note, "Motorcycle Helmets and the Constitutionality of Self-Protective Legislation," 30 *Ohio St. L. J.* 355 (1969); Henkin, "Privacy and Autonomy," 74 *Colum. L. Rev.* 1410 (1974).

Page 174 the criminal, the mentally ill, and the social misfit: Alan L. Otten, "More Psychotherapists Held Liable for the Actions of Violent Patients," *Wall Street Journal*, 2 March 1987, Section 2, p. 1.

Page 175 Cesarean sections increased fourfold: Erik Eckholm, "Curbs Sought in Caesarean Deliveries," *New York Times*, 11 August 1986.

Page 175 to undergo treatment they did not want: See "Policing Pregnancy," *Scientific American*, August 1987, p. 26.

Page 175 "right to self-determination": T. Lewin, "Courts Acting to Force Care of the Unborn," *New York Times*, 23 November 1987, p. 1; see also L. Greenhouse, "Wide Appeal Filed on Forced Caesarean Delivery," *New York Times*, 25 November 1987, p. A15.

Page 175 stop smoking or lose their jobs: S. Phillips, "Smoking Listed As New Ground For Losing Job," *New York Times*, 21 January 1987, p. A16.

Page 176 rest break, and speed change: B. Marx, "The Company is Watching You Everywhere," *New York Times*, 15 February 1987, p. E21.

Page 176 analyzing the electrical activity of the brain: Office of Technology Assessment, *The Electronic Supervisor* (Washington, D.C.: 1987) cited in "Electronic Taskmasters," *Scientific American*, December 1987, p. 32.

Notes

Page 177 amniocentesis and prenatal genetic screening: See "Genetic Promise," *Scientific American,* August 1987, pp. 30–31.

Page 178 that should also be screened out with care: M. Hunt, "The Total Gene Screen," *New York Times Magazine,* 19 January 1986, p. 33.

Page 178 inhaling certain industrial chemicals: Ibid.

Page 178 form of anemia when exposed to it: Ibid.

Page 178 countless others have since begun to do so: Ibid.

Page 179 in the check-out process: L. Reibstein, "Firms Face Lawsuits for Hiring People Who Then Commit Crimes," *Wall Street Journal,* 30 April 1987, Section 2, p. 1.

Page 179 and other atrocities: J. A. Kirchner, Letter to the Editor, *New York Times,* 16 June 1987.

Page 180 still more benefits are likely to be lost: S. Blakeslee, "Genetic Discoveries Raise Painful Questions," *New York Times,* 21 April 1987, p. C1.

Page 180 the crowded inn of human freedom: Cf. Richard E. Morgan, *Disabling America: The "Rights Industry" in Our Time* (New York: Basic Books, 1984).

Page 181 in matters of procreation: E. Connell, "The Crisis in Contraception," *Technology Review,* May-June 1987, p. 47.

Page 182 to flex their muscles against the vaccine industry: Henderson, "A Victory for All Mankind," *World Health,* May 1980, p. 3; see generally *World Health,* May 1980 (issue of the World Health Organization magazine announcing eradication of smallpox).

Page 183 its credit on the line to restore the service: D. Carmody, "Insurance Gap to Close Tram to Roosevelt I.," *New York Times,* 14 February 1986; T. Lewin, "The Liability Insurance Spiral," *New York Times,* 8 March 1986, Section 1, p. 35.

Page 183 the community lacked liability coverage: Chuck Hardwick, "Opinion: Getting Liability Coverage," *New York Times,* 15 June 1986, Section 11 NJ; p. 1.

Page 183 "guilt, anxiety and depression": *Nally v. Grace Community Church of the Valley,* 204 Cal. Rptr. 303 (Cal. App. 1984).

Page 184 bake-sale organizer, or roadside rescuer: Cf. D. Hilder, "Small Firms Face Sharp Cost Hikes for Insurance—If They Can Get It," *Wall Street Journal,* 5 August 1985, p. 23.

Page 184 on Main Street too, sooner or later: Cf. W. Olson, "A Naderite Backflip on Liability," *Wall Street Journal,* 11 March 1986, p. 30.

Page 184 $305,000 a year through 1999: *Garcia v. City of South Tucson,* 131 Ariz. 315, 640 P. 2d 1117 (App. 1981); "Police Agencies Seek Ways to Avoid Citizens' Lawsuits," *New York Times,* 3 November 1985.

Page 184 legal costs rose tenfold in the space of a decade: *The New York Times,* 14 July 1986.

Page 184 Ryan Barber case: "City and 7-Year-Old Bicyclist Collide in Court," *The Executive Letter,* Insurance Information Institute, 27 April 1987.

Page 184 demanding $149 billion: L. McGinley, "Explosive Growth of Lawsuits Against the U.S. Creates Concern Over Potential Budget Impact," *Wall Street Journal,* 14 January 1985, p. 38.

Page 186 when the legal rules are put to public referendum: "California Voters Decide to Sew Up Deep Pockets," *The Executive Letter,* Insurance Information Institute, 9 June 1986. A Nebraska poll showed that 75 percent of Nebraskans favor a cap on liability awards in lawsuits. "75 Percent of Nebraskans Polled Favor Capping Damage Awards," *The Executive Letter,* Insurance Information Institute, 2 September 1986. A Montana initiative, which would have allowed the legislature to place limits on liability, was passed overwhelmingly by voters in the fall of 1986, but later invalidated by the Montana Supreme Court on a technicality. "Montana Supreme Court Invalidates Liability Limits," *The Executive Letter,* Insurance Information Institute, 22 June 1987.

Page 188 when the discussion shifts to punitive damages: Contrary to popular belief, punitive damages most often *are* covered by insurance, along with other elements of the award.

Page 189 the real consequences of the action: I paraphrase here from an eloquent op-ed, Richard Cohen, "Blame Those Who Sue," *Washington Post,* 11 April 1986, p. A15.

Chapter 12. *Compassion by Consent*

Page 190 Compassion by Consent: Cf. E. Anderson, "Compensation, Without Lawyers," *New York Times*, 1 May 1986.

Page 190 ". . . Then he died": Paul Brodeur, *Outrageous Misconduct: The Asbestos Industry on Trial* (New York: Pantheon Books, 1985) pp. 356–57.

Page 190 ". . . deprived of her ability ever to bear a child": Morton Mintz, *At Any Cost: Corporate Greed, Women and the Dalkon Shield* (New York: Pantheon Books, 1985) p. 13.

Page 190 ". . . was to give him more Tylenol": Harris L. Coulter and Barbara Loe Fisher, *DPT: A Shot In the Dark* (New York: Warner Books, 1985) p. 140.

Page 193 other than life insurance and Social Security: Leonard L. Finz and Herbert L. Waichman, "1986 Legislative Changes in New York Tort Law: An Analysis," 59 *N.Y.S. Bar J.* 18 (April 1987).

Page 193 takes four years to resolve: My discussion here draws heavily from Andrew Chalk, "Is This Any Way to Litigate Air Crashes?" *Wall Street Journal*, 6 November 1985.

Page 194 A *neo–no-fault* proposal: J. O'Connell, "A 'Neo-No-Fault' Contract in Lieu of Tort: Preaccident Guarantees of Postaccident Settlement Offers," 73 *Calif. L. Rev.* 898 (1985).

Page 197 Sugarman and Cooter proposal: R. Cooter and S. Sugarman, A Regulated Market in Unmatured Tort Claims: Tort Reform by Contract (unpublished manuscript, August 1987).

Page 200 hosts of choice for most such facilities: Lena Williams, "Race Bias Found in Location of Toxic Dumps," *New York Times*, 16 April 1987, p. A20, drawing from a study prepared by the United Church of Christ Commission on Racial Justice.

Page 200 Kunreuther proposal: H. Kunreuther, "Hazard Compensation and Incentive Systems: An Economic Perspective," paper presented at the National Academy of Engineering, Symposium on Hazards: Equity, Incentives and Compensation, Washington, D.C., 3–4 June 1985.

Page 201 several other cities had also accepted the offer: Ibid.

Page 202 California cap: See *Fein v. Permanente Medical Group*, 38 Cal. 3d 137, 211 Cal. Rptr. 368, 121 Cal. App. 3d 135, 695 P.2d 665 (1985).

Page 202 Maryland cap: "Maryland Legislature Puts Ceiling on Personal Injury Awards," *New York Times*, 13 April 1985.

Page 202 Kansas caps: "Kansas Passes Award Caps and No-Fault Reform," *The Executive Letter*, Insurance Information Institute, 11 May 1987.

Page 202 Texas caps: "Texas Legislature Passes Tort/Insurance Reform," *The Executive Letter*, Insurance Information Institute, 8 June 1987.

Page 204 after the injury has occurred: J. O'Connell, "Neo-No-Fault: A Fair Exchange Proposal for Tort Reform," paper delivered at the APS-Manhattan Institute Conference, "New Directions in Liability Law," Columbia University, 10 November 1987.

Chapter 13. *Choosing Safety*

Page 208 Howard Hughes syndrome: Paul Johnson, "The Perils Of Risk Avoidance," *Regulation*, May/June 1980, p. 15.

Page 211 disclosure of workplace health hazards: "Debating a Bill On Job Hazards," *New York Times*, 13 July 1987, p. D2; P. Shabecoff, "Industry Is Split Over Disclosure of Job Dangers," *New York Times*, 11 October 1987, p. 28.

Page 214 as with drugs and aircraft: P. Hutt, "Unresolved Issues in the Conflict Between Individual Freedom and Government Control of Food Safety," 33 *Food Drug Cosm. L. J.* 558, 560 (1978).

Page 218 the trans-Alaska pipeline: See Office of Pesticides and Toxic Substances, U.S. Environmental Protection Agency, *Background Report for the Indemnification Report to Congress* (Washington, D.C.: Government Printing Office 1983) p. A-27; S. Taylor, "New Act Restricts Atomic Test Suits," *New York Times*, 4 November 1985, p. 26; 43 U.S.C. § 1653(a)(2) (1986).

Page 218 volunteers of charitable enterprises: "The Quality of Mercy: Charitable Torts and Their Continuing Immunity," 100 *Harv. L. Rev.* 1382, n.71 (1987).

Notes

Page 218 Little League programs: C. Conway, *Philadelphia Inquirer,* 13 May 1986, p. 1B.

Page 219 ". . . Freedom is not safety but opportunity": Zechariah Chafee, Jr., "The Press Under Pressure," *Nieman Reports,* April 1948.

Page 219 without courting the danger of rejection: Aaron Wildavsky, *Searching for Safety* (forthcoming, 1988).

Chapter 14. *Consent and Coercion*

Page 220 psychic powers after a CAT scan: "Judge Rejects Damage Award to Psychic," *Washington Post,* 9 August 1986.

Page 220 commercial laundry dryer: *American Laundry Machinery v. Horan,* 45 Md. App. 97, 412 A.2d 407 (1980).

Page 220 refrigerator-carrying footrace: *Columbo v. Transworld International* (Los Angeles County Sup. Ct., No. C223491, 23 September 1982).

Page 227 ". . . let the devil take the hindmost": Grant Gilmore, *The Death of Contract* (Columbus: Law Forum Series, College of Law, Ohio State University Press, 1974) p. 95.

Page 229 software that performs complex tasks: See D. Dimond, "Know-How or No Way?" *Ins. Rev.,* October 1987, p. 34.

Page 229 video display terminal radiation: E.g., Note, "Pink Collar Blues: Potential Hazards of Video Display Terminal Radiation," 59 *So. Cal. L. Rev.* 139 (1983).

Page 231 closest approximation to it in an imperfect world: See Robert Nozick, *Anarchy, State and Utopia* (New York: Basic Books, 1974).

Page 231 Or less?: I am paraphrasing, of course, from R. Nozick, *Anarchy, State and Utopia,* p. 334.

Page 232 ". . . There will still be business enough": John Nicolay and John Hay, *Abraham Lincoln; Complete Works, Comprising His Speeches, Letters, State Papers and Miscellaneous Writings,* Vol. 2 (New York: Century Co., 1894) p. 142.

Page 232 due process will be meticulously observed: Grant Gilmore, *The Ages of American Law* (New Haven: Yale University Press, 1977) pp. 110–11.

INDEX

A.H. Robins, 128, 131; Dalkon Shield cases, 9, 42, 50, 103–4, 108, 128–29, 131, 162
Abortion, right to, 228
Accident insurance, *see* Insurance
Accidents: shift from consent to coercion in law of, 5–10, 220–32; unintentional, 5
Adhesion, contracts of, 27–32, 204
Agent Orange case, 62, 70, 75, 82, 111–12
AIDS, 230; employment of people with, 177–78
Aircraft technology, 161
Airplane crash cases, 193–94
Albertson, Ray, *State Farm Mutual Automobile Ins. Co. v. Partridge*, 143
Alcohol–related accidents, 76
Alternative liability, 80–81
American Bar Association, 128
American Motorcycle Association (AMA), case against, 80
Ames, Bruce, 65
Annoyance, environmental tort as, 63
Antidiscrimination cases, 179
Asbestos cases, 9, 68, 70, 75, 110, 127–28, 163
Asbestos companies, liability avoidance by, 175–76
Athletes, Washington state insurance program for high school, 194–95
Auto maker liability, car crashworthiness theory of, 7, 42, 44, 129, 174; *see also* specific auto makers
Awards: caps on, 202–3; in environmental cases, 110–11; size of, 10; *see also* Compensation, Punitive damages

Bankruptcy, punitive damages and, 131
Barker v. Lull Engineering Co., 106–7
Bendectin cases, 102, 110, 112, 162, 209
Birth defects: avoidance of, 177; neocontractual insurance against, 197; suits over causes of, 101–3; *see also* Bendectin cases, Obstetrician-gynecologists
Bloomfield Motor Company, case against, 28, 73
Bolko Athletic Company, judgment against, 39

Bonsignore, Blase, 130
Boston, Massachusetts, lack of liability insurance in, 138–39
Brown, Texas & Pac. R. Co. v., 34
Buick Motor Company, case against, 74
Burden of proof, shifting the, 106–9
Bystander distress claims, 125

Calabresi, Guido, 6, 114
California Supreme Court, 132; on alternative liability, 80–81; on deep-pocket liability, 80; on DES daughters case, 81; on direct suits against insurers, 147; on express disclaimers, 31; on insurance contracts, 143; on safety improvements, 159; on strict liability, 37; on zone-of-danger rule, 124–25
Campbell v. Animal Quarantine Station, 125
Cancer, traumatically induced, 98–99, 112–13
Capronor (contraceptive), 155
Caps on awards, 202–3
Car crashworthiness, 7, 42, 44, 129, 174; Ford Pinto cases, 42, 50, 115–16, 128
Cardozo, Benjamin: *MacPherson* decision, 35, 74; on negligence of public standards, 47; *Palsgraf* decision, 72
Carson, Rachel, 65
Cause and effect, 100–105, 113–14; claims of, 137; confusing temporal coincidence with, 103
Caveat emptor, rule of, 23
Cesarean sections, frequency of, 175
Challenger (space shuttle), 128
Cheapest cost avoider, 154
Chemical abortifacient, 228
Chemical exposure, litigation over toxic, 65–70
Chevron, inadequate warning case against, 55
Chubb Insurance Corporation, 138
Church, suits against the, 77, 183
Churchill, Winston, 152
Cigarette cases, 60
Cities, *see* Municipalities

253

Index